Take the Plunge

Take the Plunge

Living Baptism and Confirmation

Timothy Radcliffe OP

BLOOMSBURY

LONDON · BERLIN · NEW YORK · SYDNEY

First published in Great Britain 2012

© Timothy Radcliffe OP, 2012

The moral right of the author has been asserted

No part of this book may be used or reproduced in any manner whatsoever
without written permission from the Publisher except in the case of brief
quotations embodied in critical articles or reviews. Every reasonable effort has
been made to trace copyright holders of material reproduced in this book, but
if any have been inadvertently overlooked the Publishers would be glad to hear
from them.

Bloomsbury Publishing Plc
50 Bedford Square
London WC1B 3DP

www.bloomsbury.com

Bloomsbury Publishing, London, Berlin, New York and Sydney
A CIP record for this book is available from the British Library.

ISBN: 978-1-4411-1848-6

10 9 8 7 6 5 4 3 2 1

Typeset by Fakenham Prepress Solutions, Fakenham, Norfolk NR21 8NN
Printed and bound in Great Britain

For David Sanders OP
Fellow novice, brother and old friend

Contents

Introduction

Christianity will flourish in the twenty-first century if we grasp that the Church is above all the community of the baptized. Baptism is the great mystery of our faith. It does not always seem so. Someone earnestly asked Herbert McCabe OP: 'But do you *believe* in baptism?' He replied, 'Not only do I believe in baptism; I have even seen it done'. His answer plays on the paradox of baptism. It is an ordinary everyday event. About a third of the world's population are baptized, 2.3 billion people. People are baptized for all sorts of reasons, perhaps because of a profound experience of conversion, or to pass on their faith to their children, but also just because it is expected, to please the grandparents, to get their children into a Christian school, or just as an excuse for a party or a new hat. So baptism may seem an unremarkable event, in essence the splashing of a little water and the uttering of a few words. When I told a friend that my next book was on baptism, he remarked: 'I suppose that it will be very short'.

Yet Christians make the grandest claims for baptism. It is our sharing in Christ's victory over death, our lives are hidden in the risen Christ and we are taken up into the very life of God. When Pope John Paul II was asked what was the most important day in his life, he replied: 'The day I was baptized'. When Martin Luther felt discouraged, he would say: 'I am baptized, and through my baptism God, who cannot lie, has bound himself in covenant with me'.[1]

Christianity faces vast challenges: indifference, aggressive secularism, the rise of religious fundamentalism, persecution in many parts of the world and so on. Our faith will only flourish if we recover a profound sense of the beauty of this simple ritual. Baptism touches the deepest dramas of human life: birth, growing up, falling in love, daring to give oneself to others, searching for meaning, becoming adult, coping with suffering and failure, and eventually death. A decent exploration of baptism would illuminate every aspect of our humanity, our deepest hopes and longings. It would need to be not a short book but a whole library.

In most Christian Churches, there are bitter arguments about who can be ordained: Married men? Women? Openly gay people? These are important questions which deserve serious debate, though this is not the place, but it would be easier to consider them calmly and intelligently if we really were convinced that the greatest dignity of any Christian is to be baptized. It is far more wonderful to share the bread of life than to be the one who consecrates it. In Cardinal John Henry Newman's church in Rome, San Giorgio al Velabro, there is a modest plaque which celebrates all his honours. It concludes with the words: '*Sed ante omnia Christianus*'; 'But before all else, a Christian'. His baptism was more important to him than being a Cardinal, or even the fellow of an Oxford College!

Christianity will be strong if all the baptized people of God are strengthened, their vocation recognized and their creativity released. In the Catholic Church, three of the great patrons of Europe – St

---

[1] 'The Holy and Blessed Sacrament of Baptism', *Luther's Works*, vol. 35 (Minneapolis, 1970), quoted in Claire Watkins, *Living Baptism: Called out of the Ordinary* (London, 2006), p. 33.

Benedict, St Francis of Assisi and St Catherine of Siena – renewed the Church in times of crisis. None of them were ordained priests.

For the first Christians in the pagan Roman Empire, the decision to ask for baptism was momentous. It transformed one's identity. Most early Christians had to break with their families and become estranged from their contemporaries and friends. Baptism often led to one's death. This is still true for Christians in parts of the world, but today in the West when ministers of religion baptize babies, they may wonder whether they will ever return to church until their funeral, and at neither event will they have an active participation. For many people, baptism hardly seems to matter.

This may be because the *real* Christians, the people who matter, appear to be the clergy. It would be unjust to blame this just on power-hungry clerics, though they have been around ever since apostles argued over who was the greatest. (Mark 9.34). But our failure to value baptism fully is due as much to the media's perception of our Churches as NGOs campaigning for political or moral values, rather than as communities of abundant life. If one thinks that the Churches exist to plug a line or push an agenda, then of course it is those in charge who really count, as in a political party or a business. But St Irenaeus of Lyons famously said in the second century that the glory of God is a human being fully alive. If we believe that, then what could be more wonderful than baptism into God's own life? Being alive, as we shall see, does involve the exercise of adult responsibility, having a voice in the affairs of the Church, but that is not the point of being a Christian.

I did write a book with that title.[2] It explored some of the qualities of Christian life which should surprise our contemporaries and make them wonder who we are: a strange joy, a puzzling freedom, hope,

---

[2] Timothy Radcliffe, *What is the Point of being a Christian?* (London and New York, 2006).

courage, a certain understanding of truthfulness, a deep peace. I have tried not to repeat myself. This book takes a rather different and complementary approach.

Every sacrament enacts a story. I have argued elsewhere[3] that the Eucharist is the story of our transformation through faith, hope and love. It is a three-act drama. The story enacted by baptism is less clear to me. Often when I baptize people I struggle to remember what comes next. But I believe that it too has an implicit narrative. It begins with us being named and claimed for Christ. This is the unconditional love which calls us into being. But, as the baptism proceeds, we discover that this love is demanding and transforming. We are invited to attend to the Lord, who summons us to share responsibility for each other and creation, to let go of all egoism, to die and to share the very life of the Triune God. This love is exigent precisely because it is true, and a true love is always transformative. I shall not try to give a systematic presentation of the theology of baptism. The challenge, rather, is to touch our imagination with the great adventure of becoming alive in God.

I write as a Catholic but in the hope that this small book will also be of use to Christians of other denominations. 'Catholic' means 'universal' and so as a Catholic I am bound to be open to the truth wherever it is to be found. It is often asserted that competition between our Churches is healthy. It keeps us on our toes. We need to improve our 'products' to retain our share of the market. The reason why America has such a lively Christian culture, the argument goes, is because no Church has the monopoly. This competition is symbolized by the famous, but probably mythical, duel between the notice boards of adjacent Catholic and Presbyterian churches:

---

[3] Timothy Radcliffe, *Why Go to Church? The Drama of the Eucharist* (London and New York, 2008).

The Catholic sign: 'All Dogs Go To Heaven'.

The Presbyterian sign: 'Only Humans Go To Heaven. Read The Bible'.

The Catholic sign: 'God Loves All His creations, Dogs Included'.

Presbyterians: 'Dogs Don't Have Souls. This Is Not Open For Debate'.

The Catholic sign: 'Catholic Dogs Go To Heaven. Presbyterian Dogs Can Talk To Their Pastor'.

The Presbyterian sign: 'Converting to Catholicism Does Not Magically Grant Your Dog A Soul'. And so on.

Of course some degree of competition is inevitable and we rightly feel loyal to our own Church and do not want to let our side down. There was a Benedictine monk who had a reputation for being a *bon viveur*. One evening he went out for dinner and drove back a bit the worse for wear, wearing his clerical collar. He was stopped by a kindly policeman who said to him, 'Now Reverend, you should not be driving in this state. Park your car and I will drive you home. Where can I drop you?' 'Outside the Baptist Church, please'. But baptism is the sacrament of our unity in Christ, and in a world which is ever more fractured by violence and conflict, our unity is more imperative than ever. I believe that it is intrinsic to our baptismal identity to long for and strive for the restoration of the full unity of the Body of Christ.

Today Christian unity seems more remote and unattainable than a few decades ago. But in other ways we are drawing closer together, including in our understanding of baptism. Maxwell E. Johnson, the Lutheran expert on baptism, wrote that 'the second half of the twentieth century has witnessed unprecedented change, recovery, renewal, and ecumenical convergence in the rites of Christian initiation and their interpretation within several churches throughout the world'.[4] For

---

[4] Maxwell E. Johnson, *The Rites of Christian Initiation: Their Evolution and Interpretation* (Collegeville, MN: 1999), p. 291.

the first time for centuries Catholics, Orthodox and many Protestants celebrate baptism and confirmation in much the same way. I shall largely follow the Catholic rite for the baptisms of babies, but I hope that this will not feel too unfamiliar to Christians from other traditions. The movement of liturgical reform has brought us together; we have returned to the same early sources; we face similar challenges.

But what about those who are not baptized? Our society has consecrated competition, and so a celebration of baptism might be thought to imply a disregard for the unbaptized. But this is not my intention at all. God is not confined within the limits of the Church. God is present in every human being, sustaining them in being and inhabiting their love, whatever their faith or none. Baptism is fascinating because it sheds light on the drama of every human life.

I thank my Dominican brethren to whose wisdom and preaching this small book owes so much. I especially thank Vivian Boland OP and Richard Conrad OP for reading the typescript, enriching it with their suggestions and rescuing me from many embarrassing errors. I am grateful to the monks of Glenstal Abbey and the bishops and priests of San Francisco, who heroically endured early versions of much of this book and encouraged me to keep on writing, and to the sisters of Mission San Jose for lending me their house on Moss Beach, California, where I could give the book a final polish. I thank other Christians who have helped me to understand our common baptism, especially the Dean and canons of Salisbury Cathedral, of which I have the honour to be a Sarum Canon. I thank Robin Baird-Smith, my publisher and friend, for his endless encouragement, and all the enthusiastic and creative team at Continuum. I give thanks to my fellow novice David Sanders OP for our forty-six years of friendship in the Order. This book is dedicated to him in gratitude.

The First Sunday of Advent 2011

1

This child?

Baptism begins with questions. Adult candidates are asked: 'What is your name?'; 'What do you ask of God's Church?'; 'What does faith offer you?'; 'What do you desire?'; 'For what reason have you come?' The parents and godparents of a child are questioned too: 'What name do you give your child?'; 'What do you ask of God's Church for this child?'

Why does baptism begin with so many questions? Surely the minister ought to know the answers beforehand. This is because baptism must be freely chosen. We are baptized into Christ's freedom: 'For freedom Christ has set us free' (Gal. 5.1). So when in the fourth century the Church ceased to be persecuted and baptism became socially acceptable and even advantageous, it became vital to establish that people sought baptism freely, knowing what it meant. An Egyptian bishop quizzed the catechumens: 'Are you in two minds, or under pressure from anything, or driven by convention? For nobody mocks the kingdom of heaven, but it is given to those who love it with all their heart'.[1]

What sense then does it make to baptize babies? Would it not be better to wait until they are old enough to choose for themselves?

---

[1] The *Canons of Hippolytus* 19, quoted by Johnson, *Rites*, p. 117.

Immediately after his birth in the seventh century, St Rumwold was supposed to have cried out three times 'I am a Christian', preached a sermon, demanded baptism, and died three days old. Most infants are not as precocious! Isn't the baptism of an infant an empty ritual?

This was the position of the Anabaptists at the Reformation and of their spiritual descendants today. Baptism 'is not something that is done *for* one by the Church as part of becoming a Christian; rather, it is something done *by* one who has *already* become a Christian *by conversion*. In such a context, *true* baptism is impossible for an infant… Baptism must wait until a person can, on his own, give an account of faith, otherwise the rite becomes magical, a mechanisation of grace'.[2] That sounds sensible. Surely that respects both the freedom of the child and the meaning of the sacrament. It is worth lingering briefly over this preliminary question because often parents are plagued by doubts as to whether it is right to have their children baptized.

Babies have been baptized since the beginning of Christianity. This is the tradition of nearly all the major Churches: Catholic, Orthodox, Anglican, Lutheran and Calvinist. There was a tendency for a while in the fourth century to delay baptism but this was not because people doubted that children could be baptized but because it was seen as the great sacrament of forgiveness and so one did not want to waste it by being baptized before one had the opportunity to commit some really serious sins. So many people, like the first Christian Emperor Constantine, delayed baptism until the last moment. When St. Ambrose was chosen as bishop at the age of 35, he had to be baptized before he could be ordained. One did not want to squander a unique opportunity to wipe the slate clean. So the delay was due to doubts

---

[2] D. B. Stevik, 'Christian Initiation: Post-Reformation to the Present Era', in *Made, not Born: New Perspectives on Christian Initiation and the Catechumenate* (Notre Dame: Murphy Center for Liturgical Research, 1976), p. 105.

about the forgiveness of sins after baptism rather than about the validity of infant baptism.

In the Acts of the Apostles adults and their households were baptized, including the children. Just as today, some people were baptized because they had made a personal decision to become Christian and others because they were born into Christian families. Both cases show something fundamental about what it means be baptized. Faith is both a gift and also something we must embrace in a free decision.

Faith is not primarily a matter of choosing what to believe, as if one were a consumer in a spiritual supermarket, filling one's trolley with religious goods to match one's personal needs and preferences. Faith is our response to the astonishing discovery that we have been chosen. Paul did not weigh up the arguments for and against Christianity and then make a mature option for Jesus. God burst roughly into his life and threw him to the ground. He heard a voice: 'I am Jesus, whom you are persecuting, but rise and enter the city, and you will be told what you are to do' (Acts 9.5). Paul did not have much say in the matter. So God's choice of us precedes our choice of God. 'In this is love, not that we loved God but that he loved us and sent his Son to be the expiation of our sins' (1 John 4.10).

Infant baptism expresses the utter primacy of God's love. This precedes anything that we do or say. God says to Jeremiah: 'Before I formed you in the womb I knew you, and before you were born I consecrated you' (1.5). The very existence of a baby is already a gift from God. The parents say 'Yes' to this gift by cherishing the baby in the womb and preparing for its birth. And they say 'Yes' when they bring the child to baptism, because their child is created for no other reason than that it might share eternal life. Eternal life is not the icing on the cake of ordinary human life. It is what it means for us to be fully alive. They prepare for its arrival by ensuring that it has somewhere to live in their home and so it is right that they prepare a place for its home in God. To buy the cot but not ask for the baptism would be a half-hearted reception of the gift of the child.

At whatever age we are baptized, whatever we have done and been is irrelevant; none of our achievements matters. We may be a famous professor of philosophy or a newborn baby or a wino at the end of a drunken life; at the font we are all at the beginning of a new life in Christ. Few of us come to the font with quite as much past as Jacqueline de Romilly, a famous French Classical scholar, who was baptized at the age of 95, saying: 'It is high time!' Whatever our age, we are offered pure and unmerited love. We come to the font, whether as a baby or an adult, empty handed, as we shall come to God at the end of our lives, offered a love which is a free and unconditional gift.

Of course each of us has to embrace the life we have received. I must accept that I am this person, with this genetic inheritance, living in this time, rather than an eighteenth-century Chinese mandarin or a reincarnation of Napoleon. Likewise I must eventually freely accept or refuse who I am as a baptized child of God. But it would be a mistake to imagine that someone can only freely choose baptism if they are free from any external influences,[3] and so that we must just let children grow up and decide for themselves.

A mythical story is told of a Belgian family who could not decide whether to teach their son Flemish or French and so did not teach him any language at all, so that he could be free to choose when he was old enough. That is an impossible freedom! We are formed for freedom in our families and by education. Our parents need to take all sorts of decisions for and about their children so that we grow into free human beings. They teach us to speak their own language, push

---

[3] I wrote at length about freedom in 'Learning Spontaneity', in *What is the Point of Being a Christian?* pp. 29–48.

us to walk, and slowly introduce us into a way of life which is that of a free grown up. If they left their children entirely free to choose how to live and what to do, then we would never grow up humanly at all but become feral animals. Likewise it makes sense for parents to bring their children to baptism so that they may grow up in Christ's graced freedom. Then they will be truly free to choose whether to embrace the liberty of the children of God or not.

It is often asserted that faith is only authentic if it is grasped in a mature, adult and individual way. In some traditions, the crucial moment is when you confess Jesus Christ to be your personal saviour. But our appropriation of our faith may take the form of innumerable small decisions to walk in the light of the gospel. My acceptance of my divine life may be as gradual and imperceptible as my acceptance of my human life, beginning long before I am mature or adult. My mother was raised in a profoundly Christian home. She never had, to my knowledge, a Damascus experience. That did not make her faith inauthentic. Her 'Yes' to God consolidated slowly as she grew in the free atmosphere of a Christian home, beginning even before she could speak a word.

We are free persons only in community. In an episode of *The Living Planet*, David Attenborough shows a vast mass of black and white Emperor penguins, like a General Chapter of Dominicans, clinging together in a great, pinguid, gelatinous, fuggy clump. Each penguin had been hatched on the feet of its own father but in that bitterly cold and hostile environment, it could only survive in the midst of the community. There was a continual flow of warm penguins taking their turn at the frozen circumference of the huddle, and of frozen penguins plodding to the centre to warm up again.

In the corrosive, chilly climate of the modern secular West, it is as hard for a solitary individual to retain their faith as it is for an isolated penguin to survive in the Antarctic winter. Some of us are born into 'the household of faith', into families whose belief sustains us until we are old enough personally to embrace the faith. People answered those questions for us at our baptisms not because of a lack of respect for our freedom, but because of the conviction that to be human is to be made for God, and so one would no more deny the child baptism than one would refuse to give it milk until it asked for it. They said 'Yes' to our liberation in Christ, in the context of a society which often sees our greatest freedom as going shopping, or which is haunted by fatalism. The Christian community should form us in true freedom, challenging the passivity of those who think that we are determined by our genes or biological urges or the market. Then we shall be able freely to choose Christ's freedom or not.

What if the child is brought for baptism by a family which shows little sign of faith? What if the minister suspects that the parents want the child to be baptized just because they want to get it into a faith school, or to please the grandparents? What if one is unlikely ever to see the family in church again? What sense does baptism have then? This is the cause of a lot of heartache for many.

In a conversation with the priests of Brixen in the South Tyrol, Pope Benedict replied to a similar question. It concerned communion rather than baptism, but the same principles apply: 'When I was younger I was rather severe. I said: the sacraments are sacraments of faith, and where faith does not exist, where the practice of faith does not exist, the Sacrament cannot be conferred either... Then I too, with time, came to realize that we must follow, rather, the example of the Lord, who was very open even with people on the margins of Israel of that time. He was a Lord of mercy, open with sinners, welcoming them and letting them invite him to their dinners, drawing them into his communion'.[4]

---

[4] Vatican website, www.vatican.va.

If there are just the smallest hints of faith in the family, then surely it is right to baptize. First of all, because we must offer Christ's open hospitality to those who hang around on the edge. Secondly, because the baptized are members of the Church, even if they keep far away. Even if we are filled with doubts and hesitations, we share dimly in the faith of the Church so long as we do not explicitly reject it. The doubters, the questioners, even the lapsed, belong in the spacious household of faith.

St Cyprian, the third-century bishop of Carthage, believed that we should baptize babies because they made such a lot of noise! 'Immediately, on the very beginning of their birth, lamenting and weeping, they do nothing else but entreat'.[5] He believed that howling babies are begging for baptism. Crazy as this may sound, surely there is an implicit longing in every human being, even prior to consciousness, for that fullness of love which we name God. The baby may not know it, and may *never* know it in this life, but it is for God that we all cry out. And isn't secularized Europe hungry for its forgotten faith, like 'an infant crying in the night, an infant crying for the light, and with no language but a cry'?[6]

Some babies may never enter a church again, and their later search for meaning may lead them away from Christianity to other faiths or even to atheism, but it is our belief that somehow God will be with them, opening ways forward where there seem to be none, never giving up. This is why parents testify to their faith precisely by *not* fretting when their children wander far from the Church. To do so would be a denial of our faith in the God who leaves the ninety-nine safe sheep to look for the one who was lost.

---

[5] Epistle 64. Quoted in Johnson, *Rites*, p. 68.
[6] Acknowledgements to Abbot Gregory Collins, of Dormition Abbey, Jerusalem, for this application of the quote from Alfred Tennyson, 'In Memoriam'.

Becoming a child

So the baptism of babies expresses something at the heart of our faith, the absolute primacy of God's love for us. But it also suggests that to be alive as Christians, we must become childlike. 'At that time the disciples came to Jesus, saying, "Who is the greatest in the kingdom of God?" And calling to him a child, he put it in the midst of them, and said, "Truly, I say to you, unless you turn and become like children, you will never enter the kingdom of God' (Matt. 18.1-3); 'I thank you, Father, Lord of heaven and earth, that you have hidden these things from the wise and understanding and revealed them to babes' (Matt. 11.25). Jesus' invitation that we become children may seem to confirm what many atheists suspect, that religion makes us infantile, that it is a flight from the complexities of adulthood. Sister Ann Willits OP was asked at confirmation, aged nine, what was the sixth commandment, and replied: 'Thou shalt not commit adulthood!' Like Peter Pan, we Christians do not want to grow up but take refuge in an illusory and pious Neverland!

Our society suffers from an obsession with lost childhood. I was in Hollywood when Michael Jackson died, whose fantasy home was also called Neverland, and millions the world over mourned the loss of someone in whose anguished search for childhood they recognized themselves. Stories about children have an immense popularity: C. S. Lewis's *Narnia Chronicles*, Harry Potter at Hogwarts, young Frodo and his pals in *The Lord of the Rings*, Philip Pullman's *His Dark Materials* etc. These enchant us not just because they are beautifully written, and even profound, but because our society suffers from a crisis of childhood. Teenagers, even children as young as seven, were caught up in the riots on the streets of British cities in August 2011, robbing, looting and attacking. These young people seemed to have missed out on their childhood, and so how could they ever become truly adult? Maybe they never had that secure space, a healthy dependency on their parents in which to ripen, but were forced into a premature independence, already consumers when they should have been playing.

In baptism even adults become children of God. This does not pander to a flight from maturity because becoming a Christian, especially at confirmation, is also about growing up and becoming spiritually adult. The paradox of Christianity is that we can only be truly adult if we become childlike and we will only be childlike in a healthy way if we are set on the road to spiritual maturity. This first chapter is about becoming childlike and the last chapter of this book, on confirmation, will be about becoming grown up. These are inseparable dimensions of becoming alive in Christ. We are freed from both infantilism and tired old cynicism. The Chief Rabbi, Jonathan Sachs, wrote that 'societies start to grow old when they lose their faith in the transcendent. They then lose faith in an objective moral order and end by losing faith in themselves. But there is an alternative. The West can rediscover what Jeremiah called "the devotion of your youth"'.[7] In a world-weary age, believers should be provocatively youthful, even when we are old. What does that mean?

Human beings need a longer childhood than any other animal. The infancy of a fruit fly is over in a moment. Even a newborn elephant must be on its feet soon if it is to avoid being eaten by a lion. Chimpanzees grow up quickly. But we human beings need years to learn to become the people we are created to be. When we are born, our brains are only a third of their fully grown size, otherwise we could never make it down the birth canal.

God came to us in a baby who had a long childhood, adolescence and youth. According to Luke he disappeared, apart from his meeting

---

[7] 'China is reversing the decline and fall of Christianity', *The Times*, 21 May 2011.

with the teachers in the Temple, until he was thirty years old. Jesus took a much longer time growing up than his contemporaries, until he was ripe to preach the gospel. The new takes time to hatch and the one who 'makes all things new', more than most. If parents today complain of their children refusing to leave the nest, think of Mary and Joseph!

> 'When I say I hate time, Paul says
> How else could we find depth
> Of character, or grow souls?'[8]

Children should spend a lot of their time playing. When he was old Picasso liked to say: 'I have spent all my life learning to paint like a child'. Wisdom played in the presence of God when she created the world, and God made the Leviathan to play with it. In the Bible animals are often at play. And in the Kingdom 'the suckling child shall play over the hole of the asp' (Isa. 11.8) and 'the city shall be full of boys and girls playing in its streets' (Zech. 8.5).

Each of us is created to be *homo ludens*, a playful human being. It is an echo of our childhood and an anticipation of our heavenly destiny. If we forget how to play, then we will never be truly grown up. St Thomas Aquinas believed that an inability to play was a sign of moral weakness: 'Therefore, unmitigated seriousness betokens a lack of virtue because it wholly despises play, which is as necessary for a good human life as rest'.[9] St John the Evangelist was said to have spent his old age playing with his favourite partridge: 'Nay, mark how this old man plays with a bird, just like a boy!'[10] The fruit of a life

---

[8] Mark Doty, *The School of the Arts* (London, 2005), p. 84.

[9] *Eth. Ad Nic, IV, 16, 854*. Quoted by Hugo Rahner SJ, *Man at Play or Did you Ever Practice Eutrapelia* (London, 1965), p. 2.

[10] Ibid., p. 3.

well lived should not be a second childhood, but an abiding childlike ability to play, that prepares us for a ludic eternity. A child lives now, in the present, utterly absorbed in its games. Czesław Miłosz wrote of his childhood: 'I lived without yesterday or tomorrow, in the eternal present'.[11] This is the wisdom of the child, for no other moment exists except now. And it is a prefiguring of the eternity of paradise.

The point of play is that it is pointless, done just for its own sake. Terry Eagleton compares it to jazz:

> What we need is a form of life which is completely pointless, just as the jazz performance is pointless. Rather than serve some utilitarian purpose or earnest metaphysical end, it is a delight in itself. It needs no justification beyond its own existence. In this sense the meaning of life is interestingly close to meaning-lessness. Religious believers who find this version of the meaning of life a little too laid-back for comfort should remind themselves that God, too, is his own end, ground, origin, reason and self-delight, and that only by living this way can human beings be said to share his life.[12]

Playing develops our imaginative life. Being made in the image of God, we can reimagine the world. Frank Ahrens, creator of the cartoon Calvin and Hobbs, stated: 'Adults lose the capacity for fantasy though we probably need it more. It is beaten out of us by things that are knowable'. I remember the imaginative richness of my own childhood, the inexpressible vibrancy of a red letter box, a dead tree trunk in the woods which was a castle to be defended or a pirate's galleon to be boarded. There were also the terrors of childhood, the dread of climbing up to my bedroom at night, avoiding horrors

---

[11] Czesław Miłosz, *Proud to be a Mammal* (London, 2010), p. 80.
[12] Terry Eagleton, *The Meaning of Life: A Very Short Introduction* (Oxford, 2007), pp. 100–1.

at every turn of the staircase. When it was my turn to lock up the chickens at night, I always took a big stick to beat off any tigers that I might meet on the way. I performed unnoticed feats of heroism. The child expresses something essential to our humanity, which is our capacity for the new. Hannah Arendt called this 'the human condition of natality'.[13] 'With each new birth something uniquely new comes into the world'. Every child is unknown at birth, even to its parents. We can only guess what he or she will be like. Arendt says that of every child we ask the question, 'Who are you?' At the font we are baptized into Christ's own newness, God's eternal freshness. We baptize children so that as members of Christ's body they may face challenges that we cannot anticipate, and build a Church which we cannot imagine. We baptize children so that they will not be like us.

Dietrich Bonhoeffer, the great Lutheran theologian, was hanged by the Nazis on 9 April 1945, 23 days before they surrendered. It was a dark time, when he could see no way forward. He wrote a letter to his newborn nephew, Dietrich Bethge, for his baptism. The baby was a sign of hope for a new world that Bonhoeffer could not imagine, a new beginning:

> All those great ancient words of the Christian proclamation will be spoken over you, and the command of Jesus Christ to baptize will be carried out on you, without you knowing anything about it... It is not for us to prophecy the day (though the day will come) when people will once more be called so to utter the word of God that the world will be changed and renewed by it. It will be a new language, perhaps quite non-religious, but liberating and redeeming – as was Jesus' language; it will be the language of a new

---

[13] Hannah Arendt, *The Human Condition* (New York, 1958), chapter V, section entitled 'The Disclosure of the Agent in Speech and Action'.

righteousness and truth, proclaiming God's peace with men and the coming of his Kingdom.[14]

Young Dietrich Bethge was to be baptized for this new world, which his uncle could not anticipate. We remain childlike by keeping our imaginations alive, refusing to be bound by the status quo, open to God's fresh grace.

Another quality of childhood is confidence. Children begin by trusting. Without this confidence, children can be neither imaginative nor playful:

> I have calmed and quieted my soul,
> Like a child quieted at its mother's breast
> Like a child that is quieted is my soul.
> O Israel, hope in the Lord
> From this time forth and for evermore (Ps. 129.2-3).

Lytta Basset, a Swiss theologian and mother, sees confidence as one of the fundamental qualities of the child which is so often destroyed: 'Sooner or later every human being knows the destruction of confidence. But to destroy in another – an adult or even more a child – its confidence in another, whether this is by lies, betrayal, abandonment or manipulation, is to attack that spiritual link which gives sense to one's earthly life'.[15]

This is why the sexual abuse of children and young people is so terrible, especially by ministers of Christ. It is an assault not just on their childhood but on what is central to their humanity: their confidence, their trust in other people, their playfulness and light-heartedness. Of course the victims of sexual abuse cannot easily

---

[14] 'Thoughts on the baptism of D. W. R.', in *Letters and Papers from Prison*, ed. Eberhard Bethge (London, 1967), pp. 171–72.

[15] Lytta Basset, *Une spiritualité d'enfant* (Paris, 2011), p. 12. My translation.

let go what has happened, because it stains every day of their adult lives. Alas, this is just part of a worldwide sexual exploitation of children, millions of children taken from their parents for prostitution, especially in Asia. Plane loads of men fly from the West and Japan to abuse children.

This, in turn, is just part of the vaster problem of the physical and emotional abuse of children all over the world. Think of the millions of young girls who suffer genital circumcision. It is estimated that between 100 million and 157 million women have undergone this dangerous, humiliating mutilation, over two million every year, 6,000 a day, mainly in Africa and the Arabian peninsula. In *What is the What*, the lightly fictionalized autobiography of a Sudanese boy, Valentino Achak Deng tells of his lost childhood, as he fled from the Sudan to Kenya.

> I know everything one can know about the wasting of youth, about the ways boys can be used. Of those boys with whom I walked, about half became soldiers eventually. And were they all willing? Only a few. They were twelve, thirteen years old, little more, when they were conscripted. We were all used, in different ways. We were used for war, we were used to garner food and the sympathy of humanitarian-aid organisations. Even when we went to school, we were being used.[16]

Thousands of child soldiers who should be playing with toys are taught to kill. Their hearts are chilled and become stone, not flesh. Take the example of James Saah, a Liberian child soldier cared for by the Catholic Overseas Development Agency (CAFOD):

> The first time James Saah fired an AK47 the recoil tossed his tiny frame into the air and he fell flat onto his back, knocking

---

[16] Dave Eggers, *What is the What* (London, 2008), p. 47.

the breath from his body. Then, he was eight years old: James has learned a lot since then. Today, at little more than nine, the emaciated and bedraggled boy is a veteran soldier of the brutal four-year war in Liberia that claimed the lives of more than four million people. He has spent the past 12 months as a drug-fuelled executioner with the government forces, and he learned to revel in his work: James's job was to finish off with his Kalashnikov the rebel captives after they had been tortured and maimed... Last week, as James crouched under a makeshift hut, sheltering from the torrential rain that marked the beginning of the country's rainy season, he plucked at the tail of his tattered and outsized T-shirt – the only clothing he possesses. His eyes glued to the ground, he says bleakly: 'I can't remember the last time anyone kissed or hugged me – but my commander would praise me when I fought well. He called me a big man.[17]

Our Churches should be places where the trust of children is cherished. Jean Vanier, the founder of L'Arche, tells the extraordinary story of how, when he was 13 years old in 1943, he went to see his father to ask if he could cross the Atlantic to train for the Royal Navy to take part in the war. His father was the Governor General of Canada. On that day he taught Jean one of the most important lessons of his life. He trusted him.

Because my father said, 'I trust that your desire is a holy desire, a desire that comes from what is right and from what is God', then I could trust myself. I believe deeply that in children and young people a light is present. We must listen to children. We must hear what they have to say. They are people in whom the light of God

---

[17] 'The boy soldiers of Liberia', Olga Craig *Daily Telegraph*, 14 September 2003. To be found on the CAFOD website, www.cafod.org.uk.

exists. They will never be able to trust themselves unless someone trusts them.[18]

Trust is often lost as children grow up in a harsh and manipulative world, but that is a trust that we must renew if we are to embark on the venture of faith. The trust of the child, perhaps asleep at its own baptism, is a sign of what we must find again.

There is an Afghani saying that 'you are not a man until you give your love, truly and freely, to a child. And you are not a good man until you earn the love, truly and freely, of a child in return'.[19] How sad it is that even parents hardly dare to hug other people's children, that teachers, doctors and nurses live in fear of accusation and that priests must always be in the presence of other adults when they talk to a child. What sort of womb will the font be for the children of God until we learn and earn trust again?

So when we bring a child to the font to be baptized, we are entrusting him to Christ, forever the child of Bethlehem and the eternal Son of the Father. We are praying that this child may indeed have a childhood and so become an adult child of God with something of Christ's fresh spontaneity. At the font we commit ourselves to build communities in which children can grow in confidence and whose trust in adults will not be abused.

> Be here, then, with the undefended child,
> Turn back the predator, the wild,
> The ruthless – kindle here
> Moments of mercy, rescue from fear.[20]

---

[18] Jean Vanier, *Images of Love, Words of Hope* (Hainesport, 1991), p. 52.

[19] Gregory David Roberts, *Shantaram* (London, 2005), p. 353.

[20] John W. Bowker, *Before the Ending of the Day: Life and Love, Death and Redemption* (Toronto, 2010).

I asked Philippe Denis, a Belgian Dominican who works with Aids orphans in South Africa, what light childhood sheds on baptism. He replied:

> We should not idealise children. They also have their problems. Yet all children are – or can become – resilient. Despite enormous challenges, they have the ability to bounce back. They can seize the opportunities which come their way. Again this is how we are in front of God. We are wounded and traumatised, yet resilient. We can seize opportunities… In that sense also we, the baptized, are like children.

Baptism is like dew on that deep human resilience. It nurtures the strength of children which helps them to endure terrible sufferings and deprivations and still grow up humanly, wounded but unbeaten. And if we come to baptism as adults, it is in the hope that God will 'renew our youth like an eagle's' (Psalm 103.5). Even the fragile come to the font to be touched by God's eternal resilience.

I become irritated when people in middle age begin to complain: 'We are getting old'. Once, at a retreat for a diocese in the United States, I came across a group of priests in their forties and fifties. I asked them what they were talking about: 'Our retirement plans!' Rabbi Nashman of Breslev rightly said 'It is forbidden to become old'.[21] This is nothing to do with running away from aging or denying our mortality. This we must face, as we shall see when we look at our immersion in the waters of death and resurrection. We grow old well when we let God's grace work within us a perpetual renewal, childlike to the end.

---

[21] Basset, *Une spiritualité d'enfant*, p. 105.

The righteous shall flourish like the palm tree, and grow like a cedar of Lebanon.

They are planted in the house of the Lord, They will flourish in the courts of our God.

They still bring forth fruit in old age, they are ever full of sap and green,

To show that the Lord is upright; he is my rock in whom there is no unrighteousness (Ps. 92.12-15).

2

What name?

Baptism begins with asking questions and the first question concerns the candidate's name. Adults are asked 'What is your name?' At the beginning of Lent, the names of those being instructed for baptism are written down in a register, for now they are members of 'the household of Christ'. They have begun to belong. One of the earliest ways of describing asking for baptism was 'to give in one's name'.[1] The first question put to the parents of a child at baptism is: 'What name do you give your child?'

One of Adam's first tasks in Genesis is to name. God brought all the animals to Adam 'to see what he would call them; and whatever the man called them, that was its name' (2.19). Naming is not just sticking labels on things, so that we remember what they are. We share in God's creation of an ordered, significant world.

Everything exists because God called it into being by name. In the beginning God says 'Let there be light' and there was light; let there be the sun and the moon; let there be trees and vegetables, birds and fish. God 'calls into existence the things that do not exist' (Rom. 4.17). This is not an explanation of the Universe in competition with

---

[1] Edward Yarnold, *The Awe-Inspiring Rites of Initiation: Baptismal Homilies of the Fourth Century* (Slough, 1971), p. 7.

theories of the Big Bang or Darwinian evolution. It is recognition of the astonishing gratuity of anything existing at all, the miracle that there is anything rather than nothing. Everything that exists says 'Yes' to God just by being itself. 'The stars shone in their watches and were glad; he called them and they said, "Here we are!" They shone with gladness for him who made them' (Bar. 3.34). Stars joyfully say Yes to God by shining. This is not a denial of any scientific explanation of the birth of stars, of red giants and blue dwarfs. In fact scientific understanding can help us to arrive at wonder, a tiny glimpse of the astonishing gratuity of existence.

We collaborate with God, giving names that bring to light what things are. The invention of languages, the seven thousand different tongues of humanity, the naming of plants and mountains, the fine nuances of words for music, medical languages, poetic language, the tender language of love, legal languages, philosophical languages, scientific languages, the obscure words for the cyber-world, jargon, dialects, all these belong to perpetual struggle to make sense of our world. God 'did not create the world a chaos; he formed it to be inhabited' (Isa. 45.18). When we name anything, we are sharing in God's creation of a meaningful world in which we can flourish.

But Adam needs more than the animals. He names Eve, who in turn will call him by name. Human beings flourish when we name each other. The creation of babies is more than just the penetration of the egg by the sperm leading to pregnancy and birth. The baby is named so that it may be addressed and come to respond. Its parents and family will hover over it, making strange faces, pinching its fat cheeks and calling it by name. One comes alive in being named in love. One's name is safe in the mouth of those who cherished you. When you love someone, it is impossible not to bring their name into conversation. Their name is on your tongue. You relish it. This is one of the ways that we give away the secret of our growing affection for someone: 'Mary loved that film too; Mary is going on holiday to Barcelona next year; Mary also loves curry'.

Father Gregory Boyle, a Jesuit who cares for the young caught up in the gang wars of Los Angeles, quickly learned that his first task was to discover their names. They are often surprised that he even wants to know, and so a frequent response is: 'Who? Me?' He has to gently persuade them to reveal their names, getting beyond their nicknames, their surnames, their formal names, to the names that their mothers call them when they are not angry. Boyle describes one such moment with a child nicknamed Sniper: 'I watch him go to some far, distant place – a location he has not visited in some time. His voice, body, language, whole being are taking on a new shape – right before my eyes. "Sometimes," his voice so quiet, I lean in – "sometimes…when my mom's not mad at me…she calls me…Napito"'.[2] No wonder the walls of our cities are covered by scrawled names. These are kids who need to remind themselves that they have names. They may 'disfigure' our cities, but each graffito recalls someone whose face awaits recognition.

Parents choose names for all sorts of reasons: because of where the child was conceived – Paris Hilton, Brooklyn Beckham – or because the name belongs to a member of the family or a friend, or because the name is that of a celebrity, a member of the Royal Family (William is a popular boys' name in Britain), or a footballer, or film star, or pop singer. Names show how we are the fruit of the past, how we belong in the present, and our parents' dreams for our future.

But names can also be used to express contempt or to denigrate people. Slave owners in the States refused to use their slaves' African names. They imposed new names: Billy, Tom, Beth. Joseph Bruchac,

---

[2] Gregory Boyle, *Tattoos on the Heart: The Power of Boundless Compassion* (New York, 2010), p. 54.

a Native American of Abenaki descent, shows in a poem called 'Baptism' how names can open us to life, or oppress us:

> Believing that people
> were or became
> what they were named,
> they rose with the Sun,
> called themselves Eagle,
> Fox, Otter, Hawk, Wild
> Bear and Deer.
>
> Then new ones came,
> those who named
> themselves for forgotten memories,
> great-grandfathers seeking
> hard dominion over rock and stream,
> ownership of forest and plain,
> with names of Farmer, Smith, and Weaver,
> Joiner, Carpenter, Stoner, Wright.
>
> Then they gave
> the first people new names,
> Government men and preachers smiled
> as they christened Washingtons,
> Wilsons, Garcias, Smiths –
> and waited for them to change.
>
> Yet even today,
> when the newest names,
> Citizen, Band, Breeder Reactor,
> Missile Range, Strip Mine and Pipe Line
> have begun to move in,
> residing where Bark Lodge, Wigwam

and Tipi, Wickiup and Hogan stood,
things have not ended as they should.

Somewhere, it is whispered,
at some ragged edge
of the unfinished land
the Sun is rising, breathing again
names which we have not yet heard,
names about to be spoken.[3]

When the Nazis came to power in Germany and Austria, they stamped the identity cards of Jews with new first names. All the men were called 'Israel' and the women, 'Sara'. These names both identified people as Jews, but also wiped out their individuality. It was a foretaste of what was to come at Auschwitz, a parody of true naming, an unmaking of God's creation.

The names of most people are forgotten a few years after their death. They disappear without trace. In Alan Bennett's *The History Boys*, Hector, the teacher, explains Thomas Hardy's 'Drummer Hodge' to one of his pupils:

The important thing is that he *has* a name. Say Hardy is writing about the Zulu wars or later the Boer war possibly, these were the first campaigns when soldiers…common soldiers…were commemorated, the names of the dead recorded and inscribed on war memorials. Before this, soldiers…private soldiers anyway, were all unknown soldiers, and so far from being revered there was a firm in the nineteenth century, in Yorkshire of course, which swept up their bones from the battlefields of Europe in order to grind them down into fertiliser.[4]

---

[3] With permission of the author.
[4] Alan Bennett, *The History Boys* (London, 2004), p. 55.

When we are baptized, our names are recorded. This is more than merely a record of our membership of the Church, as when one joins a club or receives citizenship. It is a sign that our names are treasured by God. We are enrolled as members of Christ's household and so we belong to the One who never forgets anyone: 'Can a woman forget her suckling child, that she should have no compassion of the son of her womb? Even these may forget yet I will not forget you. Behold I have graven you on the palms of my hand' (Isa. 49.15).

Herbert McCabe wrote 'We are not just human beings but human becomings… For us to be is to have a lifetime, a development…our lifetime is a life story'.[5] And we are changed by entering into conversations which stretch us open. Our names do not just identify us, they summon us to reply, to join the conversation, and so become the people whom God created us to be. St Catherine of Siena said to Stefano di Corrada Maconi: 'Be who God meant you to be and you will set Italy on fire'.[6] In the Bible God calls people by new names as a sign that they have a new vocation of the creation of his people. Abram and Sarai become Abraham and Sarah (Gen. 17) because they will become the ancestors of a vast nation, more numerous than the stars. Jacob becomes Israel (32.29) as the father of the twelve tribes, and Simon becomes Peter, the Rock, the one on whom Jesus will build his Church.

In all these ways in which we are named, we are called to flourish or we are denigrated and oppressed. Our names are called with love or with contempt. In all the loving ways in which we are addressed – by our parents, our friends, our spouses – there is an

---

[5] Herbert McCabe, OP, *God Still Matters* (London, 2002), p. 189.
[6] Quoted during the wedding of the Duke and Duchess of Cambridge, though 'the world' was substituted for 'Italy', for understandable reasons. *Lettres de Sainte Catherine de Sienne*, trans. E. Cartier, Vol. III, Paris 1858, CCLXIX (261), p. 314.

echo of God's address to us. Augustine wonders why God was silent during his childhood and then he realizes that all the time God had been addressing him through his mother: 'Then whose words were they but yours which you were chanting in my ears through my mother, your faithful servant?'[7] This is God beginning to call us into friendship and freedom.

Our personal names may be suggestive of who we are to become, our vocation. Luke's gospel begins with Zechariah in the Temple being told the name that he is to give the son shortly to be born: 'You shall call his name John' (1.13). John was not a family name. The name 'John' implies that he will be free of his family for a vocation which they could not yet understand or imagine. His father has to let him go for the Lord's work:

> And on the eighth day they came to circumcise the child and they would have named him Zechariah after his father, but his mother said, 'Not so, his name shall be John'. And they said to her, 'None of your family is called by this name'. And they made signs to his father, inquiring what he would have him called. And he asked for a tablet, and wrote: 'His name is John'. And immediately his mouth was opened and his tongue loosed and, he spoke, blessing God (Lk. 1.59-63).

'John' was a common name. It means: 'The Lord has been gracious'. Usually the graciousness was the gift of the child itself. But here it expresses the baby's vocation, to be the one who proclaims that in his cousin Jesus, God's grace is breaking into our lives. So names can be signs of our destiny.

Gregory David Roberts is an Australian who had lived a life of crime and violence before being sent to prison. He escaped and made

---

[7] *Confessions* Bk 2.7, trans Henry Chadwick (Oxford, 1991), p. 27.

his way to India. In a lightly fictionalized autobiography, he describes how he gradually discovered who he was called to be. A turning point was a stay in an Indian village. The village women gave him a new name, Shantaram, which means 'the man of peace', or 'the man of God's peace'.

He arrived in that village as a hardened criminal. His face and body said: 'Don't mess with me'. But the villagers could not read this Australian's body language, and every time that he tried to look tough, they laughed and patted him on the shoulder. And then they gave him his new name, which he received as his vocation, standing by a river in the rain:

> I do not know if they found that name in the heart of the man they believed me to be, or if they planted it there, like a wishing stick, to bloom and grow. Whatever the case, whether they discovered that peace or created it, the truth is that the man I am was born in those moments, as I stood near the flood with my face lifted to the chrismal rain. Shantaram. The better man that, slowly, and much too late, I began to be.

My parents called their children after the saints on whose feast we were born, as long as it was not too ghastly. I was born on the feast of Sts Timothy, Hippolytus and Symphorianus. I got off lightly, though my great uncle who baptized me used to write to me at school as Master Timothy Hippolytus Symphorianus Radcliffe, which caused a lot of mockery. 'Timothy' means: 'The one who honours God'. This does not describe me accurately. My name is an invitation to become that person. Not all names evoke a journey to be made. A friend of mine is called 'Graham' which I am told means 'gravel pit', which is not, I hope, his glorious destiny! *The Importance of Being Ernest*, by Oscar Wilde, plays upon how a name may or may not promise a future. The beloved would only marry someone with a dignified name like Ernest.

Members of religious Orders often take new names when they commit themselves to a new way of life. I was threatened by the novice master with the name 'Cuckoofat'. He may have been a fine Spanish saint, but I could not have survived a week as Cuckoofat Radcliffe!

So when a child is named at baptism, it is given more than a convenient label. It is being prepared for participation in the conversation of those who love it. Naming the child in love is the food that will help it grow into a human being capable of calling others in love too. But this conversation is sacramental of our entry into conversation with God, which will transform us in ways that we cannot anticipate. We may fear to get entangled with God, not knowing what will become of us. It is dangerous to let go of control of our identity. Will we be ourselves anymore, or become inhumanly pious, cardboard saints? Augustine cried out, 'O Lord, let me remain Augustine!'[8] But God's grace only transforms us so that we may indeed become fully ourselves, at the end of the journey, when we shall share in the eternal loving conversation which is the Trinity.

Jesus was named at his baptism by his Father: 'You are my beloved Son; With you I am well pleased' (Mk 1.11). At baptism, we too are taken up into the Father's delight in the Son. God takes pleasure in us. Meister Eckhart wrote: 'God is so besotted in His love for us, it is just as if He had forgotten heaven and earth and all His Blessedness and all his Godhead and had no business except with me alone, to give me everything for my comforting.'[9] We do not literally hear God speaking to us. It is said that when we address God we are praying, but if we think that we hear God addressing us, we probably have

---

[8] Quoted by Adolphe Gesché, *La Destinée* (Paris, 1995), p. 109.
[9] Sermon 79 in Maurice O'C. Walshe, *Meister Eckhart: Sermons and Treatises*, Vol. II (London and Shaftesbury, 1981), p. 307.

problems! But we begin to hear God's delight in the voice of our parents and friends, and we learn to respond.

So the baptized life is a vocation; it is to be someone who says Yes to God, and who is embarked on a journey. We are called by name not just once, at the font. We go on being called by God until we see God face to face. We are called at confirmation with a name we have chosen ourselves. This is a sign of our maturity as people who can mould their own destiny. Our names are spoken when we declare our love for someone at marriage or in moments of intimacy. Our names are called when we assume some new responsibility, or when we are ordained priests, and finally they are written on our tombs as we await the voice that calls us to eternal life. Jesus calls to his friend: 'Lazarus, come out' (Jn 11.43). I wished to use that quote as the title of a talk in Los Angeles, but I was discouraged from doing so on the grounds that it might suggest that Lazarus was gay.

Finally, the Book of Revelation writes that to the one who conquers 'I will give a white stone, with a new name written on the stone which no one knows except him who receives it' (2.17). This is one of the most mysterious passages of a mysterious book,[10] but the thrust is clear. Finally in God we shall discover who we are. Our identity is to be discovered in Christ. When we are named at baptism, it is not so as to give us a fixed identity once and for all but to invite us to enter into a conversation with God and all his friends, in which it will eventually be disclosed who we are called to be. Just as we draw closer to God by being freed of false ideas of God so the baptized become themselves by letting go of false self-images, liberated from identities which are denigrating or define us in opposition to others, or because they are too small. 'For only he who lives his life as a mystery is truly alive.'[11]

---

[10] Cf. Roland H. Worth Jr, *The Seven Cities of the Apocalypse and Greco-Asian Culture* (Mahwah, NJ:, 1999), pp. 143–53.

[11] Stefan Zweig, quoted by Ali Smith, *There but for the* (London, 2011), frontispiece.

3

Commandments and claim

Our baptism began with us being called by name. God delights in us and calls us to share his love and freedom. Our life is a vocation, a journey into the liberty of the children of God. It may seem a bit of a letdown that at a child's baptism the minister then asks the parents and godparents if they will accept the responsibility to train the child in the practice of the faith and in obedience to God's commandments. We appear to have slipped from an unconditional love to the ecclesiastical world of obedience and discipline. The child must be taught to obey the rules! At this point, people may get a little tense, wondering whether they really want this child's life to be so constrained.

And then the child is claimed for Christ and welcomed by the community. It is as if the Church wants to grab the child from its parents and enrol it in the narrow and sometimes suffocating world of the Church, with its prejudices and occasional intolerance. At this point, one might begin to wonder whether baptism is really such a good idea after all. It is fine to celebrate the God lovingly calling us by name, but do we really want to promise to raise the child to be obedient to laws and to belong to a Church? God loves everyone, and so why get stuck in some arrogant organization that seems to claim moral superiority? We must face these hesitations, and see how this stage of the baptism reveals a little more of the mystery of God's love for us.

Obedience

In the Catholic rite the parents and godparents are asked if they accept the responsibility to raise the child in the practice of the faith and to 'keep God's commandments as Christ taught us, by loving God and our neighbour'.

Why, right at the beginning of baptism, do we talk of obedience to commandments? This appears to suggest that the child is being baptized into a community of the righteous, those who do God's will. But Christ said 'I came to call not the righteous but sinners' (Matt. 9.13). Jesus ate and drank with tax collectors and prostitutes, with Pharisees and priests, with lawyers and thieves. But often our churches are not seen as offering such a welcome. They are thought to be intolerant, shutting the door on people because their lives do not conform to Christian moral teaching, because they are divorced and remarried, or because they are gay or have had an abortion. In a society which is ever more tolerant our churches are often thought of as the last bastions of prejudice, teaching a moral vision which is out of touch and shuts out most of humanity.

This same tension between moral teaching and unbounded hospitality is also found in Jesus. He was demanding. He said that if we are to be his disciples, we must take up our cross every day and follow him. We must be perfect as God is perfect. Jesus was not a wishy-washy liberal. And yet he welcomed everyone, he was a friend to those who were despised, sinners could eat and drink at his table without being required first to repent. Richard Burridge maintains that Jesus 'kept bad company while teaching good morals.'[1] How did he manage to do both at once?

Commandments in the Bible are not primarily rules to which one must submit. From the sixteenth century, the Ten Commandments began to be displayed in Protestant Churches. These were the requirements of God's will to which we must submit. People examined their consciences with reference to them. There was a Polish Dominican chaplain in the Second World War who, on the eve of the battle of Monte Casino, opened his tent and was alarmed to see thousands of Polish soldiers waiting to go to confession, preparing themselves to face death. What could he do? There was no time to see them all. He had them all lie face down, so that no one could see anyone else. And he said, 'I will go through the Ten Commandments. If you have broken one, waggle your left foot and with your right foot indicate how many times'. It was an admirable solution but it might give the impression that the moral life was about passing a test. One might feel sympathy for Bertrand Russell who said that the Ten Commandments should be treated like an examination paper: No candidate should attempt more than six.

But the Chief Rabbi of Great Britain, Jonathan Sacks, once told me that in the Hebrew Bible there is no word for 'to obey' in the modern sense of submission of one's will to an external power. When the State of Israel was founded after the last World War, it was necessary to borrow a word from Aramaic for 'obey' in this modern sense. Instead there was obedience as 'listening'. Indeed the Latin word from which we get 'obedience' means listening intently: *ob-audiens*. We are asked

---

[1] Richard Burridge, *Imitating Jesus: An Inclusive Approach to New Testament Ethics* (Grand Rapids, MI, 2007), p. 72.

to listen to the Lord our God. The commandments are not so much an external constraint as an invitation to be attentive to God: 'I am the Lord your God, who brought you out of the land of Egypt, out of the house of bondage. You shall have no other gods before me' (Exod. 20.2-3). The Ten Commandments are not the imposition of God's arbitrary will. They form us for his friendship and freedom. They are given to Israel through Moses to whom God spoke as to a friend. They are a tough apprenticeship in the freedom of friendship. Any friendship worthy of the name is demanding, and none more so than friendship with God.

Jesus revealed his new commandment to his disciples on the night before he died, that they should love one another, at just the moment that he claimed them as his friends. 'I have called you friends, for all that I have heard from my Father I have made known to you' (Jn 15.15). Commandments in the Bible are given in the context of friendship with God and each other. They are not about control but the formation of a heart and mind for mutuality. They are the vastly demanding invitation to grow up into the true, genuine, equal love which is the Trinity. We are indeed loved without condition, but God's friendship, like any friendship, transforms us.

This has profound consequences for how the Church teaches morality, which can only be done in friendship. The media often look to Church leaders to make statements on moral issues. We are expected to lay down the law. If we fail to do so, then we shall be dismissed as vague and liberal. If we do so, then we shall be dismissed as conservative and bossy. But we cannot address people from above, as it were, like God's police. It is only when we are close to people, sharing their challenges, their hopes, fears, and their temptations, that we have anything to say. Joseph Pieper paraphrased Aquinas thus: 'A friend, that is a prudent friend, can help to shape a friend's decision. He does so by virtue of that love which makes the friend's problem his own, and the friend's ego his own'.[2] So we can only discover what to say on any moral issue with people, listening together, hearing with their ears the teaching of the gospels and the Church, standing in their shoes, torn by their dilemmas, knowing their pain and joy as our own. Then, with them, the right word may be given.

Jesus' enemies often try to trap him by asking questions to which there seem to be no right answers: Should we pay taxes to Caesar or not? If he says yes, then he is a collaborator with the enemy; if he says no, then he is a political rebel. This woman has committed adultery. Should she be stoned as the law requires? If he says Yes, then he is cruel; if he says no, then he is rejecting God's own law. But Jesus' answers bring people beyond these narrow alternatives. It is not that he is cunningly evading the trap. God's friendship opens up new spaces that no one could have anticipated. Obedience is not ticking the right box, it is being summoned into a new space.

Usually our ways of seeing the world are deeply dualistic: day/night; good/bad; black/white; male/female; body/soul. Often these dualisms signal the oppositions which give people identity: us/them; right/wrong; liberal/conservative. Our politics, our sport, our loves and antagonisms are usually understood in terms of sharp alternatives. Each side wants to enlist Jesus on its side, liberals appealing to Jesus' open welcome of everyone, and conservatives to his moral demands. We go on trying to trap Jesus, as did the scribes and Pharisees before us, using the gospel for our own purposes. Jesus is right because he agrees with me! And yet the voice of the Good Shepherd calls us out of our narrow sheepfolds into the wide open space of God's vast surprising love. The Sufi poet Rumi wrote: 'Out beyond our ideas of right and wrong there's a field. I'll meet you there.'[3]

---

[2] Joseph Pieper, *Four Cardinal Virtues* (Notre Dame, 1966), p. 29.
[3] Jelaluddin Rumi Coleman Barks, *The Essential Rumi* (San Franscisco, 1995), p. 36.

A Trinitarian love liberates us beyond such binary oppositions. We are caught up into the love of the Father for the Son and the Son for the Father which is the Holy Spirit. This is a love which is utterly mutual but which overflows beyond itself. So being caught up into the life of the Trinity carries us beyond the narrow little infatuations and antagonisms that confine human beings. We are brought into an ever larger space. St Gregory Nazianzus says that we are carried from the dyad to the triad![4]

So faced with the tension between clear moral teaching and open hospitality, we offer God's friendship which may eventually bring us to new places in which fidelity to the exigent moral teaching of the gospel and Christ's unconditional welcome are reconciled, perhaps in ways that we could never have anticipated. And so training the child in the practice of the faith and in obedience to God's commandments is never a matter of suffocating a young person by narrow moral strictures. Of course every child needs to learn the security of a clear moral universe. There are moral absolutes, summed up, for example, in the Ten Commandments. But as the young grow and question the teachings of our Churches, then we must accompany them, attentive to their hesitations, as together we journey into the mystery of a love which exceeds our imagination. This is not relativism but true obedience, which is always surprising.

I claim you for Christ

Then the priest says: 'The Christian community welcomes you with great joy. In its name I claim you for Christ our Saviour by the sign

---

[4] Andrew Louth, 'St Gregory the Theologian and St Maximus the Confessor: The Shaping of Tradition', in Sarah Coakley and David Arthur Palin (eds), *The Making and Remaking of Christian Doctrine: Essays in Honour of Maurice Wiles* (Oxford, 1993), pp. 126–27.

of the cross. I now trace the cross on your forehead and invite your parents and godparents to do the same'.

Why should the baby be claimed by this cleric for Christ and the Church? I was just three days old when I was baptized. I was barely born when my parents gave me away. My mother was not even there, still in bed, as was the custom at the time. This sounds almost scandalous, baby snatching! And yet the baby's parents love their child best by giving it away at baptism, which is just a foretaste of all the times they will have to give it away, to friends, to live its own life, to belong to another in love. This is the paradox of Christian love, that it cherishes the other most in letting them go.

Jesus would have most startled his contemporaries by breaking away from his family.

> In Nazareth, family was everything: one's birthplace, life school and job security. Outside the family an individual was unpro-tected, unsafe... Thus leaving one's family of origin was a bizarre and risky decision. But at some point Jesus did just that. His family, even his extended family, must have seemed too small. He was looking for a 'family' big enough for everyone who was willing to do God's will.[5]

This was surely the root of his scandalous decision not to be married. This would have shocked his neighbours; it would have been seen as a gross dereliction of his religious duty to his ancestors not to perpetuate his family. Later rabbis said: 'Seven things are condemned in heaven, and the first of these is a man without a woman'. Jesus was close to women and cherished their friendship and dignity, but he was alive with a love that necessarily overflowed any limits.

---

[5] José A. Pagola, *Jesus, An Historical Approximation* (Miami, 2009), p. 58.

It is into this vast love that we are baptized, and so our parents love us most in heeding the claim of Christ and letting us go. This Triune love which we see at Jesus' baptism is paradoxical. The voice of the Father is heard saying, 'You are my Son, the beloved, with you I am well pleased' (Mk 1.8). The Father loves the Son in particular, he is the uniquely beloved, the chosen one. But the Spirit descends on him like a dove. This is the Father and Son's overflowing love, opening a space for us. A Trinitarian love breaks open any narrow infatuation, any introverted mutuality, so that there is a place for us all. In St John's gospel, the last words of the Son to the Father before he goes to die promise its openness. He prays 'that the love with which you have loved me may be in them and I in them' (Jn 17.26).

God's love is always particular and universal. Our loves aspire to become so. I love my wife, my husband, this person, this child, this friend in particular. My love cherishes their precious uniqueness. Love drives us to say: 'It is wonderful that you exist'.[6] In *Gilead*, the extraordinary novel by Marilynne Robinson, an elderly Protestant pastor talks to his child of his mother's love: 'She has watched every moment of your life, almost, and she loves you as God does, to the marrow of your bones. So love the *being* of someone. Your existence is a delight to us'.[7] One loves the back of the beloved's neck, the small hairs on an arm, a fierce intelligence, a laugh, and the vulnerable look on a sleeping face. The Father delights in the Son in this way, and in him takes pleasure in each of us in our particularity.

But if our love is to be Trinitarian then it must unfold, stretch itself open, become hospitable to others. The intense, mutual love of parents will have to find space for a child. When a couple have a child, then this is a sort of living of the procession of the Spirit from

---

[6] Joseph Pieper, *Faith, Hope, Love* (San Francisco, 1997), passim.
[7] Marilynne Robinson, *Gilead* (New York, 2004), p. 136.

the Father and the Son. This may be deeply painful, especially if the father is disconcerted to discover that he is no longer the centre of his wife's attention. The safe place of the home needs to be opened up to the stranger, the orphan and the widow.

Nurses, doctors, teachers, priests and religious are obvious signs of a love that is large. Think of Mother Teresa loving the dying who were brought to her home in Calcutta. They were loved before they had begun to disclose their individuality, just because they are received in faith as Christ. This is a spacious love which may be less emotional, and which demands quiet commitment, the doctor staying on after hours to see his patients, the nurse cleaning someone who is sick, a social worker visiting someone who does not even want to see them. It is a selfless love which is given even before someone is seen to be lovable. It is an unsentimental love which does what is needed. The hero of Proust's great masterpiece talks of 'the truly saintly embodiments of practical charity...the impassive, unsympathetic, sublime face of true goodness'.[8]

When I was in Angola during the civil war, I had a meeting with the Dominican postulants. They were cut off by the conflict from their families and those whom they loved. Should they leave their religious communities and go home to care for their families and tribes or stay in the Order? Africans have a deep sense of family and tribe and so this was a terrible dilemma. But one young sister stood up and said, 'Leave the dead to bury the dead; we must stay to preach the gospel'. That is a generous and open love.

Every Christian love aspires to the mystery of God's unimaginable love, both particular and universal. And so the intense love of two people for each other, or parents for their children, implies both

---

[8] *Swann's Way*, trans. C. K. Scott Moncrieff and Terence Kilmartin, revised by D. J. Enright (London, 2005), p. 97.

this delight in someone, and the painful act of giving them away. When the child was born, it began its journey from the warmth and intimacy of the mother's womb and made its way down the birth canal into our perilous world. She had to let it be separate from herself so that it may belong also to its father and their family. In the beautiful Spanish expression, she gives it to the light, *dar a luz*. Now the light shines on its face, and is visible for the first time, a face that can look back at ours in astonishment and learn to smile.

Parenthood demands many such moments of release. Each of them is a new birth pang. I was delivered to boarding school at the age of eight. I remember the alarm at being removed from the warmth of my large family and being left alone in a great crowd of strangers and frightening boys. It was years before I discovered that my mother had to stop each time at the end of the school drive and weep. Seamus Heaney describes being left at school by his parents:

I stood on in the Junior House Hallway
A grey eye will look back
Seeing them as a couple, I now see,

For the first time, all the more together
For having had to turn and walk away, as close
In the leaving (or closer) as in the getting.[9]

This closeness is surely both that of parents to each other, even closer than in the intimacy of begetting, and also a closeness to young Seamus, the gift whom they recognize precisely in letting him go. There will be other departures to be endured, for work or for University. One day the parents may have to let their child go to love someone even more intimately than themselves. At a marriage

---

[9] 'Album' *Human Chain* (London, 2010), p. 5.

the father gives away his daughter. 'Therefore a man leaves his father and mother and cleaves to his wife and they become one flesh' (Gen. 2.24).

The story of salvation tells of a love that opens doors and sets one on journeys away from home so that we can come to our true home. After the terrible stories of the Fall, the murder of Abel by Cain, the Flood, the tower of Babel, the way home begins when Abram is commanded to 'go from your country and your father's house to the land that I will show you' (Gen. 12.1). In Robinson's *Gilead* the old preacher tells his congregation of how Abraham had to give up both his children, Ishmael to God's providence in the wilderness, and Isaac on the mountain:

> Any father, particularly an old father, must finally give his child up to the wilderness and trust to the providence of God. It seems almost a cruelty for one generation to beget another when parents can secure so little for their children, so little safety, even in the best circumstances. Great faith is required to give the child up, trusting God to honour the parents' love for him by assuring that there will indeed be angels in that wilderness. I noted that Abraham himself had been sent into the wilderness, told to leave his father's house also, that was the narrative of all generations, and that it is only by the grace of God that we are instruments of His providence and participants in a fatherhood that is always ultimately His.[10]

For any parent this entrusting of the child into God's care is an anxious moment, especially when young adults distance themselves from their family and perhaps even from their faith. Often parents fret and wonder what they did wrong that their child has rejected

---

[10] Robinson, *Gilead*, p. 129.

them or God or embraced a life that they cannot understand. But we best witness to our faith by trusting in our God who never lets anyone fall outside his care, but leaves the ninety-nine sheep who are safe in the flock and goes to search out the one who has gone astray (Lk. 15.4). These, Cecil Day Lewis says, are 'the small, scorching ordeals which fire one's irresolute clay'.[11]

In Luke's gospel, Mary and Joseph receive the gift of a child whom they must learn to let go from the very moment of his birth, a child who will puzzle them, disappear when he is just 12 years old when he is found by his parents in the Temple, get mixed up with disreputable friends and finally die a shameful death. So a Christian family, paradoxically, is one that lets you go, which is why the gospels are so ambiguous about families and why discipleship often requires us to leave mother and father, brother and sister, for Christ's sake. When the rich young playboy of Assisi, our St Francis, discovered his vocation he said: 'I have called Peter Bernadone my father, but now that I have resolved to serve God, I return to him all the money he was upset over and even all the clothes which I have from his property; from now on I want to say, "Our Father who art in heaven", not "My father Peter Bernadone"'.[12]

Christian love searches for intimacy but lets people be free. We love others by drawing close, by being in touch, and yet also in offering space and letting be. Herbert McCabe OP wrote: 'What gives us elbow room, what gives us space to grow and become ourselves, is the love that comes to us from another. Love is the space in which to expand, and it is always a gift... To give love is to give the precious gift of nothing, space... To give love is to let

---

[11] Cecil Day Lewis, 'Walking Away', in *The Gate and Other Poems* (London, 1962), p. 546.
[12] Quoted in Simon Tugwell OP, *Ways of Imperfection: An Exploration of Christian Spirituality* (London, 1984), p. 127.

be'.[13] Meister Eckhart used a lovely word for this unpossessive love, *Gelassenheit*, letting be.

This tension between close union and letting the other person go is beautifully caught in a novel about the Second World War by Thomas Keneally, *The Widow and her Hero*. The widow writes a poem for her beloved husband. She loves him deeply and wants to be completely fused with him, one flesh, one life. But she also knows that loving him means accepting that he has his own life. He has an existence which precedes their love. He is a commando with his own mission which will lead him to risk his life on the sea. She must give him breathing space. The first part of the poem describes the gravitation pressure towards union:

> And in love's bed, caresses seemed
> A holy vacuum,
> Since lovers seek to force the air
> From every cavity and intervening space.
> Love's pressure is enormous,
> The normal terms of gravity become trite.

That is the vast erotic pressure towards union, squeezing out any separation. And then she describes how she must let him be, with his dreams of heroic action, his own life. To love him she must also give him space:

> But then, I catch his eye
> And see the shoals and surfs
> And archipelagos
> Which fill the other mind,
> The tides that go on running

---

[13] Herbert McCabe OP, *God Matters* (London, 1987), p. 108.

When his tide is spent.
The Projection of Mercator cannot save me
From concluding,
Love is the longest distance between two bodies.[14]

I need to sense what those whom I love need at any moment, which may not be what I want. I may feel a need for intimacy when the other needs space. I may need to breathe and be quiet when the other is desperate for a word or a hug. The asceticism and discipline of love is being alert to what the other needs now. One may long to hug one's sulky teenage child, but this might be just the wrong moment! Of course often at that age, the intimacy is oppressive and the space is terrifying, and so the parent can do nothing right.

What is in tension in us is one in God. For in this dynamic rhythm of our loving, drawing near and holding back, we enact just a faint hint of God's love. God's word is intimate to everything. Eckhart says that 'Every creature is full of God and is a book'.[15] God is present 'in a stone or a log of wood only they do not know it'.[16] And of course God is utterly intimate to each of us, even if we are not aware of him. Eckhart says, 'Even if you cannot conceive of yourself as near to God, you should still regard God as near to you'.[17] For God is utterly and intimately present to us, closer to me than I am to myself, as St Augustine said. God is more intimately settled at the core of my being than any lover could ever be. And yet God's utter intimacy is such that we can be completely unaware of God. God's presence is completely discreet, unobtrusive.

---

[14] Thomas Keneally, *The Widow and her Hero* (London, 2007), pp. 95–96.

[15] Sermon 23 in Walshe, *Meister Eckhart*, no 54, Vol. II, p. 72.

[16] Sermon 68 in Walshe, *Meister Eckhart*, no 69, Vol. II, p. 165.

[17] *Talks of Instruction no 17.* Quoted by Richard Woods OP, *Meister Eckhart: Master of Mystics* (London, 2011), p. 163.

'Truly, you are a God who hides himself, O God of Israel, the Saviour' (Isa. 45.15). Why? Karl Jaspers believes that 'it is as if God wished to give us the highest form of being, true freedom, but to do so, God is forced to hide himself'.[18] So it is out of respect for our high dignity as free people that God now only shows himself to us by hints and glimpses. A Hassidic rabbi, Reb Barukh, said, 'Imagine two children playing hide and seek. One hides and the other does not look for him. God is hiding and we are not looking for him. Imagine his distress'.[19]

More radically, God creates us to be ourselves. McCabe again:

> The power of God is pre-eminently the power to let things be. 'Let there be light' – the creative power is just the power that, because it results in things being what they are, in persons being who they are, cannot interfere with creatures. Obviously creating does not make a difference to things, it lets them be *themselves*. Creation is simply and solely the letting things be, and our love is a faint image of that.[20]

It is because God is utterly transcendent that he may be unimaginably close in a way that gives us the gift of being ourselves. Theologians often make the mistake of wanting God to be a rather emotional person, who gets upset over our suffering and is really just like us. But it is the utter transcendence of God which is the foundation of unimaginable intimacy. If God were more obtrusive, we would be crushed.

Even when God came to us in a human being, with a human face, there is an extraordinary discretion in his presence. God did not

---

[18] Karl Jaspers, 'Le mal radical chez Kant', *Deucalion* 36, no. 4 (1952), p. 123.
[19] Elie Wiesel, *Souls on Fire* (New York, 1972), pp. 83–84.
[20] McCabe, *God Matters*, p. 108.

come with drums banging and trumpets blowing, but in a child who was only noticed by shepherds. And when he drew near to people, it was often just to ask a question. God hates to intrude; he is extraordinarily respectful.

When I was flying to Sydney once, I watched again that wonderful film, *The Children of a Lesser God*, the story of a man who teaches in a school for the deaf, and falls deeply in love with a beautiful angry woman who is imprisoned in silence. Finally she signs to him, 'Unless you can let me be an "I" as you are an "I", I cannot let you into my silence to know me'. I thought 'Yes. What an insight into love; that is the incarnation, God's gentle intimacy which lets us be'. And I rushed down the aisle to beg the stewardess for a piece of paper so that I could write it down. She probably thought, 'Another nutter who has had too much to drink'.

The Christian community

So the parents love their child by giving it away to the Church, which is a sort of sign of all of humanity. The priest says 'The Christian community welcomes you with great joy'. This letting go first began in choosing godparents. This is a sharing of parenthood. They become kin of the child, their parents 'in God'. They become god-siblings of the parent, from which we get the word 'gossip', sustaining the couple with their conversation and kindness.[21]

Then the baby is entrusted to this parish community. When Jesus called people to follow him, they joined the odd crowd of his other friends, to eat and drink with sinners and tax collectors. He claims us as members of this community of people whom we have

---

[21] I confess my total failure as a godparent, and any of my godchildren are free to claim a copy of this book from me.

not chosen and with whom we may disagree and not even like. Karl
Rahner wrote 'When we attend a baptism we do not go merely to see
a spectacle... We are gathered around the newly baptized as fellow
members of the Church. We say to him: "Now you belong to us, and
we to you, in quite a new way".[22] Who I am is 'Whose I am'.[23]

Often parents prefer a private family baptism. It is pleasant to
gather this child's family around him for his christening. Aunts and
uncles and distant cousins turn up, stand around the font and take
photos. It is a family occasion. But this is a little odd, since in baptism
the child is surrendered to the larger family of Christ's boundless
love. And so it makes more sense to have a baptism at a gathering of
the parish, and even for there to be lots of different babies baptized
at the same time, surrounded by their new brothers and sisters in
Christ, the first and foremost title of every Christian.

And this parish community is just the tiniest sign of the community
of the whole Church, scattered throughout the world. When my
family went on holiday, the first thing that my father did on arrival
was to find out at what time was Mass on a Sunday in the nearest
Catholic church. We were just as much members of that community
for a couple of weeks as we were of our home parish. In fact the word
'parish' comes from a Greek word, 'paroikos', which means 'visitor'.
It is the word used of Jesus when he meets the disciples on the way
to Emmaus. A Christian community should not be an introverted,
exclusive group, but is most itself in welcoming visitors for we are all
travellers on the way to the Kingdom.

In the Catholic tradition, you dip a finger in the little bowl
of holy water as you enter the church and make the sign of the

---

[22] Karl Rahner, *Meditations on the Sacraments* (London, 1977), pp. 13–14.

[23] William C. Spohn, *Go and Do Likewise: Jesus and Ethics* (New York and London, 2007),
p. 24, acknowledges Martha Ellen Storz as the originator of this pithy formula.

cross. This may look like Catholic 'superstition', but the gesture is a reminder that one enters that church as one's home, as baptized in Christ's death and resurrection, even if you have never been there before.

And this scattered communion of communities throughout the world is sign of the whole family of humanity, which is called to be one in Christ. Derek Walcott, the West Indian poet, wrote: 'Either I'm nobody or I am a nation'.[24] We cannot be fully ourselves, as we are created to be, apart from the whole family of humanity, to which we are entrusted in baptism. The universality of God's love is symbolized, in a small way, by the unity of the Church throughout the world. This odd communion of people of every tribe and tongue and nation is an inadequate, fragile, faulty sign[25] of the mystery of God's will, 'according to his purpose in Christ as a plan for the fullness of time, to unite all things in him, things in heaven and things on the earth' (Eph. 1.9-10).

Colombia has endured years of armed conflict between the government and guerrillas, often made rich by the drug trade. The Body of Christ is torn and divided. But when the bishops have been involved in peace making, they have seen it as building up the unity of *humanity*. Bishop Jorge Leonardo Gómez Serna of Magangué, one of the principal peace makers, sees his work as the restoration of the human family: 'God as the good Father created us in his image and likeness: that is to say, He created us as a great family, as a mystery of love and peace...and He gave us the entire Universe...to be shared among all. God gave us the capacity to continue to build this great

---

[24] Derek Walcott, 'The Schooner Flight', in *Collected Poems 1948–1984* (London, 1992), p. 346.

[25] In which case, some people may ask, why does the Roman Catholic Church not invite everyone to share the Eucharist? A good question for which there is not the space to answer here. I explore it in 'The Demands of the Mass', *The Tablet*, 1 December 1990, pp. 1544–55.

family'.[26] Christ claims us for the great task of building humanity. We will not know what it means to be human until we are one.

So all the work for justice, for the elimination of poverty and the healing of division, is much more than standing up for individual human rights. It is an expression of what it means to be baptized, alive in Christ, for as long as anyone is crushed, so am I. In a speech in December 1963, Martin Luther King said: 'All life is interrelated… somehow we're caught in an inescapable network of mutuality tied in a single garment of destiny. Whatever affects one directly – affects all *indirectly*. For some strange reason, I can never be what I ought to be until you are what you ought to be. And you can never be what you ought to be until I am what I ought to be'.

This sounds lovely, but do we see any sign of that interdependence? Our magazines are filled with pictures of the very rich and their happiness does not seem to be marred by the great gap which divides most of us from the poor. Is our sense of completion in any way diminished? Do we feel the claim of Christ in the destitute? Do we feel one body with them? No happiness can be secure as long as one has to shut out awareness of the sufferings of one's kin in Christ. There must be a vast work of shoring up the defences of one's contentment against their pain, a great effort not to be touched by these 'the least of my brothers and sisters' (Matt. 25.40). There is an unending labour to sustain our insensitivity to their pain. This is resisting the claim of Christ made at baptism.

And the purest and most spontaneous joy is often to be found where nothing more is to be lost. One of my brethren, Brian Pierce, was walking through the slums of Lima feeling a little glum, and he came across two young boys playing jacks. It is a game that I often

---

[26] John Lederach, 'The Long Journey back to Humanity', in Robert J. Schreiter et al. (eds), *Peacebuilding: Catholic Theology, Ethics and Praxis* (Maryknoll, NY: Orbis, 2010), p. 46.

played as a child. You throw a ball upwards, and while it is in the air, you must pick up as many little pieces of metal as possible, in time to catch the ball before it lands. And these two boys were laughing and joking as they played; only there was no ball. They imagined the ball. They were exuberantly creating the game out of nothing. And Brian said, 'That was an image of God; with joy and laughter creating out of nothing'. Their joy could not be destroyed by the loss of the ball, because they had nothing to lose. When we are claimed in Christ, it is so that we may share their joy.

4

Listening to the Word

The baptized have been named so that they may respond to God who calls them to life. They have been claimed for Christ. Now we move to a new moment, the liturgy of the Word, which includes the reading from the gospel, the homily and the prayers of intercession. This is very similar to the first part of the Eucharist, on which I have commented at length in *Why Go to Church? The Drama of the Eucharist*.[1] I will not repeat what I wrote there, but just share some brief thoughts on what the liturgy of the Word means for us as we live our baptism.

During their preparation for baptism, adults are entrusted with the gospels: 'Receive the gospel, the good news of Jesus Christ, the Son of God'. This is known as the *traditio* of the gospels, from which we get the word 'tradition'. To be a Christian is to be entrusted with the Word of God.

When the persecution of Diocletian broke out at the beginning of the fourth century, Christians were commanded to surrender their scriptures to the authorities to be burned. Those who did so were considered by the Church to be traitors, *traditores*, literally those who

---

[1] London, 2008. I examine listening to the Scriptures on pp. 28–41, the preaching of the homily on pp. 42–62, and intercessory prayer on pp. 92–96.

had 'handed over' the words of eternal life. We tend to think of traitors as people who betray their nation, whereas for those Christians it was the very opposite; it was to succumb to the demand of the State that one betray the scriptures. One ruse was to try to fool the authorities by handing over heretical writings and enjoy seeing them burnt! And so it became important to know what was the Word of God and what was not. This gave a powerful impulse to the definition of the canon of the scriptures. The scriptures were those sacred texts for which one is prepared to die.

So at baptism we are entrusted with the Word for which we are prepared to give our lives. Why should we die for a book? The Bible is not words *about* God, a user's guide to Christianity. Indeed, the closer we draw to God and share his life, the more we discover the unknowability of God. When you draw near to someone to kiss them, they disappear from sight, and so it is with God. We are, as St Thomas Aquinas said, joined to God as to the unknown. Acceptance of the Bible is not to assent to the literal accuracy of its contents. That is a very modern and misleading idea. It was a reaction to the claim of modern science to offer the literal truth.

Rather we open ourselves to the one who is the Word of God in person and who addresses us. Yves Congar said that he had devoted his life to the truth. He loved it 'in the way that one loves a person'.[2] And that is how we love the scriptures given to us at baptism, as the Word addressed to us by someone who died for us. That is why a Christian should be prepared to die for the scriptures.

Often we may be puzzled by them. Much of the Old Testament is violent and vengeful. As we shall see in Chapter 6, this is because it took time for the people of God to be ready to be pregnant with the Prince of peace. It took centuries of men and women wrestling

---

[2] 'Reflections on Being a Theologian', *New Blackfriars* 62/736 (1981), p. 406.

to understand how God was at work in their lives before they were ready for God to be present in person. Kings, scribes, prophets and poets prayed and argued, endured exile and defeat, before the Word of God could come to us as the man who told us to turn the other cheek. Even Jesus can speak and behave in a puzzling way. When he began to speak of himself as the bread of life who must be eaten, then lots of people fled. When Jesus asked Peter whether he, like so many others, would desert him, he replied: 'Lord to whom shall we go? You have the words of eternal life; and we have believed, and have come to know, that you are the Holy One of God' (Jn 6.68-69). He had to hang in there, puzzled, waiting for the moment when Jesus' words might make some sense.

So at baptism, we are entrusted to the Word of God and learn to live with it. Isaiah said: 'Morning by morning he wakens, he wakens my ear to hear as those who are taught' (50.4). We let the Word shape our lives, give them direction, unfold their purpose, disclose our end. In Western Christianity, a traditional way of praying is *lectio divina*, reading the scriptures, slowly and attentively, letting them embed themselves in one's life.[3] Living with the Scriptures is living with someone whom you love. You do not listen to them so as to get information, but to cement a shared life. You must open yourself to surprise; if you think that you know in advance what they are going to say, then you will get them wrong, like a couple whose relationship has gone stale because each thinks that they know the other one too well.

Some early Christians thought that if one did hand over the scriptures to the authorities, then there could be no readmission to communion. One was forever marginalized. But there were so many *traditores* that those who remained strong, the confessors of the faith

---

[3] Cf. David Foster OSB, *Reading with God: Lectio Divina* (London, 2005).

who risked their lives, were perhaps even a minority. But it was this same Word of God which taught the Church the vastness of God's mercy, so that no one should remain excluded. The Church continues to live with the Word of God, forever surprised, always just at the beginning of understanding a mercy and love beyond our comprehension. Beethoven's last words are supposed to have been 'I shall hear in heaven'. We are trying to catch the voice that we shall only hear fully when we arrive at our destination.

The discipline of Christian life is mostly about learning to be still and listen. Of course if you are busy, packing kids off to school, rushing to work, then this can be hard, but we need still moments, even a minute or two of quietness, to sustain our relationship with God, just as we do to keep our love alive for our spouses and friends. The Rule of St Benedict begins: 'Listen carefully my son, to the master's instructions, and attend to them with the ear of your heart'.[4] And we go on listening. 'What dear brother, is more delightful than this voice of the Lord calling to us? See how the Lord in his love shows us the way of life'.[5] Often we seem to hear nothing but we must wait, attentively. Cardinal Hume was asked in an interview 'What do you feel when you pray?' He replied: 'Oh I just keep plugging away. At its best it's like being in a dark room with someone you love. You can't see them, but you know they're there'.

Cardinal Newman wrote, 'God has created me to do him some definite service. He has committed some work to me which he has not committed to another. I have my mission. I may never know it in this life, but will be told it in the next'.[6] I meet innumerable young

---

[4] *The Rule of St Benedict*, ed. Timothy Fry OSB (Collegeville, 1981), p. 157.
[5] Ibid., p. 161.
[6] 'Meditations on Christian Doctrine', 7 March 1848, in *Meditations and Devotions of the*

people who feel that they have a vocation but they cannot discern what it is. They know that God calls them, as God calls everyone, but it is not clear in what way they are to walk. There are lay people who want to serve God and the Church with all their strength and love but cannot discern how, and others who feel called to religious life, but cannot find the right community. They know that their life must find a shape, a narrative form, but find it hard to recognize what that is.

This is especially so since the idea of the human life as a vocation is weakening in our society. In my childhood, a number of ways of life were considered vocations. One might be called to be a teacher or a nurse or a doctor or an artist or a priest. These were 'jobs' that gave an overall sense to one's life, which is perhaps why vocational jobs were not usually very remunerative. After all, if someone's vocation is to be a teacher, then one does not need to pay them very much since they have no option but to teach!

But even this residual understanding of vocation is being weakened in a society that has largely lost any sense that our lives make sense as a whole, rather than as a succession of disconnected jobs. The average American has eleven jobs in a lifetime. Nicholas Boyle says that once we become seen as a series of consumer choices – 'first an Escort, then a Sierra, then a loft conversion' – then the idea of life as a vocation becomes meaningless.

The concept of a vocation, of a job or task – for life, that defines a large part of what a person is, loses its value, and is actively persecuted. We may still say 'she is a printer', 'he is a teacher' but what we mean, and what in future we shall increasingly say, is, 'she is doing some printing, at the moment', 'he is on a three-year teaching contract'. The question of what 'he' or 'she' permanently

late Cardinal Newman (London and New York, 1893), p. 399.

is does not arise: even gender is irrelevant – for the market what matters is the performance indicator that 's/he', the production unity, can show.[7]

So we may lose the sense that a truly human life is a story that stretches from birth to death and beyond. Enduring commitments are harder to maintain; marriages break up, people leave the priesthood and religious life. This is not to point a finger of blame. Who has the right to do that? It is to recognize that when we are entrusted with the scriptures at baptism, our lives are accepted as having a meaning as a whole, defined by their goal, life with God. Each life is a vocation, shaped by our response to a voice that we first acknowledge, perhaps, at the font, but which keeps on calling us. This is hard to grasp in a society which sees life as a series of fragmentary events, like unconnected episodes in a soap opera: *Coronation Street* rather than walking the Christian way; *Friends* rather than God's enduring friendship.

Also we can get stuck in our failures and limitations and resist being called to journey to God. Emily Dickinson wrote a poem called 'A prison gets to be a friend'.[8]

The slow exchange of Hope— For something passiver—Content Too steep for looking up— The Liberty we knew Avoided—like a Dream—

We may resist the Word of the Lord because it will disturb our plans and destroy our small contentment. God's liberty is frightening. It is safer to remain captive of some small prison with its small ambitions, little desires. C. S. Lewis tried to avoid that encounter with Christ

---

[7] Nicholas Boyle, *Who are We Now? Christian Humanism and the Global Market from Hegel to Heaney* (Edinburgh, 1998), p. 79.

[8] *The Complete Poems*, ed. Thomas H. Johnson (London, 1975), p. 652.

because he feared it would undo his easy life. He said that looking for God is like a mouse looking for a cat: 'You must picture me all alone in that room at Magdalen,[9] night after night, feeling, whenever my mind lifted for even a second from my work, the steady, unrelenting approach of Him whom I so earnestly desired not to meet. That which I greatly feared had at last come upon me. In the Trinity Term of 1929 I gave in, and admitted that God was God, and knelt and prayed'.[10] In John's gospel Pilate begins to talk to Jesus. He is fascinated. He shows him to his enemies: 'Behold your king'. He is on the verge of conversion but he is afraid and so lets the conversation lapse. When Jesus confronts him, 'Everyone who belongs to the truth listens to my voice' (19.37), Pilate dare not and hides in a weary scepticism: 'What is truth?'

The film *Of Gods and Men*[11] is the true story of a small community of Trappist monks living in Algeria who were murdered in 1996. They are deeply embedded in the life of the local Muslim village. They love and are loved, but slowly they become aware of the rising tide of Islamicist violence and know that it will threaten their lives. Are they called to stay or go? The film tells of their dawning realization that their vocation is to stay. When they share with the villagers their hesitation – they are like birds on a branch and perhaps are about to depart – a Muslim woman says, 'We are the birds and you are the branch'. So we see the painful and ultimately joyful realization dawn on them that this is what the Lord asks of them, to remain. That is to abide in his Word. One of the younger monks says to the Prior, 'But I did not become a monk to die'. And the Prior answers back, 'But you have already given away your life!' To be baptized is to live one's life

---

[9] The Oxford College of which he was a fellow.

[10] C. S. Lewis, *Surprised by Joy* (London, 1955), p. 215.

[11] In French it is the other way around, *Des hommes et des dieux*.

as a vocation, shaped by response to this Word of God, leading one slowly by unknown and sometimes tough paths towards the fullness of life and happiness.

Often it is when one appears to be going in the wrong direction that the way forward is discovered. The disciples are fleeing Jerusalem when they meet Jesus on the road. Saul was busily murdering Christians when he heard the voice choosing him to be the apostle of the Gentiles. Dante was astray on the mountain, 'the straightway was lost', when he began his pilgrimage to paradise. One may wake up in one's vomit, or be exposed in a lie, or with one's hand in the till, or sleeping with another person's spouse and then discover that there can be a new beginning, a deeper understanding of one's vocation. If we are disgraced or humiliated, then it may be the dark that precedes the dawn. And so we need not fear if we find ourselves in a mess. Sometimes we have to lose the plot so as to discover it more clearly. Ruth Bidgood wrote:

> Nothing I see here matches the map. Getting lost here
> Seems inevitable and good.[12]

It is when the old map no longer makes sense that you may find a new one that shows the way forward. In *War and Peace*, Pierre, a Russian Count and a man of vast wealth, loses everything during the French capture of Moscow. He is thrown into prison, humiliated, starved, but it is the beginning of happiness: "'People speak of misfortunes and sufferings," remarked Pierre, "but if at this moment I were asked: 'would you rather be what you were before you were taken prisoner, or go through all this again?' then for heaven's sake let me again have captivity and horseflesh! We imagine that when we are thrown out of our usual ruts all is lost, but it is only then

---

[12] Quoted by Claire Crowther, *Times Literary Supplement*, 21 August 2009.

that what is new and good begins".[13] When you no longer know who you are or why you are here, then you may be open to hear the Word of God summon you further on your journey. It was at his lowest ebb that Pierre met the simple peasant whose faith showed him the way to a new life.

Etty Hillesum, a Jewish young woman who fell in love with Christ before she was sent to her death in Auschwitz, conversed with God in the face of death, in the dreary deadness of the camp. She came to love especially Matthew's gospel, the most Jewish of the four, and Augustine's writings. It was in desolation, when the way forward had disappeared, that her conversation with God flowered. 'My life has become an uninterrupted dialogue with You, O God, one great dialogue. Sometimes when I stand in some corner of the camp, my feet planted on Your earth, my eyes raised toward Your heaven, tears sometimes run down my face, tears of deep gratitude. At night, too, when I lie in my bed and rest in You, oh God, tears of gratitude run down my face, and that is my prayer'.[14]

We do not listen to the Word of God alone. We are baptized into a community of listeners. The role of the homily is to help us to listen together, with the whole tradition of the Church and with our contemporaries. Homilies are, of course, notoriously instruments of torture, often the greatest deterrents to participation in Sunday worship. A Mexican Dominican bishop who preached with dramatic fervour but also at considerable length once noticed an old man fast asleep in the front bench. He said to his grandson: 'Please wake up your grandfather'. To which the boy replied, 'You wake him up. You put him to sleep in the first place'.

---

[13] Leo Tolstoy, *War and Peace*, trans. Aylmer Maude and Louise Shanks Maude (Kindle, 2011), p. 1204 Bk 15 chapter 17.

[14] Etty Hillesum, *An Interrupted Life and Letters from Westerbork* (New York, 1996), p. 640.

But homilies should not address us from on high, battering us with the vast superiority of the preacher's learning or boring us with platitudes. Homily comes from a Greek word which means 'to converse'. We are invited into the conversation of the Church with the Word of God, a conversation that began in the gospels and crosses generations and will continue until the end of time and which is attentive to what we think, and our response. This is the beginning of our participation in the eternal, loving, equal conversation which is the life of the Trinity. In a good conversation, you open your mind and heart to the puzzles and convictions of the other person. A good homily, one of my brethren said, swings on the horns of a dilemma. It enables a conversation between the gospel and the challenges and questions of our contemporaries.

When the first group of Dominicans arrived in the Americas five hundred years ago, the prior was a young friar, 28 years old, called Pedro de Córdoba. On his first trip across the island of Quisqueya, which Columbus appropriated under the conquering name of La Española, the Small Spain, Pedro surprised the Spanish conquerors by asking to meet with the despised indigenous people. All of them, men and women, old and young, gathered and Pedro sat himself on a wooden bench, with a cross in his hand, to talk to them face to face. This form of preaching, placing himself on the same level, looking into their eyes, challenged the Spanish conquerors' understanding of their relationship to these indigenous people, whom they considered to be barely human. Luisa Campos Villalón OP writes that this meeting led 'to a mutual communication in which Pedro was going to discover in the eyes of the indigenous people a receptivity to the Word'.[15] Jesus sat down to preach the beatitudes (Matt. 5.1), as he sat

---

[15] *Pedro de Córdoba: precursor de una comunidad defensora de la vida* (Santo Domingo, 2008), p. 53. My translation.

in the boat to preach (Mk 4.1), and sat at table to converse. Preaching only communicates the Word of God if it takes the form of a word given to one with whom one sits and to whom one listens, as Pedro sat to talk with the indigenous people.[16]

We help each other to recognize the voice of the good shepherd: 'The sheep hear his voice, and he calls his own sheep by name and leads them out. When he has brought out all his own, he goes before them, and the sheep follow him, for they know his voice' (Jn 10.3-4). When the gospels are given, the priest says: 'Receive the good news of Jesus Christ, the Son of God'. We have only heard the word of the Lord aright if we hear it as good news.

The voice of the Lord summons the sheep out of the confines of the little sheepfold into the spacious wide open pastures to feed in safety. Imagine a walled enclosure to keep out the wolves. In Africa, one often sees a circle of thorn bushes to protect the animals from leopards and lions. The voice of the Lord invites us to leave the safety of the sheepfold and trust in the Lord's voice. We have nothing to fear. One of the ways that we recognize the authentic voice of the Lord is that it invites us to be brave. We have no need to run away from the world and its complexities and challenges. The Lord invites us to leave any suffocating little ecclesiastical fortress in which we may be tempted to hide. We must not become sacristy mice. No, the Lord's voice gives us the courage to go out into the world to share our faith and outface the wolves.

One of our brethren, Bernard Kadlec, fled from Communist Czechoslovakia in danger of death. But he told his Provincial that he was ready to go back immediately if he was asked: 'If he [the Czech provincial] gave me an order to return home, I should return without any difficulty. I am not afraid. There is no doubt that I should be

---

[16] I thank Brian Pierce OP for this insight.

arrested as soon as I arrive. I am not courageous, on the contrary, I have always been a coward, but religion helps to boldness'. Religion helps to boldness!

I visited the part of Algeria where the monks lived just a few weeks after they were beheaded. Their bishop was a Dominican, Pierre Claverie. He also had received death threats and refused to leave, and was murdered just a month after my visit. One day we were driving around his diocese when he shared a worry. The diocese had opened libraries so that Muslim students could come and study, but the religious sisters who had looked after one library had been shot by terrorists. Pierre was wondering how he could keep the library open. Then an old friar in the back of the car, Jean-Pierre, offered to take their place. He had to die one day, and so why not take the risk?

So one of the ways to recognize the voice of the Lord, and under-stand Scripture aright, is that it offers us security *and* invites us to take risks. It is rather like those scary fairground rides that throw you all over the place: safe but rather frightening. The difference is that the roller coaster or whirligig really is safe and there are no risks. With Christianity, you may well get hurt, and in some parts of the world killed, but the Lord is still with you. If we trust in the voice of the Good Shepherd, we can risk everything. So we recognize the true voice of the Lord since it offers both safety and invites us to be courageous.

A few years ago, a group of English and French Dominicans went on a walking holiday on the Isle of Skye, in Scotland. One day we came to a cliff where the path disappeared. We had to place our feet in a slit and work your way along. It was all rather frightening, suspended above the waves of the sea and the rocks. When we got to the end, we realized that one brother, Gareth Moore, the philosopher and Scripture scholar, was not there. We had not realized that he suffered from vertigo. So I had to go back to find him, half-paralysed with fear, and say: 'Gareth, put your hand here. Now stretch the other foot to the right. Give me your hand'. 'No, then we shall both fall in'. Until finally he made his way to safety. When we asked him what he would like to do the next day, he said, 'Take me to a high cliff'. All our lives we call each other to have hope and to be courageous. Homilies should summon us to be brave. If they encourage timidity one might wonder if they help us to hear the voice of the Lord.

We now have the prayers of the faithful, or the bidding prayers, in which we pray to God for each other's needs, and the needs of the Church and the world. We pray for each because we depend upon each other as we shape our way to God. This is good; the mutual love of the Trinity takes human form in our reciprocal dependence. It is human to need each other. In St Catherine of Siena's dialogues, God says: 'I could well have supplied each of you with all your needs, both spiritual and material. But I wanted to make you dependent on one another so that each of you would be my minister, dispensing the graces and gifts you have received from me'.[17] It belongs to the priesthood of every Christian to minister to the needs of others and accept that we need the ministry of others too. I may need another's wisdom when she needs my courage; I may need her faith when she needs my hope.

> How could I have come so far?
> (And always on such dark trails?)
> I must have travelled by the light
> Shining from the faces of all those I have loved.[18]

In our macho, competitive world, we Christians may appear as

---

[17] *Catherine of Siena: The Dialogue*, trans. Suzanne Noffke OP (New York and Mahwah, NJ, 1980), p. 38.
[18] Thomas McGrath, 'Poem', from *Selected Poems: 1938–1988* (Copper Canyon, 1988), p. 102.

inadequate wimps who cannot make it on our own, but this is our witness to God's own humanity, which became flesh and blood as a needy and vulnerable child. And so we inhabit a world of mutual dependence, asking for each other's prayers and praying for the dead. This is not because we do not trust God but because it is thus that we share in the mutuality of God's Triune life. We even pray to the saints, to which topic we turn next.

5

The community of the saints

At this point in the Catholic ritual, we ask for the prayers of the saints. We ask Mary, John the Baptist, Joseph, Peter and Paul and other saints, such as the patron of the person being baptized or of the church where the baptism is taking place, to pray for us. This may cause Protestant hackles to rise! If we have a direct relationship with God in Jesus Christ, then why do we need any intermediaries? This attachment to the saints looks to many Christians like a betrayal of the heart of the gospel, salvation by faith alone. And so, during the Reformation, the statues of saints were pulled down, their shrines destroyed, and their feasts abolished. This devotion to the saints is not so odd as it may seem. I have received so much from my brothers and sisters who belong to other Churches, and I hope that they may be open to hear a Catholic voice on this sensitive issue which has wounded our baptismal unity.

It is true that Christians sometimes speak as if we need the saints because God is remote. If God is busy running the Universe, then it may seem hard to catch his attention. It may look as if we need people who are close to him to nudge his elbow, as it were, and remind him

that a rather unimportant Englishman is in urgent need of help.
Christians have even spoken as if Jesus were so harsh and judgmental
that we need his mother's help to obtain mercy. Mary softens up Jesus
for us. In the Romanesque cathedral at Autun, Michael the archangel
is seen tampering with the scales so as to get a favourable judgment
for a sinner.[1] We need all the allies we can get if we are to escape
punishment. No wonder the Catholic devotion to the saints is often
seen as unchristian and a lack of faith in God's infinite mercy.

No doubt much popular piety has seen saints in this way, a back
door entrance into the divine presence, but that is not the traditional position of the Orthodox or Catholic Churches. We have
already seen that God is closer to us than we are to ourselves. We
do not need the saints because God is remote; God is more intimate
with us than any saint could ever be. And so why do we ask their
prayers?

The Father's only begotten son became human in a first-century
Jewish family. He could not be truly human except as a member of a
family, and so it is natural that our relationship with him overflows
into a relationship with his family. On the cross Jesus adopts us
as members of his family, his final gift. He said to Mary, 'Woman,
here is your son' and to the beloved disciple, 'Here is your mother'
(Jn 19.27). That is why we ask for the prayers of Mary, his mother,
John the Baptist his cousin, and Joseph. In a sense his family is ours
too. We are all members of the Holy Family. To think that we could
have a relationship with Jesus that was purely individual, without
reference to his own natural kin, would be to impose on our faith a
modern, Western individualistic understanding of the person which
is inhuman and contrary to the gospels.

---

[1] David Brown, *Discipleship and Imagination: Christian Tradition and Truth* (Oxford,
2000), p. 143.

An Irish Dominican, Cardinal Browne, returned home to Ireland from Rome. He sought out the ancient nun who had baptized him as a baby when he was in danger of death, so that he could thank her. And to his horror she replied, 'Eminence, it was an honour to have baptized you…in the name of Jesus, Mary and Joseph'! For a terrible moment he wondered if he had been baptized at all, and then realized that her mind was just wandering a little. And yet it is true that to be baptized in the name of the Triune God is indeed to become a member of Jesus' family, since he became human so that we might become divine and no one can be human alone.

God is the eternal, equal love of the Trinity. This Triune love lives in our love of each other: 'Beloved, let us love one another; for love is of God, and whoever loves is born of God and knows God' (1 Jn 4.7). Our relationship with God flourishes in mutual friendship with each other. Erasmus said of St Thomas More that he was a man made for friendship. The saints are people who are evidently and beautifully God's friends. We are attached to them not because God is remote but for the very opposite reason, because God is close. We are caught up in God's friendship and so, of course, we are friends of his friends.

This is not because we do not trust God but because it is thus that we share in the mutuality of God's Triune life. Pope Benedict was asked by a German journalist how he prayed: 'Naturally I always pray first and foremost to our Lord, with whom I am united by old acquaintance, so to speak. But I also invoke the saints. I am friends with Augustine, with Bonaventure, with Thomas Aquinas. Then one says to such saints also: Help me!'[2] Augustine's help is not a substitute or a supplement to that of the Lord, but an expression of it.

---

[2] *The Light of the World: The Pope, the Church, and the Signs of the Times. A Conversation with Peter Seerwald*, trans. Michael J. Miller and Adrian J. Walker (London and San Francisco, 2010), p. 17.

In January 2011, I was at a meeting of the Global Christian Forum with the Ecumenical Patriarch of Constantinople. He was filled with joy that Pope John Paul II had returned the relics of St. Gregory Nazianzus and St John Chrysostom. They had been stolen by the Latin looters in 1204 and now at last they had come back home. On his feast day, the bones of Chrysostom are placed on the throne in the Cathedral and the saint is back with his people. The Patriarch wrote: 'From now on we will have them both [Gregory and Chrysostom] with us. This will be a great support for us, strengthening us, and bringing us consolation during our tearful and sorrowful days'. To a modern Westerner, this delight in the return of a few old bones may seem a little eccentric, even crazy. But it expresses a profound sense of how our Christian community is knit together, even across the barriers of death, by reciprocal love, a sacrament of that Trinitarian friendship which is our home.

The Trinity is an equal love, and the communion of saints is wonderfully egalitarian. It overthrows the social barriers between men and women, the rich and the poor. Even the humblest Roman peasant could choose a grand saint as his patron. In a rigid, patriarchal world, God's friends were of every sort: Popes and slaves, women and men, rich and poor. When Christians gathered at the tombs of the martyrs to feast, then everyone mixed freely, rather too freely for some! The social barriers dropped, a sign of our equality in Christ.

Gregory of Tours describes an extraordinary scene in the south of France when the relics of St Julian came in procession through fields where men were ploughing. They shouted: 'Look at the most blessed Julian drawing near to us! Behold, his power! Behold his glory! Run, lads, leave your ploughs and oxen; let the whole crowd follow him.'[3]

---

[3] *Liber de passione et virtutibus sancti Juliani martyris*, quoted by Peter Brown, *The Cult of the Saints* (Chicago, 1981), p. 122.

Peter Brown says that the presence of the saint 'had brought to these tired men the touch of an ideal dependence that could set them free, if only for a moment, from the harsh demands of Gallo-Roman landowning in a labour intensive cereal-growing area'.[4] They might be peasants, but they were the friends of God and of God's friend Julian.

In Ireland many homes had images of St Martin de Porres, the sixteenth-century Dominican brother, son of a Spanish nobleman and a black slave, famous for his love of the poor and the sick. In a society which used to be entirely white, this 'mestizo' was a beloved friend. And when I visited the Dominicans in Ho Chi Minh City, Vietnam, I found that already by 5 a.m. Martin's shrine was filled with people asking for his prayers: A man of a different colour, a different culture, a different century, and so a fitting symbol of God's wide friendship given in Christ 'in whom there is neither Jew nor Greek, slave nor free, there is neither male nor female, for you are all one in Christ' (Gal. 3.28).

G. K. Chesterton asserts that we easily forget just how bizarre it is to honour someone for no other reason than that they are recognized as good. This is a scandalous subversion of any understanding of greatness which was based on power and wealth:

> The notion of an eminence merely moral, consistent with complete stupidity or unsuccess, is a revolutionary image grown unfamiliar by its very familiarity, and needing...some almost preposterous modern parallel to give its original freshness and point. If we entered a foreign town and found a pillar like the Nelson Column, we should be surprised to learn that the hero on the top of it had been famous for his politeness and hilarity during a chronic toothache. If a procession came down the street with a brass band

---

[4] Ibid.

and a hero on a white horse, we should think it odd to be told that he had been very patient with a half-witted maiden aunt.[5]

The saints are signs of hope. Heroic holiness *is* possible. God's grace is in us to triumph over fear and despair. 'Therefore, since we are surrounded by so great a cloud of witnesses, let us also lay aside every weight, and sin which clings so closely, and let us run with perseverance the race that is set before us' (Heb. 12.1). Pagan Rome was deeply fatalistic. Our lives were ruled by the stars. But when the baptized took the name of a saint, they believed that they were touched by Christ's freedom as it had broken through in that saint. Usually we celebrate the day upon which the saint died, often the day of the martyr's courageous perseverance in the face of Imperial power.

Our society also is tempted by fatalism. We may think that we are the victims of our genes, of our parents and their mistakes, of circumstances beyond our control, of the stars, of the market, of prejudice or whatever. And so holiness may seem impossible, as if we are doomed to moral mediocrity. But the saints witness to how God's liberating grace frees weak people like ourselves. St Paul says that he prayed that he would be freed from weakness, but the Lord 'said to me, "My grace is sufficient for you, for my power is made perfect in weakness." So I will boast all the more gladly of my weakness, so that the power of Christ may dwell in me' (2 Cor. 12.9). And so we ask for the prayers of the saints, that God's strong grace can work in weak people like us too.

Their friendship breaks through the barriers of death, a resurrection friendship. The pagans were shocked by the Christian attitude to the dead. For them, the dead were dangerous. They were buried outside the city walls where they could do no harm. But Christians

---

[5] Quoted by Ian Ker, *G. K. Chesterton: A Biography* (Oxford, 2011), p. 380.

loved to gather at the tombs of the martyrs, and after the conversion of Constantine, the dead began to find their way into the centre of the city from which they had been excluded. First of all the relics of the martyrs were brought back into the city churches, and then the bodies of those who wished to be buried near them. Bernard Green OSB wrote:

> People continued to be buried in the catacombs during the fifth century but by then they were being superseded by graveyards within the city. The old taboo against being interred within the sacred limits of the city gave way to an entirely new Christian attitude to burials and bodies so that it was increasingly common for Christians to be buried inside the city walls. The catacombs had expressed a belief in the solidarity of the living with the dead, all united together in the Christian community which made up the Body of Christ, which was very different from pagan attitudes to the afterlife and the polluting danger of the corpse.[6]

This was a slow-motion fulfilment of Matthew's account of the consequence of Christ's resurrection: 'The tombs also were opened, and many bodies of the saints who had fallen asleep were raised, and coming out of the tombs after his resurrection they went into the holy city and appeared to many' (27.52-53). By the Middle Ages, virtually every church was surrounded by the dead. They were not buried in a necropolis, literally 'a city of the dead', but a cemetery, which means a place to sleep, a dormitory, awaiting the Kingdom. When the living gathered to celebrate the Eucharist, the dead were present, the outermost circle of the congregation, faithfully there at every Mass,

---

[6] Bernard Green OSB, *Christianity in Ancient Rome: The First Three Centuries* (London, 2010), p. 194.

never late, always on time! They are God's friends, and the saints are heroic examples of that friendship.

Baptism initiates us into the community of the living and the dead. In Christ, death's dominion has been destroyed and so our community is not just the 2.3 billion Christians who happen to be wandering the planet at this moment. We belong to the vast community of everyone who has ever been baptized, all the saints and sinners who are in Christ, 'and all who seek you [God] with a sincere heart',[7] of any Church or faith or none. We accept that we are brothers and sisters of the Borgia Popes as well as Pope John XXIII, of the worst Inquisitors as well as St Thomas Aquinas. As James Joyce said, 'Here comes everyone'. We are bound to this great multitude by prayer, praying for the sinners and asking for the prayers of the saints for us. It is no more bizarre to ask for the prayers of the saints than it would be to ask for those of the person next to you in the pews. Prayer is the conversation of the resurrection, sustaining the bonds of community.

In Chapters 13 and 14, we shall explore further what it means for us all to be called to holiness. For now, it is enough to see that when we ask the saints to pray for us, it is not a lack of trust in God's love and mercy but an expression of it. They are a sign of that spacious Triune friendship into which we are baptized. Devotion to the saints could only be seen as in competition to our relationship with God if we have a very diminished view of God, as if God were a very powerful being who is afraid of rivals. Because Jesus is truly human, he enters the web of kinship and friendship, and because he is truly divine, then our devotion to the saints is no threat to our relationship with God.

---

[7] Eucharistic Prayer IV.

6

Fight the good fight

Baptism is our initiation into the mystery of love, God's love for us, and our love for God, others and ourselves. As we move closer to the pivotal point in the drama of baptism, the pouring of the water and the invocation of the Trinity, this love is gradually shown to be more beautiful and demanding than one could ever have imagined. It involves accepting obedience to God's commandments. This is not a constraint on one's behaviour, submission to the dictates of a divine policeman, but our formation in friendship. Then the candidate for baptism is claimed for Christ. The parents of a child give it away to belong to the Church and, ultimately, to the whole of humanity which is being gathered into unity in Christ. The love into which we are baptized is not just my particular delight in this or that person or even God. We are baptized into the mystery of God's universal love which has no boundaries.

Now we enter choppier water with the prayer of exorcism. We invoke Jesus who 'came into the world to cast out the power of Satan, the spirit of evil'[1] and pray that the person being baptized be 'set free

---

[1] Roman Catholic Rite of the Baptism of infants.

from original sin'. This may well make our contemporaries feel uneasy. 'Exorcism' conjures up films such as *The Exorcist* or *Rosemary's Baby*: terrible battles with Satan, furniture flung all over the place, hideous laughter and terrible screams. This is not what we expect at baptism where the only screams are likely to be the baby's shocked reaction to being splashed by a frightening stranger.

We may also feel uneasy with the association of religion with combat with Satan. Our world is torn apart by violence and much of it is rooted in belligerent religious belief. Oliver McTernan wrote: 'From Indonesia to Northern Ireland, the Middle East to Kashmir, India to Nigeria, the Balkans to Sri Lanka, Christians, Buddhists, Jews, Hindus, Muslims and Sikhs justify the use of violence on the grounds that they are protecting their religious identity and inter-ests.'[2] In March 1995 I whisked through an underground station in Tokyo minutes before there was a nerve-gas attack by members of Aum Shinrokyo, a Buddhist sect. It is true that the unprecedented violence of the last century was largely due to atheist regimes led by Stalin, Lenin, Hitler, Mao Tse Tung, Pol Pot *et al.*, but violence today is associated with the resurgence of religion. Linking religion and conflict seems perilous even if the enemy is Satan. The Church militant has justified terrible violence by claiming to be combating people seen as the enemies of Christ, often Jews and Muslims.

Then these prayers speak of freeing us from 'original sin'. The very mention of 'sin' tends to make people shift nervously in their seats. When Clare Watkins tried to talk about the forgiveness of sin to her students, they were unhappy. One of them said: 'All this talk about sin makes me feel like I'm not *worthy* or something'. She was asked by the school authorities not to use the term 'sin' but rather talk of weakness,

---

[2] Oliver McTernan, *Violence in God's Name: Religion in an Age of Conflict* (London, 2003), p. ix.

peccadilloes, 'anything that gets us away from the dark psychological damage of guilt-complexes, low self-esteem, and self-hatred. To speak of sin is, many think, to risk instilling these negative and destructive feelings in people'.[3]

Is this talk of combat and original sin a hangover from a primitive form of religion that we should have left behind, or does it reveal something more about the mystery of the love into which we are baptized? In the New Testament, the Christian life is seen as warfare (2 Cor. 10.4), a struggle (Phil. 1.30), an athletic contest (1 Cor. 9.24), and a boxing match (1 Cor. 9.27).[4] We are caught up in a conflict between good and evil (Jn 5.29), light and darkness (Jn 3.19), truth and falsehood (Jn 8.44), life and death (Rom. 6.13, 23). This combative religious language seems to infect our faith with an inescapable violence. Surely this is one reason why so many people feel more drawn to a nice, gentle spirituality rather than to religion which, it is often claimed, is inherently aggressive.

The Bible is filled with violence. In the Old Testament God is often seen as a bloodthirsty warrior eagerly slaughtering the enemies of Israel. Many psalms are filled with cries for vengeance. Early in the morning at Blackfriars, I often wonder what is going through the sleepy heads of my brethren, as we sing that 'Moab I will use for my washbowl; on Edom I will plant my shoe' (Ps. 60.8). Psalm 137 notoriously ends with a horrible cry of revenge against Babylon: 'Happy shall they be who take your little ones and dash them upon the rocks'. What are we to with such a text? In the modern Roman breviary it is discreetly dropped. A Scottish paraphrase has:

O happy shall that trooper be

---

[3] Clare Watkins, *Living Baptism: Called out of the Ordinary* (London, 2006), p. 114.
[4] Cf. Vivian Boland OP, *Spiritual Warfare: Fighting the Good Fight* (London: CTS, 2007), p. 5.

Who riding on his naggie
Shall take thy wee bairns by the toes
And ding them on the craggie.[5]

We must place such texts in the slow evolution of Israel's faith, the long preparation for the appearance of Jesus, who refused to summon God's armies to his side when he was arrested in the garden of Gethsemane and commanded that if we are struck, we must turn the other cheek. The Bible is not, as we asserted above, a collection of literal, factual statements about God. It is the encounter with the Word of God in person. We read these raw and bloody texts as moving towards the dawning of Easter morning, when the wounded Jesus would appear to the disciples and say 'Peace be with you' (Jn 20.19). Centuries of reflection, of prayer and song, of painful exile and liberation were needed before the language was ready for the conception of that Word of peace.

We can only assent to these texts as true, as revelation, by placing them within the movement towards a truth who always remains, even today, beyond our complete grasp. The truth with which we are concerned is not captured by plodding literal statements, but unfolds organically, like a child growing out of childish tantrums and adolescent infatuations into mature, peaceful adulthood. To suggest how this happened, I will offer an extremely abbreviated history of violence in the Bible. Scholars would dispute the details, the dates of biblical texts are not agreed, but that does not matter. I just wish to evoke the dynamic nature of biblical truth, the gradual process by which the non-violence of God was uncovered. Given that the constant accusation against religion is its complicity with violence, it is worth lingering a little on this topic.

---

[5] David Brown, *Tradition and Imagination* (Oxford, 1999), p. 133.

The most obscene violence in the religion of our forebears in faith is already fading by the time the earliest texts came to be written. James Alison writes: 'It is now increasingly clear that for a very long part of their history, the people we now call the people of Israel, had as a regular part of their basic culture the sacrifice of first born children.'[6] Their neighbours still killed their firstborn and it came to be regarded by Israel as an abomination but there are hints that this may have been part of a cruel religion that they grew out of. God says to Israel on Mount Sinai: 'The first born of your sons you shall give to me' (Exod. 22.29). Probably in the earliest days, they literally fulfilled this command, just as their neighbours continued to do so. The strange episode when God tries to kill Moses (Exod. 4.22-26), and the story of Abraham taking Isaac to the mountain to offer him as a sacrifice, are possibly vestiges of a terrible violence that Israel has left behind. Shocking as this might sound, surely this horrible practice embodies a valid religious insight, waiting to be purified of its cruel embodiment, which is that all is a gift from God and so all is owed to God. Israel had to awaken to the insight that giving everything to God does mean that it has to be slaughtered.

Then there is the bloodthirsty tradition of Holy War. During the Easter Vigil, we sing Miriam's song of victory after the Egyptians are routed at the Red Sea, and their bodies are left dead on the seashore. She sings: 'The Lord is a man of war; the Lord is his name. The Pharaoh's chariots and his host he cast into the sea. The flood covers them; they go down into the depths like a stone' (Exod. 15.3-5). And when the people of Israel win the Promised Land, it is again with violence. Joshua recalls how God gave his people this land through war: 'And you went over the Jordan and came to Jericho, and the men of Jericho fought against you, and also the Amorites, the Perizzites,

---

[6] James Alison, *The Forgiving Victim*, chapter 3 (London, forthcoming 2012).

the Canaanites, the Hittites, the Girgashites, the Hivites, and the Jebusites; and I gave them into your hand' (Josh. 24.11).

This image of our God as a warrior may be repulsive to us, but Israel was developing its understanding of God in a religious world in which every nation had its gods fighting on its side. The clash of nations was a reflection of the battles of the gods. And so Israel's faith that God was on its side naturally took this form. We can see here a true insight waiting for liberation from its militant form, which is God's commitment to us: 'If God is for us, who is against us? He who did not withhold his own Son, but gave him up for all of us, will he not with him also give us everything else? Who will bring any charge against God's elect? It is God who justifies' (Rom. 8.31-33).

As Israel settled down in the Promised Land and evolved the worship of the Temple, the priests evolved another understanding of conflict. God's great battle is with the waters of chaos. The battles against the Philistines and the Canaanites are part of a larger and more fundamental drama, with all that threatens the stability of the world. Victory was the creation of an ordered, habitable world. The enemy was turbulent disorder, often symbolized by the roar of the sea. Outside the Temple was a great basin of water which probably reminded the worshippers of God's victory over the powers of destruction. We can detect echoes of the creation myths of Israel's neighbours which told of the slaughter of water monsters when the gods established the world.

Our ordered world, with its separation of the waters above from the waters below, the land from the sea, day from night, male from female, was always threatened by the forces of chaos, which God holds at bay: 'When the waters saw you, O God, when the waters saw you, they were afraid; the very deep trembled' (Ps. 77.16). We believe that the waters of chaos did overwhelm God's own Son on Good Friday. The ordered world broke down. The sun was darkened at midday. God's victory was not in imposing his will on the forces of chaos but in raising his Son from the dead. The chaos of Good Friday was pregnant with Easter Sunday.

So these different forms of combat and conflict are not to be dismissed as simply untrue, as if we could simply shed the Old Testament as an inheritance of which we are ashamed. Here are the first hints of the victory that would happen through a defeat on the cross. The way is prepared by an earlier defeat, when in the summer of 586 BC the Temple was destroyed, the ruling class was deported, and the ordinary people left to live in the ruins under Babylonian rule. Paradoxically it was this traumatic experience of the collapse of all sacred order that took Israel another step closer towards the non-violence of Jesus. The Kingdom of Israel had been wiped off the map so either Israel's God was a complete failure and the gods of the other nations more powerful, or else our God must be the only God, the one who rules all history, and whose purpose is worked out even through this moment of humiliation.

So the crushing of Israel led to the transformation of her faith. God was not just one of the gods, even if stronger and better than the others. Our God was the only God, who had no enemies worth speaking of. We see the seeds of an extraordinary idea, that creation was out of nothing. God spoke a word and the world sprang into being. God creates without having to defeat anything or anyone. This is another step towards the non-violence of Jesus.

So, even in this absurdly simplified sketch, one can see the slow journey by which Israel was being liberated from violence against its own children, from the image of the warrior God smashing its opponents, and on its way towards a new creation which was born of a man who refused violence but bore it with forgiveness.

It seems odd, then, that when we come to the New Testament, we are back into battle again. Jesus came into conflict with the scribes and the Pharisees and with the Roman authorities, but this was but the backdrop to a more fundamental battle, which was with the powers of evil: 'For our struggle is not against the enemies of flesh and blood, but against the rulers, against the authorities, against the cosmic powers of this present darkness, and against the spiritual forces of evil in the heavenly places' (Eph. 6.12).

What is going on in this struggle with the forces of evil? All around the Mediterranean at this time there is a new obsession with demons. They hardly crop up in the Old Testament. They are peripheral beings who hang around the desert. In the classical literature of the Greeks and Romans, demons are neutral; they could be good or bad, but now nasty demons are everywhere. Demons were blamed for every misfortune, for bad harvests, for illness and even for bad book reviews. According to Peter Brown, they were as commonly invoked as microbes today. Brown asserts that 'the sharp smell of an invisible battle hung over the religious and intellectual world of Late Antique man. To sin was no longer merely to err; it was to allow oneself to be overcome by unseen forces. To err was not so much to be mistaken; it was to be unconsciously manipulated by some invisible malign power'.[7]

Brown sees this new concern with demons as symptomatic of an anxious world. Small nations and city states had been swallowed up first in the Empires of Alexander the Great's generals and then in the Roman Empire. Local identities were undermined, and small communities felt embattled and insecure. This sense of uncertainty found expression in an obsession with demons. This is not to dismiss the demonic but to suggest why they were suspected of being under every bed. Demons were chaotic beings who were invoked to explain the experience of a world that was uncertain and threatened. They

---

[7] Peter Brown, *The World of Late Antiquity: AD 150–750* (London, 1993), p. 53.

articulated people's sense of being powerless. They were associated with dirt and dung, with ruins and graveyards. Exorcists protected the community, defended the territory, and gave people amulets and magic words to keep them away. They manned the battlements against demonic assault.

So Jesus is born into a demon-ridden world. He was seen as an exorcist but an unusual one. First of all his exorcisms are part of his healing ministry. The gospels use words that suggest that he is more like a doctor than a warrior. Even more fundamentally, he is not protecting the community by repelling the enemy which menaced its defences. He is beginning to redefine the community. His cures are not so much defensive as creative, bringing a new community into existence. He cures the Gentile man afflicted with a legion of demons and, reluctantly at first, the possessed daughter of the Syro-Phoenician. He refuses to stay behind the walls, but opens the community to foreigners and lepers and all sorts of other frightening people. Exorcism in the gospels is not a matter of taking pot shots from the trenches, but opening up a community beyond its old boundaries. And this is surely why he was seen as a frightening and even demonic figure by his contemporaries: 'And the scribes who came down from Jerusalem said, "He has Beelzebul, and by the ruler of demons he casts out demons"' (Mk 3.22). To these frightened, anxious people, who felt assaulted on every side, this man's outreach to sinners and the sick and foreigners must have felt chaotic and menacing and so he must be on the side of the demons. In a world of exorcists, he was seen as an exorcist, but a strange one, in whose conflicts with the demons something new is coming to be.

But the exorcisms of Jesus were mere preliminary skirmishes. The showdown is on Calvary. This is the final combat, which begins in the garden of Gethsemane, when his enemies come to arrest Jesus. 'This is your hour and the power of darkness' (Lk. 22.53). But the apparent 'defeat' of Jesus on the cross is his victory. He wins by apparently losing, by refusing to return violence for violence.

Jesus conquers through his radical renunciation of violence, and by refusing to be caught in reactions of hatred. This great victory over evil is won by bearing it in hope. In the 'Dream of the Rood', the Anglo-Saxon poem in which the cross tells its tale, we hear of how the young warrior prepares for war by mounting the cross:

> The young hero stripped himself – he,
> God Almighty – Strong and stout-minded.
> He mounted high gallows,
> Bold before many, when he would loose mankind.
> I shook when that Man clasped me.
> I dared, still, not bow to earth,
> Fall to earth's fields, but had to stand fast.
> Rood was I reared. I lifted a mighty King,
> Lord of the heavens, dared not to bend.[8]

He is Christus Victor, the Victorious Christ, usually shown holding up the cross as his trophy of victory. He wins this last great battle through his nonviolence. But what is marvellous is that we are only brought to this astonishing insight by enduring at least two great defeats, that of Exile and that of the cross. The battle is against violence, and above all the violence that lurks within our own hearts. John Paul II described the meeting of religious leaders in Assisi to pray for peace as 'the great battle for peace'. Judaism has made a similar journey. At the Seder when the ten plagues are recounted, the Jews drop ten drops from the wine goblets because the sufferings of the Egyptians diminish their own joy.

---

[8] Quoted by Boland, *Spiritual Warfare*, p. 52.

Oliver McTernan, in *Violence in God's Name*, has traced how for two thousand years Christianity has swung between collusion in violence and its renunciation. The earliest Church was profoundly pacifist. At baptism, one renounced any complicity with war or even capital punishment. One could not be a soldier and a Christian. Tertullian asserted that the Lord 'in disarming Peter disarmed every soldier'.[9] No public official who could execute people, such as St Ambrose, could be baptized until he renounced his post. And yet it was in people like Ambrose, after the conversion of the Empire, that we see the beginning of the Church's complicity in warfare. Once Christianity became the religion of the State, then its primal renunciation of violence began to wane.

In the eleventh century, the pendulum swung again: the Church led a vigorous campaign against the brutality of war. Pope John XV proposed in 985 what became known as the Truce of God. Brutal weapons were forbidden, and on most days of the year no war was permitted for any reason at all. No violence in the name of religion was justified. Cardinal Peter Damiani wrote: 'In no circumstances is it licit to take up arms in the defence of the faith of the universal church; still less should men rage in battle for its earthly and transitory goods'.[10] And then the pendulum swings back and we find ourselves in the age of the crusades, of armies raised to fight for Christianity, and violence is condoned and even blessed.

If there was space, we could trace this waxing and waning in detail in the succeeding centuries: the Spanish conquistadors murdering and enslaving the indigenous people of the Americas in the name of Christ, and yet friars, like the Dominican Bartolomé

---

[9]Quoted by Oliver McTernan, *Violence in God's Name: Religion in an Age of Conflict* (London, 2003), p. 56.
[10] McTernan, *Violence in God's Name*, p. 60.

de Las Casas, battling, also in Christ's name, for the human rights and dignity of these same people, leading eventually to the condemnation of all slavery by Pope Paul III in 1537,[11] almost three hundred years before the cause was taken up in Britain. And then the pendulum swung again. At the beginning of the twentieth century, rival Christian Empires each claimed that God was on our side in the Great War: Gott mit uns! By the end of the century, you find an ever deepening Christian resistance to all war, leading to Paul VI's famous address to the United Nations in 1965: 'No more war, never again war. If you wish to be brothers, drop your weapons'.

Why has Christianity swung to and fro between violence and non-violence? Human beings are violent. Even after baptism and our immersion in Christ's death and resurrection, violence lurks in our hearts. When you want to beat up an enemy, then the battle cries of the bloodier parts of the Old Testament seem to offer a good religious justification for doing exactly what you want to do anyway. So these violent words hang around in our culture waiting to be misused. Satan quotes the Scriptures to Jesus when he tempts him in the wilderness, and these words can still tempt us to unleash the violence in our hearts.

When Jesus met the disciples on the way to Emmaus on the day of the Resurrection, 'beginning with Moses and all the prophets, he interpreted to them the things about himself in all the scriptures' (Lk. 24.27). All of Scripture must be read in the light of Jesus, and those bloody texts must be read in the light of his peace. But in the heat of the moment, we may fall back into a conveniently literal reading of those early battle cries, to justify the imposition of our will. 'Oliver Cromwell had few scruples about brutally crushing the

---

[11] Roger Ruston, *Human Rights and the Image of God* (London, 2004), p. 80.

Irish in the name of the Kingdom of God'.[12] One of my brethren, on his way for his doctoral viva, met his supervisor, Henry Chadwick, who urged him: 'Go and smite the Amalekites!' (1 Sam. 15.18). Chadwick realized that Amalekites would be hard to find in Oxford on a summer's afternoon.

Secondly, we are always mere disciples, which means 'students'. We are forever at the beginning of understanding Jesus' non-violence. It is so radically counter-cultural that we never get hold of it once and for all. It swims against the tides of violence churning in our hearts. And so the combat against violence is never won once and for all, this side of the Kingdom. When someone makes a breakthrough into a deeper glimpse of one aspect of the mystery then he or she may let go another. St Bernard of Clairvaux had a profound understanding of God's love affair with humanity, and his commentary on the Song of Songs is of incomparable beauty, and yet he was an enthusiastic promoter of the crusades. During recent years, the Church has been moving towards a consensus that capital punishment is a violence that is never justified and which harms societies that practise it. What is it that we today simply do not get? One day people may look at us and be astonished at some aggression in our lives of which we are hardly aware. We are just beginning to open our eyes to the violence that we commit against creation, plundering it at the risk of our own future, and our cruelty against animals for the sake of cheap meat.

But the struggle carries on, and for that we are anointed with the oil of exorcism. Adam and Eve run from God's presence because they have awoken to the violence of their act in grabbing the fruit, and to its destructive, death-dealing consequences. They are confronted with a slither of negativity which sours their lives. There is an element

---

[12] William C. Spohn, *Go and Do Likewise: Jesus and Ethics* (New York and London, 2007), p. 69.

of wilful self-harm in the act. This lingers in our lives and needs healing. The man possessed by a legion of demons lives among the dead: 'Night and day among the tombs and on the mountains he was always howling and bruising himself with stones' (Mk 5.5). We are touched by 'something of the night'.

Confronted with evil and violence, it is tempting to see it as being the fault of other people, their aggression, their intolerance. If only we could get rid of them then all would be well. But we must confront our own violence. Etty Hilesum, the young Jewish woman, discovered Christ while waiting to be sent to her death in Auschwitz. Here more than anywhere else in human history, surely it must be right to see the demonic in others. But she says: 'Human beings you say, but remember that you're one yourself... The rottenness of others is in us, too... I really see no other solution than to turn inward and to root out all the rottenness there. I no longer believe that we can change anything in the world until we have first changed ourselves. And that seems to me the only lesson to be learned from this war'.[13]

Jean Vanier, the founder of the L'Arche communities, is one of the gentlest people I have ever met but, with typical courage and honesty, he faces the violence that haunts his own heart. He describes his reaction to the incessant screaming of a mentally disabled young man called Lucien:

> The pitch of Lucien's scream was piercing and seemed to penetrate the very core of my being, awakening my own inner anguish. I could sense anger, violence, and even hatred rising up within me. I would have been capable of hurting him to keep him quiet. It was as if a part of my being that I had learned to control was exploding.

---

[13] Hilesum, *An Interrupted Life*, p. 245.

It was not only Lucien's anguish that was difficult for me to accept but the revelation of what was in my own heart, – my capacity to hurt others – I who had been called to share my life with the weak, had a power of hatred for a weak person.[14]

Mahatma Gandhi was our great master of non-violence in the last century. When India was boiling with conflicts between Muslims and Hindus, he said: 'Each of us should turn the searchlight inward and purify his or her heart as much as possible'. When the Prior of the Trappist monks in Algeria realized that their lives were in danger from the terrorists, he prayed: 'Lord, disarm me and disarm them'.[15]

What is it that has to be healed in our hearts and minds? What is this rottenness, which brought shame to Adam and Eve and made them run away and hide from God's smile? Terry Eagleton claims that we must confront what Freud calls a death drive.

At the core of the self is a drive to absolute nothingness. There is that within us which perversely clamours for our own downfall. To preserve ourselves from the injury known as existing, we are even ready to embrace our own disappearance. Those who fall under the sway of the death drive feel that ecstatic sense of liberation that springs from the thought that nothing really matters. The delight of the damned is not to give a damn... The death drive is a deliriously orgiastic revolt against interest, value, meaning and rationality. It is an insane urge to shatter the lot of them in the name of nothing whatsoever.[16]

---

[14] Jean Vanier, *Essential Writings*, selected and introduced by Carolyn Whitney-Brown (London, 2008), p. 87.

[15] Bernado Olivera OSCO, *How Far to Follow? The Martyrs of Atlas* (Kalamazoo, 1997), p. 19.

[16] Terry Eagleton, *On Evil* (New Haven and London, 2010), pp. 108–9.

And so we come to the font asking for liberation from original sin. It is a doctrine which is so obviously true. G. K. Chesterton says 'it is the only part of Christian theology which can really be proved'.[17] One just has to walk down the street to see it. It does not mean that we are utterly depraved, but that we are born bearing the traces of estrangement from God and each other. It is evident that children born in the Middle East or Northern Ireland, for example, carry the burden of the past, of old prejudices and hatreds. A newborn child is not a *tabula rasa*. It carries within itself an inheritance of anger. Terry Eagleton wrote: 'Original sin is not the legacy of our first parents but of our parents, who in turn inherited it from their own. The past is what we are made of. Throngs of ghostly ancestors lurk within our most casual gestures, preprogramming our desires and flicking our actions mischievously awry'.[18]

Perhaps it would better be called 'unoriginal sin'. In Flann O'Brien's *At Swim-Two-Birds* we meet John Furrisky who 'had one distinction that is rarely encountered – he was born at the age of twenty-five and entered the world with a memory but without a personal experience to account for it'.[19] He was not such an exception. We are all old even before we leave the womb, and our deepest impulse to love must be liberated from the burden of history and a tendency to hit and hurt carried in our genes. Judaism calls it 'the evil impulse'.

In the night Jacob wrestles with a mysterious figure. Jacob will not let him go until he blesses him, which he does and gives him a new name: 'You shall no longer be called Jacob but Israel for

---

[17] G. K. Chesterton, *Orthodoxy* (London, 1996 [1908]), p. 10.
[18] Terry Eagleton, *The Meaning of Life: A Very Short Introduction* (Oxford, 2007), p. 35.
[19] Flann O'Brien, *At Swim-Two-Birds* (London, 2001), p. 9.

you have striven with God and with humans and have prevailed'
(Gen. 32.28). Israel is born, as it were, of God's defeat which is
a blessing. In every church we see Christ on the cross, put there
by ourselves. He bore all of humanity's anger at creation, at our
own existence. That destructive urge was focused on the Son of
God, who died and lives. We are blessed by his defeat. As we
prepare ourselves to be baptized into that death and resurrection,
it is good to recognize that in our own hearts there remain
seeds of violence and that we might well have been in the crowd
shouting 'Crucify him!' We did our damnedest to hurt both God
and ourselves and yet we are alive in him. Maybe our toughest
striving is still with God, whom we try to wrestle to the ground,
but who blesses us.

At baptism today, we are not 'exorcized' in the strict sense of the
word. Satan is not violently cast out of the baby or adult with hideous
screams. The baptized is not 'possessed' but still needs to be liberated
from the chains of 'unoriginal sin', so as to begin afresh in Christ.
In a fifth-century inscription in the Lateran Basilica, the bishop of
Rome's cathedral, we read: 'The water receives the old person, and in
his place makes the new arise. You wish to become innocent; cleanse
yourself in this bath, whatever your burden may be, Adam's sin or
your own'.

We are rejuvenated in Christ, truly young for the first time,
touched by Christ's new creation. In Christ, the child and the
adult can be younger even than the newborn. Our hearts are
strengthened by the Holy Spirit, shaped by God's love and wisdom
and made pure. This does not mean that we shall never again have
'impure thoughts' but that we are touched by Christ's unfailing
newness. Simon Tugwell wrote: 'To have a pure heart is to have a
life which wells up in us from a source too deep for us to plumb.
To have a pure heart is to have a heart that is not just created by

God and then abandoned to us for us to make the most of it; it is to have a heart which is constantly being created and sustained by the newness of the life of God'.[20]

---

[20] Simon Tugwell OP, *The Beatitudes* (London, 1984), p. 97.

7

The oil of gladness

The combat against violence, especially the violence that lurks in our own hearts, sounds rather grim. But we are anointed for this struggle with 'the oil of gladness' (Ps. 45.7). Oil is also a fundamental part of our bodiliness. 'Oily membranes differentiate the smallest parts of our bodies, govern the flow in and out of each cell, protect our skin, and communicate sensations throughout our bodies.'[1] And this olive oil makes the face shine with joy (Ps. 104.15). We are liberated from the power of gloomy old Satan, constantly pondering on past resentments, accusing us of old sins, never forgetting anything, the infernal accountant. He is defeated by Christ's joy, symbolized in the olive oil kept for times of communal celebration:

> How good and pleasant it is, brothers dwelling in unity!
> It is like precious oil on the head, running down upon the beard, on the beard of Aaron,
> Running down over the collar of his robes.
> It is like the dew of Hermon, which falls on the mountains of Zion.
> For there the Lord ordained his blessing, life for evermore.
> (Psalm 133)

---

[1] Gibler, *From the Beginning to Baptism*, p. 45.

At the Chrism Mass on Maundy Thursday, when the oils are consecrated by the bishop in the cathedral, we sing a sixth-century Irish hymn which describes the oil as the fruit of the sun:

> Blest by the sun, the olive tree
> Brought clusters of fair fruit to birth,
> Whose ripeness now we bring with prayer,
> Lord Jesus, redeemer of the earth.

Cyril of Jerusalem says that we were grafted into Christ, the olive tree. Olive oil is distilled sunshine. It is the joy of summer. I do not suppose that in sixth-century Ireland there were any olive trees, but in this anointing we share in the Mediterranean warmth of Christ's own native land. It is a sort of anti-suntan lotion. Our holiday oil protects us from the sun, whereas our holy oil protects us from darkness. We are rubbed down in the oil of Christ, the rising sun who has overcome the power of the night. When Judas goes to betray Jesus, John tells us that 'it was night' (Jn 13.30). We are anointed in the fruit of the sun of Easter morning.

'It was in Antioch that the disciples were first called Christians' (Acts 11.26). We are the disciples of the Christ, which means the Anointed One. He was anointed with the Holy Spirit, and now at this stage of baptism we are anointed with his joy to combat the gloom of evil. According to Denis Minns:

> 'Christos' in ordinary pagan usage was a word used to describe a particular quality of olive oil. It was an adjective meaning 'suitable for anointing'. *Christos* oil was of a lower quality than oil suitable for human consumption, which was called *pistos* – 'trustworthy', or 'safe', but of a higher quality than the oil you would put in a lamp to burn. The kind of olive oil, in other words, that you can buy in Boots, for medicinal purposes. To pagan ears, then, calling

someone Christ would be like calling him ... 'Low Grade', or 'Product of More than One Country'.[2]

This is suitable for the oil that symbolizes the unity of all nations in the humble Christ.

Today there is usually just a dab of olive oil but the earliest Christians were rubbed all over 'from the hair of your head to your toes',[3] says Cyril. It must have made those about to be baptized rather slippery. They were Christ's athletes[4] in the wrestling match with the powers of darkness, which could not get a grip on them.

In the Old Testament, the Lord's anointed was protected from violence. Saul hunts David to kill him, but when he falls into David's hands, he refuses to kill Saul: 'The Lord forbid that I should put forth my hand against the Lord's anointed' (1 Sam. 26.11). 'Who can put forth his hand against the Lord's anointed and be guiltless?' We, the baptized, are the Lord's anointed, and are safe under the Lord's protection. We may be hurt and even killed, but the 'violent one' cannot take our lives in Christ. We glisten with the oil of gladness that is Christ's joy, who for 'the joy that was set before him, endured the cross, disregarding its shame and has taken his seat at the right hand of the throne of God' (Heb. 12.2). And so one of the characteristics of the baptized should be our joy. A French TV team came to S. Sabina, the Order's Headquarters in Rome, to make a programme about the Dominicans. After a week of interviews, the producer said to me: 'We have talked of so many challenges that the Order faces around the world: persecution, civil war, sharing the lives of the destitute, and yet you all seem so happy!'

---

[2] Denis Minns OP, Unpublished sermon.
[3] Cyril of Jerusalem in Edward Yarnold SJ, *Awe-Inspiring Rites*, p. 75.
[4] E.g. Ambrose of Milan in Johnson, *Rites*, p. 136.

Lent is traditionally the time when people are prepared for baptism, and the baptized get ready to renew their baptismal promises during the Easter Vigil. It is described in the first preface for Lent as 'this joyful season'. This is because the traditional disciplines of Lent overcome the violence in our hearts and awaken in us true Christian joy. This is our 'jihad' in the proper sense of the word. In Islam the 'greater jihad' is the personal struggle with oneself to be obedient to God. Vivian Boland OP has helpfully suggested that one can understand this struggle in terms of the threefold command, to love God, one's neighbour and oneself. And the three traditional practices of Lent – prayer, almsgiving, and fasting – heal each of these loves. Lent is the time when Christ's athletes go into training at the spiritual gym and learn again his joy.

Love of God

Our prayer makes us mindful that God is God. We ask for things from God and gives thanks for what we have received, reminding ourselves that God is the source of everything that is. When we pray we are liberated from the terrible burden of thinking that we are tremendously important, and that everything depends on us. This is not a licence for irresponsibility, as we shall see in the final chapter on confirmation, but a prerequisite of proper responsibility. Adam and Eve lost the joy of paradise because they did not trust in God whose only desire was to give them more than they could desire. They grabbed at the fruit because they would not let God be God and so destroyed their own happiness.

Dictators are usually gloomy people because they carry the weight of the world on their shoulders. Hitler was a notoriously boring, self-obsessed conversationalist. He longed to be played in a film by his hero Clark Gable, but instead he got Charlie Chaplin making fun of him in *The Great Dictator*. In *The Last King of Scotland*, Idi Amin starts off as a genial and even lovable figure, but as he claims total power, he too becomes grim and humourless. We tend to have messianic expectations of even democratically elected leaders. Presidents and Prime Ministers are expected to solve all problems within months, and when they inevitably fail to do so, they are despised, because they did not turn out to be God after all. This is why every politician is ultimately regarded as a failure.

This has become acutely so in the West with the rise of what Charles Taylor has called 'the culture of control'.[5] Beginning in the sixteenth century with the rise of the modern centralized state, there was a fading of trust in God's discreet and providential guidance of humanity towards its destiny. God's rule of the world came to be seen in unbending scientific laws rather than in care for his people. It was present in the laws of nature rather than at work intimately in our lives, healing us and nudging us home, redeeming our errors. If God's grace is not at work in our lives, ordering them to our final end, then we must take control instead. The apparent absence of God is no longer sensed as the intimate presence of the one who is closer to us than we are to ourselves, but just at a distance. Having constructed the great clockwork Universe, the divine clockmaker could forget about us and so became irrelevant to our daily lives, our fumbling after goodness. The seeds of secularism are sown and we are on the way to the sadness of the nanny state, in which everything must be policed, watched, measured, administered, taxed, and distrust becomes endemic.

Even in the Church we take ourselves too importantly. Once I had to insist to a senior Vatican Cardinal, who was fretting over

---

[5] Charles Taylor, 'The Rise of the Disciplinary Society', in *A Secular Age* (Cambridge, MA and London, 2007), pp. 90–145.

troublesome Dominicans, that if the Holy Spirit has been poured on the Church at Pentecost, then there was no need to worry! A few rather loose Dominican cannons cannot bring the Church to ruins. Relax!

Pope John Paul II gave Mother Teresa's nuns some space to build a home for poor elderly women, right up against the walls of the papal audience chamber. A senior Vatican archbishop came to preach at a ceremony of its inauguration, attended by Mother Teresa. Paul Murray OP, who was there, describes what happened:

> He spoke for a minute or two, I remember, of the great kindness of Pope John Paul who had originally taken the initiative in making land available, several years before, for the building of the home for the poor. We must, he said, be very grateful to the Pope first, for that original generosity, but also for the new initiative he had taken in offering more space for the building of the dormitory... At this point there was, all of a sudden, an interruption from the front row. Mother Teresa spoke, and I thought I heard what she said. But I could scarcely believe it. Then, with a smile on her face, pointing her finger straight up into the air, she again repeated her original statement: 'We must thank the Lord first!' ... In the wake of Mother Teresa's intervention the Bishop looked, understandably, a bit bewildered. But then, after a moment's hesitation, smiling a little to himself, he continued on with his homily. For her part, Mother Teresa – to my astonishment – continued to keep her index finger pointing straight up into the air. And, while she did this, she glanced over for a second to where I was standing, and in a voice, a half-whisper, at once serious and playful, she exclaimed, 'The *Lord*!' ... Finally, when at last Mother Teresa took down her finger – the homily of the good Bishop having continued on, all

this while, unabated – I noticed she was wearing a very impish grin on her face.[6]

In Murray's book, there is a wonderful photograph of Mother Teresa, taken at that very moment, with her finger pointing upwards: First the Lord! Her impish joy broke through the self-importance of those who mistakenly think that they run the show.

Whenever I visit countries in earthquake zones, earthquakes tend to happen. I have experienced earthquakes in the United States, Japan, Taiwan, Mexico, New Zealand and even Italy. They have never been so severe as to threaten lives. The most dramatic was in San Francisco in 1989, at 6.4 on the Richter scale. But they shook me up enough to remind me that I was really very insignificant. This was strangely liberating. All my silly pretentions to be important were demolished, and I remembered that I was not even a minor angel. We cannot as yet engineer minor earthquakes to keep us sane, but we pray, remembering that God alone is God.

Love of neighbour

The second traditional discipline of Lent is almsgiving. It heals our alienation from each other, and is also inseparable from joy. Charitable giving is an all-pervasive part of our culture. The Charity Commission for England and Wales registers more than 160,000 charities with a combined annual income of £50 billion. There is even a secular humanist charity. It is easy to forget that the giving of charity is deeply rooted in our Christian past, and before that in the

---

[6] Paul Murray OP, *I Loved Jesus in the Night: Teresa of Calcutta, a Secret Revealed* (London, 2009), p. 72.

Old Testament concern for the poor, the stranger, the widow and the orphan.

Wealthy pagans also gave food for the poor. It was a social obligation. But for early Christians almsgiving was central to their baptismal life. The bishop interrogated candidates for baptism, asking 'Have they honoured the widows? Have they visited the sick? Have they done every kind of good work?'[7] Today bishops spend a lot of time ensuring that the diocesan budgets balance. In the early days, one of their most important tasks was to seek funds for the poor. A good bishop was known as a 'beggar lover'.[8] Baptism was initiation into a web of charity. This was the special task of deacons, the most famous of whom was the third-century martyr St Lawrence. Ambrose of Milan tells us that the prefect of Rome was greedy for the Church's supposed wealth – a myth that continues to this day – and commanded Lawrence to surrender it. Lawrence asked for three days, and gathered all the poor and sick supported by the Church and said to the prefect: 'This is the Church's treasure'. According to the legend, he was grilled to death, telling his torturers, 'Turn me over. I am done on this side'!

Christian charity had a fundamentally different meaning from the pagan benefactions for the poor.[9] The poor were seen as our brothers and sisters in Christ. There was a reciprocal relationship between the donor and recipient; the poor prayed for the rich and welcomed them into heaven. The gospels underline the moral perils of being wealthy, and so the rich need the help of the poor, the sick, the homeless, prisoners, who are Christ (Matt. 25.40). When Christ

---

[7] W. Cavanaugh, *Torture and Eucharist: Theology, Politics, and the Body of Christ* (Oxford, 1998), p. 238.
[8] Richard Finn OP, *Almsgiving in the Later Roman Empire* (Oxford, 2006), p. 126.
[9] Finn, *Almsgiving*, pp. 176–220.

claims us in baptism, then the poor claim us. The beggars on the street call on us in the name of Christ and are him. The millions of young people who have no job, or prospect of one, the swelling 'underclass', who are often despised as lazy, living off state benefits, reckless and feckless, are Christ to whom we are bound in baptism. Mother Theresa was once going to a party of important people in Rome, when she stopped to talk at length to a beggar at the door. People began to come out to look for her, and urge her to go in since the great and the good were waiting for her, but she said, 'Can't you see that I am talking to Christ?'

Once the Church became the official religion of the Empire, bishops began to channel money towards big churches and elaborate vestments. But St John Chrysostom preached that it was absurd to spend money on chalices and vestments when Christ was poor and naked on the street:

> Do you wish to honour the Body of Christ? Then do not disdain him when you see him in rags. After having honoured him in Church with silken vestments, do not leave him to die of cold outside for lack of clothing. For it is the same Jesus who says, 'This is My Body' and who says 'I was hungry but you would not feed me. Whenever you refused to help one of these least important ones, you refused to help me'. The Body of Christ in the Eucharist demands pure souls, not costly garments... Give him the honour which he himself has asked for, by giving your money to the poor. Once again what God wants is not so much golden chalices but golden souls.[10]

So almsgiving is an intrinsic part of our life, an expression of who we are in Christ. It is not surprising that the two biggest charities in the

---

[10] 'On the Gospel of St. Matthew', 50, iii, in *Patrologia Graeca*, ed. J.-P. Migne, pp. 58, 508.

world have Christian roots: the International Red Cross and Caritas Internationalis, the federation of Roman Catholic charities which has an annual budget of $5 billion. Christians care for the poor and the sick because we are incomplete without them. Nicholas Berdyaev wrote: 'If I am hungry, it is a biological problem; if my brother or sister is hungry it is a spiritual problem'.

It is not a question of giving just from my surplus, of what I can spare without affecting my standard of living. I should give because in Christ the person who starves is my flesh and blood, my kin. This is hard for us to imagine because most of us have never been hungry. We see children with swollen bellies on the TV news, but it is hard to register that this comatose child is just like us and our children.

I am grateful for one brief experience of hunger. In the late sixties I went to study German in Munich in a time of currency control. I did not think that I would need much money since I had been promised accommodation in the house of the wealthy parents of a university friend. Alas, it turned out that, understandably, they did not love the English and so I had to leave. For six weeks I had to survive on a slice of pizza a day. I gazed into restaurants and was tempted to rush in and grab the food off the diners' plates! I lost a lot of weight and it took some weeks for me to be able to digest much again. I am grateful for that experience, short and relatively painless as it was, since I glimpsed briefly that the starving really are us, and not aliens from another world.

Christian almsgiving should therefore be joyful. When St Paul started the first ever Christian fund-raising campaign, for the poor Christians of Jerusalem, he quoted a proverb: 'God loves a cheerful giver'[11] (2 Cor. 9.7). The gift which is grudging, the result of moral

---

[11] Actually he misquotes the LXX version of Proverbs 22.8: 'God blesses a cheerful man who is also a giver'.

blackmail or guilt, is not really an expression of the baptized life. We rejoice to help our brother and sisters stand on their own feet with dignity. When Peter comes across a beggar at the gates of the Temple, he says to him: 'Look at me! I have no silver or gold, but what I have I give you; in the name of Jesus of Nazareth, stand up and walk' (Acts 3.4-5). Even when we do give silver and gold, still the purpose of the gift is helping someone to their feet. As Jesus was raised from the dead, so too people should be raised to stand up straight. This is our joy.

I visited the diocese of Tombura-Yambio in southern Sudan as part of a CAFOD delegation in November 2010 just before the referendum on independence. It is on the border with the Democratic Republic of the Congo, and is subject to constant violence from the Lord's Resistance Army, a bizarre sect which has killed and mutilated thousands. We always had to travel in close radio contact with another car, in case we were attacked. Already people were streaming home from the north in anticipation of independence. There were terrible food shortages. Some people walked miles just for a few kilos of food. We arrived at a diocesan meeting during a speech which was explaining how the diocese could cease to be dependent on external aid, and stand on its own feet. It was exhilarating, profoundly joyful, to know that the aid that we brought was helping liberate our brothers and sisters in one of the poorest places on earth from degrading dependence.

Ian Linden talks of 'the apartheid of inequality' which wounds the unity of the human family. It is true that poverty has decreased in recent decades in some parts of the world, especially China and India, but we see growing inequalities of wealth within these countries as well as in the West: 'Inequality has intensified both nationally and internationally, forming a network of wealth, expertise and information – all interlinked – and disconnected poverty, a patchwork of affluent nodes surrounded by black holes of marginality'.[12] Humanity suffers not just from the poverty of a third of the planet's population but from an inequality which subverts the unity of the human family and so alienates us from our own flesh and blood. This does violence to us all and adds fuel to the violence of terrorism.

To return to earthquakes: Dorothy Day's life was changed by the experience of the terrible earthquake that destroyed San Francisco on 18 April 1906. It flattened the walls of millions of homes, but it also knocked down the boundaries that separated people from each other. She wrote, 'While the crisis lasted, people loved each other. It was as though they were united in Christian solidarity. It makes one think of how people could, if they would, care for each other in times of stress, unjudgingly in pity and love'.[13] Paul Elie asserts that 'all her life she would try to recapture the sense of real and spontaneous community she felt then, and would strive to reform the world around her so as to make such community possible'.[14]

Almsgiving is an essential part of the preaching of the gospel. It shines the light of Christ on the faces of our kin in Christ. Christian charity is influencing other religious traditions, such as Hinduism, who have seen the extraordinary witness of missionaries caring for the poor, the sick and the dying. When Mother Teresa began her work, initially she encountered stiff resistance. One of her first homes was an abandoned temple of Kali and the Hindu priests wanted her expelled. The police commissioner said, 'Listen to me, I shall not get her out of this temple until you get your mothers and sisters to do

---

[12] Ian Linden, *A New Map of the World* (London, 2003), p. 86.

[13] *The Long Loneliness*, quoted by Paul Elie in *The Life you Save May be your Own: An American Pilgrimage* (New York, 2003), p. 4.

[14] Ibid., p. 5.

the work these nuns are doing. In the temple you have a Goddess in stone; here you have a living Goddess'.[15]

We are anointed at baptism with the oil of gladness. Charity overthrows the sadness of isolation, the loneliness of both the rich and the poor, and heals the wounds of inequality. Mean old Scrooge, in Charles Dickens's *Christmas Carol*, is given a glimpse of his lonely end, unmourned, robbed even of his burial clothes. He wakes up on Christmas Day, determined to give away his wealth, and the first fruit of his conversion is wild, unrestrained joy: 'I am as light as a feather, I am as happy as an angel, I am as merry as a schoolboy. I am as giddy as a drunken man'.[16]

Love of oneself

The third traditional discipline of Lent is fasting, whose purpose is to help us to love ourselves in a proper way. It heals us of greed which, in the story of Adam and Eve, undid humanity: 'So when the women saw that the tree was good for food, and that it was a delight to the eyes, and that the tree was to be desired to make one wise, she took of the fruit and ate: and she also gave some to her husband, who was with her, and he ate' (Gen. 3.6). They were greedy for the delicious fruit, greedy for knowledge, greedy for power and status. Adam and Eve are undone by their unmeasured greed and its voracious power and so lose the joy of paradise.

Of course, human beings have always been greedy but our Western society, which is becoming the planetary culture, is surely unique in seeing greed as good. It is greed that drives the market, which gets

---

[15] Edward LeJoly, *Servant of Love* (New York, 1977), p. 58.
[16] Stave five. First published 1843.

us shopping, and so leads to growth, they say. Greed seduces us with desires that can never be satisfied, for there is always something more to buy. We are consuming the planet, and are ourselves consumed by greed.

Gordon Gekko, in the 1987 film *Wall Street*, made his famous speech to the Teldar Paper Stockholders:

> The point is, ladies and gentleman, that greed – for lack of a better word – is good. Greed is right. Greed works. Greed clarifies, cuts through, and captures the essence of the evolutionary spirit. Greed, in all of its forms – greed for life, for money, for love, knowledge – has marked the upward surge of mankind. And greed – you mark my words – will not only save Teldar Paper, but that other malfunctioning corporation called the USA.

Fasting addresses our greed, and frees us from its violent power. It is not about self-denial. On the contrary it is self-affirmation, the realization that the 'real' Timothy Radcliffe does not *have* to have that extra slice of cake or glass of wine to flourish. It is liberation from a false sense of self, defined by tiny and peripheral desires. Christianity has a long and rich spirituality of fasting. Indeed the radical Muslim fasting of Ramadan probably derived from the strict fasting of Christians in the time of Mohamed. In an age obsessed with eating, too much or too little, we have an ancient tradition which could be of much help. It is paradoxical that just when consumerism was taking off in a big way in the sixties, the Church began to let go of fasting as an intrinsic part of Christian living. Abstaining from meat was abolished and the fast before the Eucharist greatly diminished.

Fasting is not about punishing the body. It is not even primarily about what and how much you eat. It is the liberation of our minds from small compulsions and obsessions, from tendencies to gorge or to anorexia. These crush our joy. Dom Christopher Jamison wrote that 'when they went to live a simple life in the silent sanctuary of the desert, the first thing the desert fathers and mothers noticed was that food was one of the main items looming large in their minds'.[17] It is more about what we think than what we eat. Our thoughts about food become detached from the needs of our bodies. We eat to fill the void in our souls. The monastic discipline of fasting was not so much about *not* eating, as being at ease in eating, eating what was put before you, eating together in gratitude, eating no more than your body needs. It is opening one's eye to the food on one's plate. It is just food to be enjoyed. And if one's boiled egg is slightly overdone, then this is not symbolic of a world that has gone disastrously astray, and the fundamental injustice of life. We love ourselves properly when we are liberated from greedy minds more than greedy tummies! Chefs and babies who hurl food on the floor in rage need to grow up.

So we have been anointed with the oil of gladness. Every Lent we are invited to learn more of that joy, as through prayer we learn to let God be God. By almsgiving, we learn the joy of reaching out to our brothers and sisters, trying to heal the violence of inequality, and, through fasting, tame the violence of our appetites.

---

[17] Dom Christopher Jamison, *Finding Happiness: Monastic Steps for a Fulfilling Life* (London, 2008), p. 67.

8

A fertile word

Baptism is the unfolding story of our entry into the life of God. Each moment responds to what has happened before and takes us one step further. The earlier moments – calling by name, claiming for Christ – reveal that to be human is to have a vocation; we are called into the mystery of love which is the Trinity. But realism forces us to recognize that this vocation involves a struggle. The baptized do not immediately become holy and loving people. Christian life is a continuing conflict with profound forces of selfishness and violence. And so now having faced the negativity that lurks in us, anointed with the oil of gladness, we must prepare for immersion in the fertile and healing waters of baptism.

Every springtime of the Northern hemisphere, Christians perform a fertility ritual. We gather around a tall, phallic candle in the night as it is lit to celebrate the defeat of the winter darkness at the Easter Vigil. The candle penetrates the waters of the font so that they might be made fecund for our regeneration. Flowers hung all over the church show the triumph of fertility. The Easter liturgy, especially in its older form, was, McCabe asserts, 'a very sexy affair'.[1] This is odd

---

[1] McCabe, *God Matters*, p. 103.

because Israel's prophets objected bitterly to the fertility cults of its neighbours. They were always berating the Israelites for whoring after mother goddesses, sleeping with temple prostitutes and ritualizing sexuality to bless their crops. The God of Israel had no sex life to help the coming of rain and the harvest of the wheat, unlike the other gods. In this chapter, when we look at the blessing of the water of the font, we shall see that our faith is indeed about fertility, but we are caught up in a more radical springtime than the religions of the mating gods and goddesses could ever have conceived. This is a fecundity that can heal the darkest twists of our hearts. We come to these waters to be freed from the burden of 'unoriginal sin' and become fertile in Christ.

Philip Larkin wrote:

> If I were called in
> To construct a religion
> I should make use of water.[2]

Alas, he was extraordinarily unoriginal. Nearly all religions make use of water. The story of creation in Genesis links the origins of humanity with the springing up of water.

> In the day that the Lord God made the earth and the heavens, when no plant of the field was yet in the earth and no herb of the field had yet sprung up – for the Lord God had not caused it to rain upon the earth, and there was no one to till the ground; but a stream would rise from the earth, and water the whole face of the ground – then the Lord God formed man from the dust, and breathed into his nostrils the breath of life; and the man became a living being (Gen. 2.4-7).

---

[2] Philip Larkin, 'Water', in *Collected Poems*, ed. Anthony Thwaite (London and Victoria, Australia, 2003), p. 91.

Obviously this is not an historical account of the origins of humanity, since the writers had little understanding of history in our sense. But it is true in a more interesting and profound sense, as an exploration of what it means to be human, and this is seen to be inseparable from water. Our own emergence from dry dust is linked to the flowing of water. The human body mostly consists of water.

In *Crow Lake*, a gem of a novel by Mary Lawson about watching pond life, the hero says, 'there is something about water, even if you have no particular interest in the life forms within it. It is the medium we came from, after all. We were all rocked by water at our beginnings'[3]. Humanity's first vocation was inseparable from water. We were formed to till the soil, to irrigate the first Eden, watered by the river which divided into four branches which gave life to the whole world. 'Without water there is no life; there are no stars, no living planets, no clouds, no mountains, no prairies, and no children of any species'.[4] But those first gardeners failed and were thrust out of the garden.

The sign of our alienation is that the ground became sterile and brought forth thorns and thistles. But when Abraham was about to sacrifice his son Isaac, and so destroy the fruit of his loins, he found a ram caught in a thorn bush. According to Jewish tradition it was in a thorn bush, burning but not consumed, that Moses encountered the living God and the summons to journey to the Promised Land, flowing with milk and honey. Finally the one who would free the land from sterility and bring the springtime of grace, carries on his head a crown of thorns.[5] So it is in this symbol of the badlands, weeds that

---

[3] London 2003 p. 101
[4] Gibler, *From the Beginning to Baptism*, p. 2.
[5] I owe this insight to a sermon by Neil Fergusson OP, 7 March 2010, on torch. op.org.

are neither beautiful nor useful, that we find the promise of a new fertility. It is fitting that when, on Easter morning, Mary Magdalene comes looking for the corpse of the one whom she loves, she meets someone whom she mistakes for a gardener.

The new Adam, Christ our gardener, begins his ministry by coming to the waters of the Jordan through which the Israelites passed to come home to the Promised Land. Through his immersion, the early Christians thought that all water was blessed. Ephrem the Syrian even sees Christ himself as a great flood of fertile water:

> Blessed are you, little Jordan River,
> Into which the Flowing Sea descended and was baptized.
> You are not equal to a drop of vapour
> Of the Living Flood that whitens sins.
> Blessed are your torrents, cleansed by His descent.[6]

Israel lived between the desert and the sea, between death through too little or too much water, dehydration and drowning, the two threats to the future of the planet today. Life-giving water was dew or stream, water that flowed and did not flood, which could be channelled and used for irrigation. So the early Church insisted that, if possible, we should baptize in running water.[7] The water that rejuvenates us is 'living water', the stream of God's grace, not stagnant water or the chaotic threatening water of the sea.

The promise of Jesus to the Samaritan woman at the well is that we shall be sources of living water ourselves: 'The water that I will give will become in them a spring of water gushing up to eternal life' (Jn 4.14; 7.38). When Jesus dies, his side is pierced by the lance of

---

[6] Trans. and Intr. Kathleeen E. McVey, *Ephrem the Syrian* (New York and Mahwah, NJ 1989), p. 326.

[7] Cf. Johnson, *Rites*, p. 36.

the soldier and he becomes a spring of living water (Jn 19.34). And on Easter morning, the dead wood of the cross is often portrayed as flowering. The old thorn bush becomes a tree of life.

At the Easter Vigil, we bless the waters and say, 'Father, look now with love upon your Church, and unseal for her the fountain of baptism'. We bless the waters of the font, a word which comes from the Latin *fons*, a fountain or a spring, so that we may be renewed in the springtime of God's grace. Or if it does destroy, as in the Flood, then it is only so that we can truly live.

Christians naturally speak of God's grace in terms of fertility. The desert of our lives blooms again. St Hildegard of Bingen, the twelfth-century mystic and theologian, speaks of God's *viriditas*, his greenness. The Holy Spirit has 'poured out this green freshness of life into the hearts of men and women so that they might bear good fruit'.[8] 'There is nothing in creation that does not have some radiance – either greenness or seeds or flowers, or beauty – otherwise it would not be part of creation'.[9] God is green. Meister Eckhart, a couple of centuries later, wrote: 'So Our Lord promised to feed his sheep on the mountain of green grass. All creatures are green in God... In the height all things are green: on the "mountain top" all things are green and new. When they descend into time they grow pale and fade. In the new "greenness" of all creatures, Our Lord will feed his sheep'.[10]

The blessing of the waters evokes our nostalgia for Paradise.

Their life will be like a watered garden.

They will never be weary again.

---

[8] The Book of Divine Works, 10, 2, cited by Woods, *Meister Eckhart*, p. 13.
[9] *Hildegard of Bingen: An Anthology*, eds Fiona Bowie and Oliver Davies, trans. Robert Carver (London, 1990), p. 96. Cited in Woods, *Meister Eckhart*.
[10] Sermon 23 in Walshe, *Meister Eckhart*, Vol. II no. 95, pp. 327–28 cited by Woods, *Meister Eckhart*.

Then the young girls will rejoice and will dance,
The men, young and old, will be glad.
I will turn their mourning into joy,
I will console them, give gladness for grief.
The priests I will again feed with plenty,
And my people shall be filled with my blessings.[11]

Notice that while the young are dancing and singing, the clergy are settling down to stuff themselves!

The Jordan entered into the songs of the slaves of the American south, expressing their longing for liberation. Often it was a symbol of the northern states to which they hope to escape to freedom, but more profoundly of the entry into a land where slavery will be no more, and humiliation will be ended and we shall be at peace. In song after song, Jordan is the water of liberation: 'I stood on the river Jordan', 'Roll Jordan, roll', 'You gotta march down to Jordan'.

Get away, Jordan
I want to cross over to see my Lord.
One of these mornings bright and fair
I want to cross over to see my Lord
Going to take my wings and fly the air
I want to cross over to see my Lord.

These blessed waters evoke the desire of every human being for our final home in which there is no threatening sea, for all death and destruction are ended. At the very end of our New Testament, John is shown a vision of 'the river of the water of life, bright as crystal, flowing from the throne of God and of the Lamb through the middle of the street of the city. On either side of the river is the tree of life

---

[11] Jeremiah 31.12-14 **Breviary translation** Morning Prayer Thursday 1.

with its twelve kinds of fruit, producing its fruit each month, and the leaves of the tree are for the healing of the nations' (Rev. 22.1-2).

Water in the Bible is a rich and varied symbolism, some of which I will look at in chapters ten and eleven, on our immersion at baptism. Now I wish to focus on how we are to live our vocation as God's gardeners, stewards of God's fertility. We must care for water in the most literal sense. We are largely made of water. Our future flourishing is inseparable from water. It is our natural element. In *Shantaram*, that lightly fictionalized autobiography of an Australian who fled from prison and found his soul in India, we hear of the hero sitting on the seashore of Mumbai, and discussing with a friend how we remain creatures of water:

> In a way you can say that after leaving the sea, after all those millions of years of living inside the sea, we took the ocean with us. When a woman makes a baby, she gives it water, inside her body, to grow. That water inside her body is almost exactly the same as the water of the sea. It is salty, by just the same amount. She makes a little ocean, in her body. And not only this. Our blood and our sweating, they are both salty, almost exactly as the sea is salty. We carry oceans inside of us, in our blood and sweat. And we are crying the oceans in our tears.[12]

Although water covers 75 per cent of the earth's surface, less than 1 per cent is usable by human beings and as the world population grows – we have just reached seven billion – we shall compete for less water.[13] Wars in the future may be fought over water as in the past they have been fought for oil. Little Jordan is literally running

---

[12] Roberts, *Shantaram*, p. 373.
[13] For the statistics in this paragraph see John L. Allen Jr, *The Future Church: How Ten Trends are Revolutionizing the Catholic Church* (New York, 2009), pp. 313–16.

dry. Nations compete for the water of the Tigris, the Euphrates and the Nile, three of the original rivers of the Biblical paradise. The CIA reckons that by 2015 more than half of the world's population will be 'water-stressed'. The western plains of the United States and much of China are likely to suffer from acute water shortages. Newsweek noted in 2007 that 'the average amount of water used daily by one person living in Ethiopia, Somalia, Eritrea, Djibouti, Gambia, Mali, Mozambique, Tanzania or Uganda equals that used by someone in a developed country brushing his or her teeth with the tap running'.[14] Water is the basis of human community, and the peace of the world will in part depend upon whether we share it or grab it. The Catholic *Compendium of the Social Doctrine of the Church* asserts that 'by its nature water cannot be treated as just another commodity among many, and it must be used rationally and in solidarity with others… Without water, life is threatened. Therefore the right to safe drinking water is a universal and inalienable right'.[15]

Genesis tells the story of how Adam and Eve failed as gardeners and so the land became sterile. This is not, as I said, an historical account, but we may make it come historically true. We have it in our power to end the fertility of our planet and so end human life. We can destroy our small Eden. How we care for water will be symptomatic of whether we are faithful to our human vocation as tillers of the earth. Czesław Miłosz claimed that the best definition of Communism is 'enemy of orchards'.[16] Alas that could be applied to raw capitalism as well. What sort of economy and politics might serve gardens?

---

[14] Ibid., p. 314.

[15] www.vatican www.vatican.va? and quoted by Allen, *Future Church*, p. 315.

[16] Czesław Miłosz, *Proud to be a Mammal* (London, 2010), p. 84.

A fertile word

So the Easter Vigil, the traditional setting for baptism, looks like a fertility rite, but it is not literally one. The God of Israel had no earth goddess with whom to mate. Eventually God's creativity came to be seen as the speaking of a word, and the first word that God speaks is: 'Let there be light'. The word is spoken effortlessly. No sea monster has to be carved up so that the 'void and darkness' be tamed. It is a word that lets whatever is created be itself. Just by being what it is, it points to the one who gives it existence. God is shown in a bush that burns and yet is unconsumed. His fire does not destroy the bush because God created it.

We are created to be God's gardeners above all by speaking God's fertile word. 'The Lord God formed every animal of the field and every bird of the air, and brought them to the man to see what he would call them; and whatever the man called each living creature, that was its name' (Gen. 2.19). Adam is trusted to choose the names rightly because he lives in harmony with the Creator. He sees what every animal is and so knows its name.

We are given 'dominion' (Gen. 1.28) over the whole world. Often this is claimed to have justified our voracious exploitation of the earth which is leading us towards an ecological catastrophe. All the plants and animals exist for our benefit, to be used as we wish. This is a very late interpretation of the text, which went with the rise of State power and the culture of control in the sixteenth century. But in the Old Testament we are seen as servants of the God who 'who loves the living' (Wis. 11.26). Being God's gardeners requires that we exercise stewardship over creation because everything sings of God just by being itself.

The pastures of the wilderness overflow, the hills gird themselves
with joy,
The meadows clothe themselves with flocks, the valleys deck
themselves with grain,
They shout and sing together with joy. (Ps. 65.12-13)

Our vocation is to hear that silent song and bring it to word. We
discover, uncover, how things praise God by their existence. Meister
Eckhart said: 'All things speak God. What my mouth does in speaking
and declaring God is likewise done by the essence of a stone, and this
is understood more by works than by words'[17];'Someone who knew
nothing but creatures would never need to attend to any sermon, for
every creature is full of God and is a book'.[18]

But Adam betrays his vocation. The north porch of Chartres
Cathedral shows the story of creation. God is in the outmost circle,
creating the world with Adam and Eve and Eve as co-creators. After
the fall, they have become part of the problem. They move to an inner
circle because they have learned to speak destructively, to call what is
evil good, to see the fruit as to be grabbed and to point the finger in
accusation. Redemption heals our tongues, so that we can regain our
role as God's partners in creating a flourishing world.

The King's Speech tells the story of how King George VI overcame
his stammer with the help of an Australian speech therapist, Lionel
Logue. The plot revolves around a gentle paradox. He must learn to
speak well because he is the King. His royal words are needed to give
strength to the nation in a time of war. He must speak like a proper
King who will inspire his people. But he can only learn to do so with
the help of this Australian commoner who insists on treating him as

---

[17] Sermon 53, in Walshe, Vol. 1 no. 22, 1979, p. 179. Quoted in Woods, p. 55.
[18] Sermon 9, in Walshe, Vol. II no. 67, p. 155 quoted in Woods.

an equal. He may be His Majesty elsewhere but in Lionel's rooms, he is just Bertie. And the King must learn to call him Lionel. This is deeply painful for the King but it is only in the context of equality that his stammer can be cured.

This is a parable of the healing of our stammering tongues. We too have a royal vocation. We are the children of the Most High God and so we have the vocation of speaking words that give strength, which encourage and build the Kingdom of God. George VI is healed by befriending a commoner. With us, it is the other way around. It is Christ the King who comes to offer us his friendship, and whose grace heals us of rivalry, of bitterness and accusation.

We are immersed in the fertile waters so that we may learn to speak again words of blessing. The first time that the word 'blessing' is used in the Bible is immediately after the creation of humanity. 'God blessed them, and God said to them, "Be fruitful and multiply"' (Gen. 1.28). Blessing makes us fecund and our words of blessing are the most fundamental way in which we are fertile.

After Mass at Manaoag, in the northern Philippines, people bring their pens to be blessed before exams, and their cars and their friends, everything! In Guanuaqil, on the coast of Ecuador, every Monday there is the blessing with the water of St Vincent Ferrer. He was a famous fourteenth-century Dominican preacher. It is fitting that a preacher's words are thought to be powerful to bless. Indeed one of the mottos of the Dominican Order is 'To praise, to bless, to preach'. People come for his blessing with their illnesses, their worries, and even their TV antennae so that 'St Vincent will give me a better reception'.

All these priestly blessings may look like 'Catholic superstition', but every human being is called to bless. Until recently, all baptized Christians blessed. It belonged to the priesthood of all believers. I visited a Flemish family forty years ago with a friend of mine, a young

Dominican priest. Before he went to bed he went to seek his father's blessing, who made the sign of the cross on his son's forehead. People blessed each other when they met. 'Hail' is a word of blessing. They blessed each other as they parted: 'Vaya con Dios' (Go with God); Adieu (To God). Dominicans used to go to the Prior and ask for a blessing before leaving on a journey and receive one on their return. Every meal was blessed before it was eaten and thanks given at the end. At the end of the day, in Ireland, there was a prayer to be said for the preservation of the fire in the embers overnight: 'I preserve the fire as Christ preserves all. Brigid at the two ends of the house, and Mary in the centre. The three angels and the three apostles who are highest in the Kingdom of Grace, guarding this house and its contents until day'.[19]

Gregory Boyle SJ recounts celebrating Mass for indigenous people in the mountains near Cochabamba, Bolivia. He was a young priest who had almost no Quechua, and at the end, as he began the long walk home, he feels that he has been a failure and failed to communicate at all. But an old peasant, poorly dressed, appears and thanks the young Jesuit for having come:

> Before I can speak, the old campesino reaches into the pockets of his suit coat and retrieves two fistfuls of multicoloured rose petals. He's on the tips of his toes and gestures that I might assist with the inclination of my head. And so he drops the petals over my head, and I'm without words. He digs into his pockets again and manages two more fistfuls of petals. He does this again and again, and the store of red, pink and yellow rose petals seems infinite. I just stand there and let him do this, staring at my own huaraches

[19] John Scally, 'The Spiritual Legacy of John McGahern', *Doctrine and Life* Vol. 60, no. 10 (December 2010), p. 19.

(leather sandals), now moistened with my tears, covered with rose petals. Finally, he takes his leave and I'm left there, alone, with only the bright aroma of roses.[20]

All this can easily slip into superstition, but it is our baptismal vocation to speak words of blessing. An Irish Catholic bishop complained recently 'we clergy have taken over the power of blessing, and it is as if no one else can bless'. Perhaps the tide is turning. When a Vatican archbishop went to a meeting of religious sisters in Madrid in 2010, they asked him for a blessing. He said that in his country, it was the mother who blessed the son, and asked for theirs instead. John O'Donohue, the Irish poet, commented, 'It might sound old-fashioned, but the blessing might be the coolest thing of all. It has a democracy and equality in it, a sense of intention and well-wishing that is concerned more with the destiny of someone rather than their destination'.[21]

Moses says to the people of Israel, 'I call upon heaven and earth to witness against you today that I have set before you life and death, blessings and curses. Choose life so that you and your descendants may live' (Deut. 30.19). Our daily choice is whether we offer words of blessing to others or words that curse, words that offer life or death. This is the choice that we make a hundred times a day as we talk about each other, gossip, joke, exchange the news, share our hopes and fears. It is sad that today most people use 'God' and 'Jesus Christ' as curses rather than blessings. Our language is so filled with crude expletives that we are in danger of becoming a race of Calibans: 'You taught me language; and my profit on't is I know how to curse'.[22]

---

[20] Boyle, *Tattoos on the Heart*, p. 38.
[21] Interview with Martin Wroe, *The Church Times* (14 January 2011).
[22] William Shakespeare, *The Tempest* Act 1, Scene 2.

Think of the vacuous boasting, the puffed-up words with which we bore and crush each other. St Bernard of Clairvaux talked of the monk who is so full of himself that he cannot stop speaking: 'He is full of words, and the swelling spirit strains within him. His hunger and thirst are for listeners, someone to listen to his boasting, on whom he can pour out his thoughts, someone he can show what a big man he is. At last the chance to speak comes. The discussion turns on literature. He brings forth from his treasury things new and old. He is not shy about producing his opinions; words are bubbling over'.[23] His brethren must have fled when he was in full flight!

Think of how our words can be reductive, blinding us to the gratuity of creation. I have often written of the commodification of language in the seventeenth century, of how things that previously had been seen as gifts of God – water, land and, indeed, human beings for example – came to be thought of as objects for sale.

Think of the snobby ways in which we speak of others. A now dead Duchess famously declared that she considered anyone who took a bus after the age of forty to be a failure. But we belong to *hoi polloi*, 'the many', 'a great multitude which no one can count' (Rev. 7.9), and the omnibus (literally 'for all') is our natural form of transport![24]

Think of the violence that is implicit in words. Shortly after the Republican politician Gabrielle Giffords was shot at her home town in Arizona in January 2010, Catherine Philip wrote of how the language of the hard right had been becoming ever more aggressive: 'At a Tea Party Rally in Las Vegas in October, I stood in a crowd that

---

[23] *The Steps of Humility and Pride*, trans. J. Leclerq and H. Rochais, cited by Stephen Cherry, *The Barefoot Disciple: Walking the Ways of Passionate Humility* (London, 2011), p. 60.

[24] Forgive this slightly laborious jeux d'esprit, which I could not resist.

cheered "lock and load" as people vowed to do away with Harry Reid, the Senate majority leader. His Republican challenger in the midterm elections, Sharron Angle, had already spoken of a "Second Amendment solution" to the frustrations with Washington – the right to bear arms'.[25] A potential presidential candidate had marked a map with gun sights on those whom she believed needed to be eliminated. This is not to say at all that these people were intending violence, but violent words have a terrible tendency to become flesh. P.J. Harvey released an album in 2010 with a track called 'The Words that Maketh Murder'.

Think of the malicious gossip which we so enjoy circulating, with feigned sadness, of other people's failures or disgrace, the glee with which we hear of the fall of celebrities. The story is told of a rabbi who was driven mad by a woman in the synagogue who was always gossiping about everyone, spreading nasty stories. And so one day he took her to the top of a high tower and asked her to empty the contents of a pillow. The feathers drifted all over the town. And then he said, 'Now go and collect all the feathers'. She replied, 'Rabbi, that is impossible; they are everywhere'. And he said, 'It is the same with your nasty words'.

It is the vocation of the baptized to speak good, healing, blessing-filled words. We are called to purify the words of even their implicit poison, the little unhelpful metaphors that lurk unnoticed. When a priest visiting Mother Teresa in Calcutta heard that she wished to send missionaries to China, he asked if there was any particular group that she wished to 'target'.[26] She replied: 'My great desire is to meet anyone who has nobody'. She purified the language of its implicit aggression.

---

[25] *The Times*, 10 January 2010.
[26] Murray, *I Loved Jesus in the Night*, p. 79.

I pointed out earlier that Jesus' opponents often try to trap him in alternatives that lead nowhere. Jesus' wit finds a way through to a new space in which we can live. His wittiness, his quickness of mind, is a participation in God's creativity. Wit can crush and deflate, but it can also liberate and renew. It can subvert divisive language, undoing its poisonous categories. Herbert McCabe, visiting South Africa during the years of apartheid, provocatively sat in the wrong part of a bus. When he was told to move, he asked why. 'Because you are white'. 'No, I am not. I'm Irish'. Once Archbishop Desmond Tutu, walking along a pavement in South Africa, came face to face with a white man who said: 'Get out of my way. I don't give way to gorillas'. To which Tutu replied, 'Ah, yes, but I do', and let him pass. The Duke of Edinburgh shouted at a group of tabloid journalists who were pestering the Royal Family, 'You are all scum'. To which one replied, 'Sir, we may be scum, but we are the *crème de la* scum!'

The Wisdom tradition taught that the wise person often refrains from speech: 'Whoever belittles another lacks sense, but an intelligent person remains silent' (Prov. 11.12). When I was Master of the Dominican Order I look back with most regret on the times when I forgot to control my tongue and said something that hurt a brother or sister, or failed to cherish their dignity. I would lie in bed at night wanting to do anything to take back the word, to replay the scene and edit out the word that slipped out, or search for an occasion to put balm on the wound, but it was too late.

There is a Mexican proverb: *Dios habla por el que calla.* God speaks for the one who keeps silent. Barbara Kingsolver's novel *The Lacuna* revolves around the importance of words that are spoken or left unsaid, lost and found. Diego Rivera, the Mexican muralist, welcomes Lev Trotsky when he flees into exile. But their friendship is destroyed by careless words, words which were never intended to hurt, which ought to have had no consequence but had been left around and discovered:

> Why did Diego call his friend a goat? He expected the word to vanish with the afternoon past, that's why. Bitter words normally evaporate with the moisture of breath, after a quarrel. In order to become permanent, they require transcribers, reporters, complicit black hearts. Diego meant nothing by that letter; his respect for Lev is undying. He had an eye infection that week, a cramp in his stomach after too many pork sandwiches. From somewhere in that roil, a few poisonous sentences erupted. Now the world has them.[27]

Once they are spoken, they are out of his control. When the hero of the novel has a harmful thought, his secretary says: 'Mr Shepherd, ye cannot stop a bad thought from coming into your head. But ye need not pull up a chair and bide it sit down.'[28]

Silence also liberates us from the chain reaction of violent speech and opens a space for some new word to be spoken. When the mob come to Jesus with the woman caught in adultery, they demand to know what he thinks should be done with her. Whatever answer he gives will bring him trouble. But he begins by saying nothing at all; he bends down and writes with his finger in the dust. When they kept on questioning him, he straightens up and says, 'Let anyone among you who is without sin be the first to throw a stone at her' (Jn 8.6-7). His silence slows the mad rush of events that was carrying her towards her death. It defuses their blind indignation and opens a space in which they might each hear his words, no longer as a mob but as individuals who must face their own sin. Rowan Williams

---

[27] Barbara Kingsolver, *The Lacuna* (London, 2009), p. 271.
[28] Ibid., p. 440.

commented: 'He hesitates. He does not draw a line, fix an interpretation, tell the woman who she is and what her fate should be. He allows a moment, a longish moment, in which people are given time to see themselves differently, precisely because he refuses to make the sense they want. When he lifts his head, there is both judgement and release'.[29]

The most beautiful words of blessing are surely those of forgiveness. They do not annihilate the past but are God's fertile words which can make even the barren wilderness of our lives blossom again. And so when someone comes to the sacrament of reconciliation in the Catholic Church, to ask for forgiveness, their first words are: 'Bless me father for I have sinned'. Forgiveness is not the scrubbing out of our sins, pretending that they never happened. Forgiveness is a blessing through which even our failures are taken up into God's grace and become part of our way to God. The priest offers this blessing on behalf of the whole community. They express the priestly forgiveness of the whole people of God. St Augustine says that the act of forgiveness gives that person's turbulent heart the community's peace.[30] We cannot all crowd into the room, and so someone is ordained to represent the whole Body of Christ.

That is why it is such a terrible disgrace if anyone is humiliated when they confess. Herbert McCabe OP once went to confession in Dublin and was given a terrible dressing down by the priest. Herbert came out of the box, said his penance, and then waited for the priest to come out of his side. He grabbed him and said to him 'You are a disgrace to the priesthood. Never ever speak to anyone like that again!'

---

[29] Rowan Williams, *Writing in the Dust: After September 11* (London, 2002), p. 80.

[30] Paul Philibert OP, *At the Heart of Christian Worship: Liturgical Essays of Yves Congar* (Collegeville, MN, 2010), p. 20.

It belongs to the priesthood of every Christian to forgive. This may be done explicitly, or else by finding healing words that offer the other person a way forward. Jim Campbell was an American who had been a navigator on a plane that bombed Japan during the Second World War. After the War he became a Dominican but he was always tormented by his part in the destruction of innocent people. And so he decided to go to Japan to ask for forgiveness. He had met Oshida, a Japanese Dominican, at a conference in the States and so he went to see him at Oshida's Ashram on the slopes of Mount Fuji. He said to him, 'Father Oshida. I bombed your people during the War. I have come to ask your forgiveness'. And Oshida replied, 'And I was in the Japanese anti-aircraft force in those days. I tried to shoot you down and I am sorry I missed!' Brian Pierce OP comments: 'They both laughed and embraced each other! The way in which Father Oshida, this holy man, had shown Jim that they had both been part of the same evil, was very liberating for Jim. "I am sorry I missed!" was the cry that set Jim free after forty years of carrying this pain from the war'.[31]

Some people, presumably Jews, even managed healing words in the aftermath of the obscenity of the Holocaust. A prayer was found next to the body of a dead child at Ravensbruck concentration camp:

O Lord, remember not only the men and women of good will, but also those of ill will. But do not remember all the suffering they inflicted on us; remember the fruits we have borne, thanks to this suffering – our comradeship, our loyalty, our humility, our courage, our generosity, the greatness of heart that has grown out of all this, and when they come to judgment let all the fruit which we have borne be their forgiveness.[32]

---

[31] Lucette Verboven, *The Dominican Way* (London, 2011), p. 48.
[32] Quoted by Michael Sadgrove, 'A Sermon: Holocaust Memorial Day', www.durhamcathedral.co.uk.

Often the baby being brought to baptism remains asleep through this most important event of its life. We might think this odd, but often God's creative fertility enters our lives when we sleep. 'So God caused a deep sleep to fall upon the man, and he slept; then he took one of his ribs and closed up its place with flesh' (Gen. 2.21). And so Adam is given Eve, flesh of his flesh. This is more than a convenient anaesthetic. It is while he sleeps that Adam is transformed and becomes someone new in his relationship with his partner. When Abraham falls into a deep sleep, the Lord makes a covenant with him. At Bethel, Jacob puts a stone under his head, sleeps and is granted the vision of angels ascending and descending and receives a new promise from the Lord. Daniel sleeps and has visions. As the psalm says, 'he puts gifts on his beloved while they slumber' (Ps. 127.2). Jesus sleeps in the boat during the storm, and finally he will sleep in the tomb on Holy Saturday and wake to Easter Day.

Why all this sleeping? Surely because it is in sleep that the new germinates. 'The kingdom of God is as if someone should scatter seed on the ground, and would sleep and rise night and day, and the seed would sprout and grow, he knows not how' (Mk 4.26). And so it is entirely appropriate that some babies slumber in this moment of rebirth.

In the depths of the earth, out of control, the seed unfolds and the new is born. Rilke wrote:

> In spite of all the farmer's work and worry,
> He can't reach down to where the seed is slowly
> Transmuted into summer. The earth bestows.[33]

In sleep we let go of control, take our hands off the steering wheel, and let God be God. The Spirit is discretely at work in our lives. If

---

[33] 'The Sonnets to Orpheus XII', in *Selected Poems with Parallel German Text*, new translations by Susan Ransom and Marielle Sutherland (Oxford, 2011), p. 195.

one is monitoring everything all the time, checking that everything is correct, then nothing new can happen. Plants cannot flourish if you pull them out of the earth all the time to inspect their roots. And so in the Church we need to do a bit more sleeping, trusting in the Lord of the harvest. Ian Stackhouse, a Baptist minister, wrote: 'Night time commits the ultimate heresy for moderns: getting us to stop. To sleep one has to relinquish, to let go. And since letting go is not something we are good at, many of us don't sleep well.'[34] We do not always need to be monitoring, managing, seeing what people are up to, fretting that they might make a mistake or get it wrong. The Church will only be renewed if we rest, trusting in the Lord, and sometimes look the other way, let be. Love, remember, let's be. When I was Master of the Order, I gave thanks to God that I had one deaf ear, to which the brethren could address things which I did not need to know or fret about.

---

[34] Ian Stackhouse, *The Day is Yours: Slow Spirituality in a Fast-Moving World* (Milton Keynes, 2008), p. 79.

9

The moment of choice

All that has happened so far – the naming of the candidate, the claiming for Christ, exorcism and anointing, the blessing of the water – all prepare us for this moment of decision. The baptized must now formally choose Christ rather than Satan. Now is the moment to take the plunge.

We begin with the rejection of Satan.

Do you reject sin, so as to live in the freedom of God's children?
I do
Do you reject the glamour of evil, and refuse to be mastered by sin? I do.
Do you reject Satan, the father of sin and prince of darkness? I do.

This should be done with bold enthusiasm. One of my brethren, Austin Milner, asked to renew his baptismal promises on his deathbed: 'Do you renounce Satan?' 'I most certainly do!' A member of our parish in London answered even more decidedly: 'I do, the old bastard!'

For our Christian ancestors in pagan Rome it was a dramatic moment. They turned to face the West, the place of the setting sun.[1]

---

[1] David Bentley Hart, *Atheist Delusions: The Christian Revolution and its Fashionable Enemies* (New Haven and London, 2009), p. 113.

They blew on Satan. This was an act of contempt, like that of the Iraqi man throwing a shoe at President Bush at a press conference in Baghdad. To blow on a statue of the Emperor was an act of treason.[2] When devils appeared to St Antony, the founding desert father, he drove them away by blowing on them. Jesus breathed the life of Holy Spirit into the apostles; the baptized blew away the powers of death. In some places, they spat on Satan. They broke with the religious culture of their society, which is why they were considered to be atheists who must die.

Then they turned east towards the rising sun and proclaimed their faith in the Risen Christ. They recited the Creed which they had learned by heart over the previous weeks, helped by their godparents. St Augustine reassured those who were nervous that they might forget it on the big day, that he would help them to remember the words.[3]

The renunciation of Satan had profound consequences for the daily lives of the early Christians. They promised not to go to the theatre or any other works of the Devil. They had to give up the horse races, which would have been tough for my father. They avoided public baths, places for meeting one's colleagues and for civilized conversation. Going to the baths was part of the life of a citizen. So they dropped out of polite society. Paradoxically the baptized might have been considered by their pagan neighbours as belonging to the great unwashed, uncivilized and smelly.

Declarations of belief are considered embarrassing in our secular society. Many feel that faith is a private matter, best not shared in public. Virginia Woolf was shocked when she discovered that T. S. Eliot had become a Christian:

---

[2] Yarnold, *Awe-Inspiring Rites*, p. 6.
[3] Ibid., p. 12.

I have had a most shameful and distressing interview with poor dear Tom Eliot, who may be called dead to us all from this day forward. He has become an Anglo-Catholic, believes in God and immortality and goes to church. I was really shocked. A corpse would seem to me more credible than he is. I mean, there's something obscene in a living person sitting by the fire and believing in God.[4]

So we may be tempted to keep our beliefs to ourselves, or at least not express them with too much conviction. They may be lightly aired as a personal preference, something that works for me, rather than making a bold claim that they are true. As Ronnie Knox put it:

When suave Politeness, temp'ring bigot Zeal
Corrected 'I believe' to 'one does feel'.[5]

Cardinal Innitzer preached a sermon in Munich in 1938, proclaiming that 'Christ is our Führer'. His house was trashed and thousands of priests and religious were sent to death in Dachau concentration camp. The Anglican Bishop of Singapore was imprisoned by the Japanese during the Second World War and tortured. He lived it as a repetition of his baptismal vows:

In the middle of the torture they asked if I still believed in God. When, by God's help, I said 'I do', they asked me why God did not save me. By the help of his Holy Spirit I said, 'God does save me. He does not save me by freeing me from pain and punishment, but he saves me by giving me the strength to bear it'; and when they asked me why I did not curse them I told them that it was because

---

[4] Quoted by Peter Hitchens, *The Rage against God* (London and New York, 2010), p. 12.
[5] 'Absolute and Abitofhell', Oxford Magazine 1913.

I was a follower of Jesus Christ who taught us that we were all brothers and sisters.[6]

Who knows how we may have to renew our baptismal promises one day? Baptism is unlikely to have drastic consequences for us in the West today, though for people in many parts of the world, Communist or Muslim, it can still mean exclusion from community, imprisonment and even death. 250 million Christians still face persecution or at least active discrimination because of their faith.[7] The silence of Western governments over the persecution of millions of Christians is hard to understand.

So what does it mean for us to renounce the 'glamour' of evil? The seduction of evil is that it looks fun. Wicked people seem to be really alive, having a good time, unlike timid, boring Christians. In *The Eustace Diamonds* by Anthony Trollope, Admiral Greystock is said to have lived life to the full until his last day, which meant 'whist, wine and wickedness'. Terry Eagleton was asked by his young son what he was writing about. When he replied, 'Evil', his son said 'Wicked!'

The myth that evil is fun and virtue boring is still seductive. Helen Gurley Brown, the editor of *Cosmopolitan*, famously said: 'Good girls go to heaven; bad girls go everywhere'. The abiding fascination of horror movies testifies to the attraction of evil. Kenneth Tynan, a flamboyant aesthete, had C. S. Lewis as his tutor at Oxford. This was profoundly challenging because Lewis made goodness seem attractive. Tynan wrote in his diary of feeling 'a genuine tug of war with my recent self. How thrilling he makes goodness seem – how tangible and radiant!'[8] Terry Eagleton argues that 'evil is philistine,

---

[6] John Bowker, *Problems of Suffering in the Religions of the World* (Cambridge, 1975), p. 96.

[7] Cf. Rupert Shortt, *Christianophobia* (London, forthcoming 2012).

[8] Paul Tankard, 'Forbidden Art', *Times Literary Supplement* (11 March 2011), p. 13.

kitsch-ridden, and banal. It has the ludicrous pomposity of a clown seeking to pass himself off as an emperor. It defends itself against the complexities of human experience with a reach-me-down dogma or a cheap slogan... Hell is being talked at for all eternity by a man in an anorak who has mastered every detail of the sewage system of South Dakota.[9]

How can we show that the deepest joy is to be a saint, and that wickedness is not as jolly as it is cracked up to be? It is often imagined that pagan Rome must have been exuberantly joyful, beautiful people having guilt-free sex, the streets flowing with wine, an admirable intellectual life, lots of sport, entertainment in the circuses, and even sunshine. The suspicion lurks that the early Christians who renounced this must have been puritanical and grim people, obsessed with death. But, according to David Bentley Hart, pagan Rome was a sad place. Recent historians have drawn attention to 'the darkness haunting much of its mythology, the capriciousness and brutality of the pagan divine, the misery and despair with which death was contemplated, the fear of occult forces within nature, the religious reliance upon sacrifices of appeasement and impetration, the violence of many sacral practices, and above all a nearly universal acquiescence to the law of fate.'[10]

Baptism was the renunciation of this dismal world. The baptized claimed their freedom in Christ, renouncing pagan resignation to inexorable fate and rejected the extraordinary variety of ways by which pagans tried to discover what lay around the corner. Theodore of Mopsuestia required candidates for baptism to give up divining the future by reading the stars, or inspecting the entrails of animals, the

---

[9] Eagleton, *On Evil*, p. 124.
[10] David Bentley Hart, *Atheist Delusions: The Christian Revolution and Its Fashionable Enemies* (New Haven and London, 2009), p. 133.

pattern of birds' flight, or hanging up fermenting dough![11] In Christ we are called to take charge of our own destiny. The pagan gods had no power over us and we could mock their pretensions. In 389, a Christian noblewoman strode into the Temple of the Great Mother Cybele, on the Palatine Hill in Rome, and snatched the necklace from the neck of the idol, walking away to the curses of the last Vestal Virgin! This was a victory over fear and fate.

Christians renounced the sadism of pagan Rome, the gladiatorial contests, the shows in which criminals were tossed to the wild beasts, the human sacrifices made to the gods, the crucifixions and burnings which were part of everyday pagan life. The word pagan possibly comes from army slang for non-combatant, someone who refused to fight.[12] The baptized promised fealty to Christ, and enrolled in his battle against violence. The renunciation of Satan and the adhesion to Christ at baptism was, Bentley Hart wrote, 'an act of cosmic rebellion' against fatalism, cruelty, violence and despair. 'The "new thing" that the gospel imparted to the world in which it was born and grew was something that pagan religion could only occasionally adumbrate but never sustain, and that pagan religion would, in most cases, have found shameful to promote: a deep and imperturbable joy'.[13] When we deny Satan, we reject fatalism, resignation, violence and despair.

But what do we affirm with the Creed? The Creed offers another way of telling the story of humanity, which leads to the Kingdom and our sharing in God's own happiness. The Creed is a love story with which we pledge our lives to God. Nicholas Lash compares the recital of the Creed to the marriage vows: The Creed 'promises that life and love, mind, heart and all my actions, are set henceforth steadfastly on

---

[11] Yarnold, *Awe-Inspiring Rites*, p. 182.

[12] Diarmaid MacCulloch, *A History of Christianity* (London, 2009), p. 152.

[13] Hart, *Atheist Delusions*, p. 145.

God, and on God alone. "William James, do you take Mary Montague to be your lawful wedded wife?" "Mary Montague, do you believe in God the Father almighty, creator of heaven and earth?" The grammar of these two declarations is the same'.[14] We bind ourselves to God for better for worse, for richer for poorer, in sickness and in health till death do us finally unite. Every Easter Vigil, we renew our marriage vows to God. Belief in God is not assenting to a number of propositions about God; it has been translated as believing 'unto God'. We cleave to God as to the Beloved.

When I was preparing a young couple for marriage recently, they wanted to know how much of the Creed they must accept if they were to 'count' as Christians. Should one aim for at least 100%? Can one scrape by with 51%? But in *Why Go to Church? The Drama of the Eucharist* I suggested that the Creed teaches us to see the world with gratitude, as the gift of the Father, to delight in its intelligibility as the work of the Word, and to see it lovingly in the Spirit.[15] In the context of baptism, it is the declaration of our confidence that God calls us to himself. This is the meaning of our lives. It proclaims that human history is a love story, leading from the creation of everything by God the almighty, to the forgiveness of sins, the resurrection of the dead and life everlasting.

St Thomas writes: 'What is it, therefore, to believe in Him? It is in believing to love, in believing to delight, in believing to walk towards him, and to be incorporated amongst the limbs and members of his body'.[16] When St Peter of Verona, the first Dominican martyr, was murdered by Cathars in 1252, he was reputed to have written in the

---

[14] Nicholas Lash, *Believing Three Ways in One God: A Reading of the Apostles' Creed* (London, 1992), p. 18.

[15] Radcliffe, *Why Go to Church?* pp. 64–91.

[16] Nicholas Lash's translation of St Thomas' commentary on St John xxix PL 35, 1631, quoted in *Believing Three Ways in One God*, p. 20.

sand with his blood: 'I believe in one God'. This was more than a declaration of orthodoxy. It was an exclamation of love.

Every article of the Creed tells us something about what it means for God to be love and to love us. If we do not read it as bringing us deeper into the mystery of God's love for us, we have misunderstood it. So when we assert that we believe in God who created the heavens and the earth, we are not offering an explanation for the existence of the Universe. We assert that all that exists is a fruit of God's love. We reject the position of early gnostic Christians that the universe was created by an evil God, that our bodies are bad, and that salvation is an escape from evil materiality. When we proclaim that the Son is true God from true God we are saying that Jesus does not just tell us about God's love, but that in sharing his life we are taken up into the divine love. Christianity is not a moral theory, but a love story between God and humanity that was consummated in Christ. And when we say we believe in the forgiveness of sins, we are saying that this love can overcome all hatred, all the negativity of the human heart and will have the final victory. So if one article of the Creed is rejected, then the meaning of the whole story is changed and our Christian understanding of love is diminished.

Baptism is a sacrament, and one of the meanings of 'sacramentum' is a binding oath. But we live in what Zygmunt Bauman has called 'Liquid Modernity'. It is a world of short-term commitments, whether at work, at home or in one's religion. The average American has 11 jobs in a lifetime.[17] 'One does not plant a citrus-tree grove to squeeze a lemon'.[18] Divorces are frequent. People drift from one religion to another, like bees getting nectar. But being baptized is not like enrolling in a gym with temporary membership. One is pledged to

---

[17] Zygmunt Bauman, *Liquid Modernity* (Oxford and Malden, 2000), p. 147.
[18] Ibid., p. 122.

Christ, bound by one's word given in the Creed. Of course children will one day have to own that commitment, but we make it on their behalf because it is a sign of our human dignity, that we may give our word for ever.

We dare to pledge ourselves to Christ once and for ever, because God has bound himself unconditionally to us. Martin Luther wrote: 'I am baptized, and through my baptism God, who cannot lie, has bound himself in covenant with me'.[19] As God's own children, we have the freedom and the dignity to promise ourselves to God unconditionally. In *A Man for all Seasons*, Robert Bolt's play about St Thomas More, Thomas struggles to convince his daughter of the importance of an oath: 'When a man takes an oath, Meg, he's holding his own self in his own hands. Like water (He cups his hands). And if he opens his fingers then – he needn't hope to find himself again. Some men aren't capable of this, but I'd be loathe to think your father one of them'.

Of course, we may find ourselves in commitments that we are unable to sustain. In this mobile, liquid world, it is hard to remain wedded to one person and the best of couples may find that they have drifted apart and cannot find a way to stay together. Wonderful priests and religious are unable sometimes to remain faithful to the vows that they have pledged. We must therefore never allow ourselves a hint of superiority. Any of us might find ourselves in the same situation. But this should not lead us to renounce the glorious freedom that we have as the sons and daughters of God to pledge ourselves to God as God has pledged himself to us. Supermarkets give people loyalty cards, to try to hold on to our custom. A baptismal certificate is the pledge of loyalty until death.

---

[19] Cf. Introduction note 1.

Sometimes we talk of Christians as 'the faithful'. This implies fidelity to our pledge at baptism, hanging in there, dragging ourselves out of bed on a Sunday to honour the Lord's day, because he is faithful to us: 'If we are faithless, he remains faithful, for he cannot deny himself' (2 Tim. 2.13). St Aelred of Rivaulx writes: 'A friendship which can cease to be was never true friendship'. We are called to respond to the Lord's true friendship for us, which can never cease. Surely it resonates in our fidelity to all friendships. We may lose contact with friends, not see them for decades, but if friendship was ever true, then it waits to be revived, like seeds long buried in the sand of the desert waiting for the rain to bloom again.

But....

When I was a child my nickname in the family was 'Ah-but', which suggests that I must have been very irritating. And here I must acknowledge a big 'but'. Most Christians do not look as if they are caught up in a love story with God. We do not usually seem to live very differently from anyone else. Jamie Whyte expressed his perplexity that so many well-educated people in the West, children of the Enlightenment, go on believing in Christianity. He concludes that we do not. If we did we would behave differently:

> When everlasting bliss is on offer, nothing else matters at all. People who believed in Heaven would surely act quite unlike those who do not. Yet the expected behavioural difference is not to be observed. The vast majority of Christians display a remarkably blasé attitude toward their approaching day of judgment, leading lives almost indistinguishable from those of us open non-believers. Put simply, they fail the behavioural test for belief.[20]

---

[20] 'I don't believe that believers really believe', *The Times*, 16 September 2008.

We do not behave as if our faith is true and nor, I suspect, have most Christians during the last two thousand years. Jesus' disciples shared his life, ate with him, saw his miracles, listened to his parables, and yet, faced with the cross, one disciple betrayed him, Peter the rock denied him, and most of the rest ran away. In the High Middle Ages, I suspect most people did not do too well in 'the behavioural test'. Faith was part of the air that they breathed. They went on pilgrimages and prayed vastly more than most contemporary Christians but there was much murder, sleeping around and robbery. How is it possible that people believe and yet act in ways that contradict their belief? Like Paul, we can say: 'I do not understand my own actions. For I do not do what I want, but I do the very thing I hate' (Rom. 7.15).

The history of humanity does not look like the love story of God and humanity. The history of the twentieth century, with its world wars, its terrible genocides, beginning with the Armenians, the incomparable horror of the Holocaust, the awful massacres in Rwanda and Cambodia, hardly suggests that human history is leading to the Kingdom and the triumph of love. What sign is there of that today, as we become ever more mired in economic crisis and so many young seem doomed to lifelong unemployment? How can one have hope for the future when we seem to be drifting towards ecological catastrophe? So to read the Creed as a love story and the promise of love's victory seems to go against the evidence of our experience.

This is the theme of the first book of the Bible. At first glance, Genesis looks like a story of endless rivalry and competition, leading to exile in Egypt. Satan, whom we have just renounced, traps Adam and Eve into thinking of God as a rival. After the fall that seems to become the thread of history, the endless fight for power and the upper hand: Cain and Abel, the tower of Babel, Sarah and Hagar, Isaac and Ishmael, Jacob and Esau, Joseph and his brothers. Genesis probably found its present form in a later exile, when there seemed to be no future for Israel.

But Genesis gives us little glimpses that this is only the superficial plot. Deep down something else is happening. God's fertile hand is making out of all this rivalrous violence a story that leads back to himself. Adam and Eve are thrust out, but they are clothed by God in skins and are still under his protection. Cain is a murderer, but God protects him from vengeance. Jacob usurps the inheritance of Esau, but becomes the founder of Israel. Most beautifully, Joseph discloses that when his brothers sent him into exile it was so that he might preserve their lives: 'I am your brother Joseph, whom you sold into Egypt. And now do not be distressed or angry with yourselves because you sold me here, for God sent me before you to preserve life' (45.4). So Genesis shows that there is an obvious, negative way of reading history, as about a vicious struggle for power, which lands the people of God in exile. But clues are left for those who have eyes to see that this is not the true story. In faith, we sometimes glimpse that God is leading his people home. When we proclaim the Creed and renew our baptismal promises we are claiming that, despite all the evidence to the contrary, we are taken up into a love story that will bring us to the fulfilment of all our hopes.

So the Creed invites us to resist a crude Darwinian reading of events as being about the survival of the fittest and the elimination of the weak who are 'unfit for purpose'. Perhaps that is fine as an explanation of natural selection in evolution, but not as the key to human history. In Niall Williams's *As it is in Heaven*, Stephen, a history teacher, falls in love and learns to see the world afresh:

When Stephen drove into Gort and across into Clare he carried in the cage of his heart the ease of accepting love, and felt it lightly like a white bird of promise and hope. It was the most ordinary thing after all. It was the fulcrum of life, and if the years he had spent studying history had shown him that the world turned not on love but on hatred and greed then this was the new unwritten history of the marvellous of which he himself could be the author.[21]

The baptized are called to be, each in our own small ways, authors of this 'history of the marvellous'.

The house in which I grew up faced woods. I spent many a dusk wandering in the woods, learning to find my way around in the encroaching dark without bumping into the trees. I learned to see in the dark, and I still find it useful when I negotiate my way through a room without having to turn on the lights. It is not that I can see anything that people brought up in a town cannot see. It is just that country people learn to interpret the little clues that show you where the path in the wood is going. Faith is a seeing in the dark. It detects the small clues of God's providence, the signs of love's little victories, the glimmers of hope. The first name for Christianity was 'the way' (Acts 9.2), and faith sees hints of the way forward, even in the dark.

Faith is not a matter of deciding to opt for a more optimistic understanding of history, as if one hovers between two ways of seeing things, and then plunges for the more hopeful version, however unlikely it seems. To recite the Creed is boldly to proclaim a certainty. One says 'I do believe that Jesus is risen from the dead', not that 'I will gamble on this as the happier option'. I might not understand clearly what it means to believe that Jesus is risen from the dead, and have all sorts of puzzles about the conflicting accounts in the gospels and what actually happened on Easter morning, and yet at the Easter Vigil I proclaim my sure faith.

---

[21] Niall Williams, *As it is in Heaven* (London, 1999), p. 99.

We discover the truth of our faith in daring to live it. In Zoe Heller's novel *The Believers*, Rosa, who has been brought up as an atheist, begins to wonder if the Judaism of her ancestors is true. But she is not certain. She says to the rabbi: 'What am I meant to do? I can't join in before I'm completely sure'. He replies, 'You may never be sure *unless* you join in'. Rosa was shocked. 'Surely you don't want me to go through the motions without really–' The rabbi smiled. 'Do you remember what the Israelites said at Sinai? "We shall do and we shall hear." Their choice of syntax was meaningful, Rosa. They were expressing their willingness to do God's will before they really understood it'.[22] This is exactly what our recital of the Creed implies, that we have the courage to embark on an adventure before we know where it will take us and what it will mean.

It is rather like getting married. You cannot know in advance what will be the cost, who you will become, and yet you say 'Yes' firmly, and not 'I will give it a go'. Faith is the conviction that this strange story of death and resurrection reveals the meaning of my life. I cannot get my mind around it, and yet it's true or nothing is. Either life is 'the history of the marvellous' or it is nothing at all, and I know that is not so. The words of Stefan Zweig again: 'For only he who lives his life as a mystery is truly alive'.[23]

Towards the end of Leo Tolstoy's *Anna Karenina*, Levin is tormented by questions that make his life seem pointless and empty: 'Without knowing what I am, and why I am here, it is impossible to live. Yet I cannot know that and therefore I can't live'.[24] Then he has a conversation with a peasant, Theodore, about an old man of the

[22] Zoe Heller, *The Believers* (London, 2008), p. 276.

[23] Stefan Zweig, quoted by Ali Smith, *There but for the* (London, 2011), frontispiece.

[24] Leo Tolstoy, *Anna Karenina*, trans. Louise and Aylmer Maude; intro. W. Gareth Jones (Oxford, 1988), p. 782.

village who does not live for his own needs but remembers God. This seems to Levin to be both incomprehensible and yet also indubitably true, and the whole meaning of his life. Nonsense and the only sense:

> What could be more senseless than what he said? He said that we must not live for our needs…but we must live for something incomprehensible, for God whom no one can understand or define. Well? And did I not understand those senseless words of Theodore's? And having understood them, did I doubt their justice? Did I find them stupid, vague, or inexact? No, I understood just as he understands them: understood them completely and more clearly than I understand anything in life.[25]

We believers may often feel that contradiction. Our faith may seem crazy, against the obvious and gloomy reading of human history, and so unsurprisingly we often live as if it were not true. But at the same time, in moments of clarity, we can affirm that this mad hope is the only sense of our lives.

We can no more fully understand what it means to be caught up in God's love affair with humanity than can a child completely grasp the love between its parents. When I was 11, a shy monk tried to explain to me the 'facts of life'. He was so confused that I concluded that it had something to do with Winston Churchill. When my contemporaries explained in graphic detail what it meant 'to make love', I was puzzled in a different way. Why on earth would anyone want to do that? It is only as one grows up that the whole business comes to be understood as an act of love. And so it is when God makes love to us in Christ. If we are spiritually prepubescent, then it will seem too odd for words. How on earth could God's love be consummated in the gruesome

---

[25] Ibid., p. 789.

death of a man on the cross? We belong to a story which we can deeply know to be true, but which often just seems crazy.

Love always demands one's death, and we fear to die. If we give ourselves to another person, then the person whom I have been until then must die. I must become a new person, my old habits broken, my identity transformed, my control of my life lost. If I love my children, then they will never again let me be as I was. Who knows in advance what it will mean? I may have to care for a spouse with Alzheimer's, or a child with a profound disability, or leave behind my country and home. How much more if we fall in love with Love itself? Peter loved the Lord with all his heart and mind and promised that he would be faithful, but of course when the time came he was afraid to die. And so no wonder Christians often do not look all that different from other people.

A man was once driving along a cliff top, wondering whether God existed or not. In fact he got so carried away that he went over the cliff, fell out of the car and found himself hanging on to a tree over the abyss. So he shouted out, 'Help, help. Is there anyone there?' And then he heard a voice from heaven calling, 'My son, I am here. Just let go of the branch and I will save you'. So he thought for a while and said, 'Is there anyone else there?'

To let go we need the sustenance of people whom we trust. Rowan Williams wrote: 'Faith has a lot to do with the simple fact that there are trustworthy lives to be seen, that we can see in some believing people a world we'd like to live in'.[26] Such witnesses help us to take the plunge.

The bold decision of faith is perhaps harder to understand today because our Christianity has been largely domesticated. For the first

---

[26] Rowan Williams, *Tokens of Trust: An Introduction to Christian Belief* (Norwich, 2007), pp. 21–22.

one and a half thousand years all Christians believed that baptism engaged us in the most wonderful and terrifying adventure. We were being taken up into the Godhead. As the early fathers said, 'God became human so that humans might become divine'. Leo the Great, the fifth-century Pope, said in his sermon for Christmas Day: 'Christian, remember your dignity, now that you share in God's own nature'. Baptism was the beginning of a process of profound transformation whereby we come to share the very life of God. We can only find fulfilment in what is more than human, nothing less than life in the Trinity. This was a bold vision which undergirded the startling excess of our Christian ancestors, and was expressed in radical generosity, in heroic virtue and in the flourishing from the fourth century onwards of religious life. Once the risk of martyrdom was over, and being baptized was less dangerous, men and women fled to the desert so as to give themselves entirely to God.

Charles Taylor links the birth of secularism with the loss of this adventure. After the seventeenth century, it gradually came to be accepted that it is enough to be human: 'A secular age is one in which the eclipse of all goals beyond human flourishing becomes conceivable'.[27] The gain is that ordinary life is seen as a place of grace: 'Ordinary life, the life that the vast majority cannot help leading, the life of production and the family, work and sex, is as hallowed as any other'.[28]

The sanctification of ordinary, married life was a wonderful leap forward, but Christianity lost something of its glorious lunacy. If ordinary human flourishing is enough, then why not settle down to a life of domestic bliss and prosperity? Religious life or any heroic Christianity becomes harder to understand:

---

[27] Taylor, *A Secular Age*, p. 19.
[28] Ibid., p. 179.

If God's purpose for us is simply that we flourish, and we flourish by the judicious use of industry and instrumental reason, then what possible use could he have for a Saint Francis, who in a great élan of love calls on his followers to dedicate themselves to a life of poverty. At best, this must lower GNP, by withdrawing these mendicants from the workforce; but worse, it can lower the morale of the productive. Better to accept the limitations of our nature as self-loving creatures, and make the best of it.[29]

Heaven ceases to be imagined as our divinization. It becomes an eternal contented retirement to the celestial equivalent of Brighton. A journalist, taking down an obituary notice over the phone, transcribed 'Requiescat', as in RIP, as 'Requires a cat'. An understandable need but hardly the summons to a heroic adventure. C. S. Lewis's grandfather looked forward to having civilized conversations in heaven with St Paul, like two clerical gentlemen chatting in their club.[30]

This is surely one reason why Jamie Whyte might wonder whether we Christians do indeed believe. Our religion is tamed to the point of being inoffensive and unremarkable. It is no longer an invitation to death and resurrection, but is often reduced to morality which easily slips into an unattractive moralism or a spirituality with a touch of psychology. If we are to excite the world with our faith, to puzzle and intrigue our contemporaries, then we need to recover a sense of how God's call will shake us up, undo and remake us, wring us out and renew the very core of our being. The only Christianity that is likely to appeal to the young is one in which we discover that we are called beyond all that we can imagine, beyond all the limitations of our humanity as we are conformed to God. We owe the young the

---

[29] Ibid., p. 230.

[30] Sheridan Gilley, 'Holiness in the Roman Catholic Tradition', in *Holiness Past and Present*, ed. Stephen Barton (London and New York, 2003), p. 337.

best, the undiluted, startling claim of Christ. One of my American brethren, who was a little too fond of drink, went to see his doctor who said to him: 'Now Father, the very best thing that you could do would be to give up drink altogether'. To which he replied: 'Doctor, I am not worthy of the very best. What is the second best?' We must offer our young the very best.

Religious life has become diminished in the life of our Churches in the West in the last few years. I am convinced we are soon due for a dramatic revival of religious life. This tends to happen every couple of centuries and is overdue. Our crazy vows of poverty, chastity and obedience are a wonderfully provocative sign of the great adventure of Christianity. This is not in any way to deny the sanctification of ordinary life – there can be no competition between these vocations – but the life of the vows speaks boldly of the Kingdom because it has no sense at all unless we are made for God. It is shockingly counter-cultural. As is tattooed on the flank of the actress Megan Fox of the film *Transformers*: 'Those who danced were thought to be quite insane by those who could not hear the music'. We need people touched by Christian folly, fools for God. They need not be members of religious orders. A married couple who took their children to East Timor, to work with the Maryknoll Missionaries, were an eloquent sign of love's wild adventure. Maybe we need to invent new forms of Christian folly.

Whatever form our Christian life takes, the pledge of baptism should surely turn it upside down, or at least shake it about a bit. The proclamation of the Creed, this great love story, invites us to have the courage to become entangled with God and be led beyond all that we know. Clement of Alexandria wrote in the third century, that we must 'take the beautiful risk of passing over into God's camp'.[31] We

---

[31] Protrepticus X, 93. Quoted in Gesché, *La Destinée*, p. 128.

must give each other courage for the adventure. Too often Christian leaders are paralysed by timidity, fearful of new experiments or of disapproval from above or below. The Church should be a school of courage.

Being courageous does not mean being unafraid. One of my brethren, Columba Ryan, was sent to prepare for the foundation of a new community in a dangerous part of Glasgow where there was a strong possibility that his flat would be violently broken into. To protect himself he invented some intimidating flat mates to discourage unwanted visitors. He put up a sign which said, 'If you want Big Charlie, ring three times. If you want little Jim, ring twice. If you want Columba ring just once'.

Now that we have decided to take the plunge, we must strip ourselves.

10

Stripped

For us, baptism usually involves no more than having a little water poured over our heads but, according to a fourth-century rubric, the bishop enters the baptistery and gives the command: 'Take off your clothes!'[1] Our ancestors were then immersed in the water of the font. Often men and women were separated at this point, with deaconesses attending to the women. Baptisms were usually conducted during the Vigil in the middle of the night and so, the experts reassure us, it would have been pretty dark![2] Right up to the beginning of the sixteenth century, babies continued to be immersed.[3] The custom died out because of concerns for the health of the baby, a cooling of the weather, and there tended to be accidents![4]

Immersion is a powerful symbol of the meaning of baptism and so is undergoing a certain revival, though when the present Archbishop of York announced that he would restore it, one newspaper reported

---

[1] Aidan Kavanagh OSB, 'A Rite of Passage', in Gabe Huck (ed.), *The Three Days: Parish Prayer in the Paschal Triduum* (Chicago, 1992), p. 171.

[2] Yarnold, *Awe-Inspiring Rites*, p. 20.

[3] Austin Milner OP, 'When did the Baptism of Babies by Immersion Cease?' Unpublished paper.

[4] Milner, op. cit., refers to a rubric in the York Manual: 'If the infant shits in the font, throw out the water. If it only pees let not the water be disturbed!'

that he was returning to the ancient custom of baptizing with water. Even if most of us are not literally stripped and immersed, it speaks eloquently of what it means to live as baptized people. First of all, we are stripped in the eyes of the Lord. We can stand in the presence of our God naked and without shame. When Adam and Eve sinned, they hid themselves because they were ashamed to be naked before God and each other, and so God in his mercy clothed them with skins. Now we can face God as we are. Gregory of Nyssa wrote: 'Casting off these fading leaves which veil our lives we should once again present ourselves before the eyes of our Maker'.[5]

Of course God always sees us as we are and looks on us lovingly. Our clothes are no more effective a screen from his eyes than they are from those alarming scanners at airports which reveal all. 'If I say, "Surely the darkness shall cover me, and the light around me become night", even the darkness is not dark to you; the night is as bright as the day' (Ps. 139.11-12). So, even if we keep on all our clothes at baptism, we are asked now to accept ourselves as we are, without fear. As Spike Milligan said of someone: 'Under his clothes he was completely naked'.

Samuel Wells wrote:

> Clothes provide not just warmth but pockets – places for the necessities of life, the marks of independence – wallet, diary, keys, handkerchief, make up, contraceptives, mobile phone. In the stable and on the tree Christ was without the comfort of clothing and the necessities of independent life. In the stripping of the body for Baptism, the candidate comes face to face with God, face to face with his frail nakedness, realizes all the lies we tell ourselves

---

[5] De Virginitate XIII 1,15f, quoted in Simon Tugwell OP, *The Way of the Preacher* (London, 1979), p. 92.

about our bodies. He has no clothes, to make himself look better than he is. He has no pockets, in which to store secrets or vital necessities. And he smells.[6]

James Alison suggests that this might be why, after conversion, we may have the impression that we have become worse, because we can let drop the masks. We no longer have to put on a show of being wonderful, moral people:

> Once people start relaxing into the gift of faith, they apparently become worse people. Why? Because they are no longer concerned with tidying up their story... The result is that one of the first fruits of the relaxation that comes with faith is a loss of a story of goodness, a loss of a self-innocenting story, a loss of a story about how right you are. You are being given a story about how loved you are. And this is what it means to be able to see yourself as a sinner: far from 'seeing yourself as a sinner' being some sort of moralistic demand that you browbeat yourself and come up with a list of alleged failings, being able to see yourself as a sinner is merely the sign that you are able to hold yourself peacefully, and realistically as being who you are, non-defensively, because you know yourself loved. You are no longer frightened of being seen to be, or actually being, a failure.[7]

We will fall again and again but no longer do we need to hide in the bushes. It would be a waste of time, and we are seen with love and mercy. A woman who had dabbled in prostitution came to see one of our brethren. 'But father', she said, 'I am a fallen woman!' 'No my dear', he replied, 'you merely tripped'.

---

[6] Samuel Wells, *God's Companions: Reimagining Christian Ethics* (Oxford, 2006), pp. 71–72.
[7] Alison, *The Forgiving Victim*, forthcoming, chapter 5.

We can let go of all sorts of props that delude us into thinking we are important. We are freed of the silly idea that we have value because of what we have. The first and easiest possession to let go is probably that of wealth. Anthony de Mello, an Indian Jesuit, tells a parable of a sannyasi, a wise man,

> who reached the outskirts of a village and settled down under a tree for the night when a villager came running up to him and said, 'The Stone! The Stone! Give me the precious stone!' 'What stone?' asked the sannyasi. 'Last night the Lord Shiva appeared to me in a dream,' said the villager, 'and told me that if I went to the outskirts of the village at dusk I should find a sannyasi who would give me a precious stone that would make me rich forever.' The sannyasi rummaged in his bag and pulled out a stone. 'He probably meant this one,' he said, as he handed the stone over to the villager. 'I found it on a forest path some days ago. You can certainly have it.' The man gazed at the stone in wonder. It was a diamond, probably the largest diamond in the whole world, for it was as large as a person's head. He took the diamond and walked away. All night he tossed about in bed, unable to sleep. Next day at the crack of dawn he woke the sannyasi and said, 'Give me the wealth that makes it possible for you to give this diamond away so easily'.[8]

Pilgrims on the way to the Kingdom walk more easily if they carry little luggage. Every time I move to a new community, I must get rid of stuff, ask whether I really do need so many books, and feel light hearted as I let things go. Parents often divest themselves of possessions and of wealth for the sake of their children. We do not

---

[8] Quoted by James Martin SJ, *The Jesuit Guide to Almost Everything: A Spirituality for Real Life* (New York, 2010), pp. 177–78.

need to prop up our identity as the children of God with valuable objects or status symbols.

We can let go of whatever we imagine make us matter, pretensions to dignity. Churches often bestow extraordinary titles on high-ranking clergy. I have met Eminences, Beatitudes and Serenities! I would like to be Pope just for one day, to replace the title 'Monsignor' (My Lord), with 'Your Servant'. Jean Vanier calls us 'to descend the human ladder of promotion'.[9] We live every day as the baptized, who have been, as it were stripped, and stand before God with no greater title than 'Brother' or 'Sister'. Remember the plaque to Cardinal Newman which concludes: 'Ante omnia Christianus', 'Before all else, a Christian'.

As the baptized, we can free ourselves from the crutches of our achievements, the important positions that we hold in life, even our wonderful moral qualities. Standing before the Lord, these are irrelevant. Simon Tugwell wrote: 'Most of us probably spend quite a lot of time "editing" our autobiographies, so that we shall have the "official version" of the story ready for judgement day. But does it really matter? Are we not just wasting our times? Is it all really not just designed to safeguard our complacent contemplation of our own picture of ourselves?'[10]

In a story by H. G. Wells, a terrible sinner, King Ahab, Elijah's old opponent, is placed in the palm of God for judgment. And he squeals and tries to flee as the recording angel reads out all of his sins, until finally he flees up God's sleeve and finds refuge. And then a saintly prophet comes, presumably Elijah, and he too sits in the palm of God and listens complacently as his good deeds were read out. And then the Recording Angels get to some unsavoury stuff:

---

[9] Vanier, *Essential Writings*, p. 103.
[10] Tugwell, *Beatitudes*, p. 7.

It seemed not ten seconds before the Saint also was rushing to and fro over the great palm of God. Not ten seconds. And at last he also shrieked beneath that pitiless and cynical exposition (of the recording angel), and fled also, even as the Wicked man had fled, into the shadow of the sleeve. And the two sat side by side, stark of all delusion, in the shadow of the robe of God's charity, like brothers. And thither also I fled in my turn.[11]

Perhaps the most difficult thing to let go is control of our lives, a recurrent theme of this book. When Jesus descended into the waters of baptism, he entrusted himself to the care of his Father. When we give our lives away – in marriage, or in ministry, or in some service of the community – we do so with an initial and unconditional generosity. We place our lives in the hands of someone whom we love, or a religious order, or some cause, happy to do whatever we are asked. But after a while we may be tempted to try to reclaim our lives, to take back the gift. In baptism we entrust ourselves to God's unknown providence. We do not have to run the show. When Pope John XXIII went to bed he used to joke, 'God, the Pope must go to sleep now. I leave you to run the Church now'. We do not know where we shall be sent. We reject a mother's advice to her daughter: 'My dear, never go anywhere you have not been before'. This is not irresponsibility, as if we were just leaving everything in the hands of our Celestial Daddy. It is accepting that we are caught up in that adventure of love which is beyond our imagining, and which leads to our sharing of the very life of God. We take the plunge and surrender to love's gravity.

Since our society is infected by the 'culture of control', then we today are especially afraid to trust in God's providence. We want

[11] H. G. Wells, 'A Vision of Judgement', http://www.online-literature.com/wellshg/2880

to keep our lives in our own hands. Paradoxically the explosion of regulation and bureaucracy means that we often feel that we have little control. *The Reader* is a novel that tells the story of a German teenager who has an affair with an older woman who worked as a ticket collector on a tram. Later when he is studying law, he discovers that she had been a guard in a Nazi concentration camp. She is taken to court and accused of having failed to release some prisoners who had been locked in a burning church. They all died. Her justification is that the guards had to control them and they could not if they got out.

> 'How could we have restored order? There would have been chaos, and we had no way to handle that. And if they tried to escape...' Once again the judge waited, but Hanna didn't finish the sentence. 'Were you afraid that if they escaped, you would be arrested, convicted and shot?' 'We couldn't just let them escape! We were responsible for them... I mean, we had guarded them the whole time, in the camp and on the march, that was the point, that we had to guard them and not let them escape.'[12]

This is control for its own sake, even if it results in death.

Our baptism therefore invites us to let drop all the fig leaves without fear, be stripped of all that we delude ourselves into thinking gives us importance: possessions, achievements, status, and power, and stand naked before the face of God who delights in us. If we accept to be naked in the presence of God, then perhaps we shall begin to dare to be seen by each other as we are, and share our ridiculous fears, our insecurities, even our shameful failures. The tradition in some Churches of confessing one's sins is expressive of one's freedom in Christ to face oneself and one's sins in the presence

---

[12] Bernhard Schlink, *The Reader*, trans. Carol Brown Janeway (London, 1997), p. 126.

of another who stands for the whole Body of Christ. We dare to be naked as we bring to word our humbling weakness. We claim our dignity as those who dare to be naked before God and his people. We are relieved of the awful burden of pretending to be better than we are. One takes the risk of being viewed as absurd, as David did when he danced almost naked before the ark, seen by his wife who 'despised him in her heart' (2 Sam. 6.16).

Stripped for touch

Being naked in the presence of God is also a sign of intimacy. Cyril of Jerusalem links our baptismal nudity to the Song of Songs: 'I had put off my garment; how could I it put it on?'[13] So we draw near to God in love, with the bodies that we are: old or young, saggy or beautiful, tired or fresh. We come nakedly into God's presence as his beloved. We must therefore be at ease in our bodies. Jesus was unafraid of touching other people's bodies and being touched by them. He touched the sick, the lepers, and let himself be touched by the woman (Lk. 7.36-50) who wet his feet with her tears and dried them with her hair. He washed the feet of the disciples on the night before he died, a ceremony that was re-enacted in some early baptismal liturgies. It is a tender and intimate gesture. Once when I was Prior, I was washing the feet of one of our Dominican students, and I smiled to see that he had written a letter on each toe, which spelt: 'Hello'.

In baptism we are, as it were, touched by Christ. Baptism makes us members of the Body of Christ, and so it is right that at this transforming moment, we are touched in our very physicality. In

---

[13] Yarnold, *Awe-Inspiring Rites*, p. 75.

his Apologia of 208 AD, Tertullian has the wonderful phrase: Caro
cardo salutis;[14] 'The flesh is the hinge of salvation'. Again and again,
the Church has defended the beauty and goodness of the body
against those who despise it. This led to the foundation of the
Order of Preachers by St Dominic, in the face of the dualism of the
Albigensians. In the library of Glenstal Abbey, there are glorious
depictions of Adam, Christ and Paul naked, by the young monk,
Brother Emmaus O'Herlihy.

Simeon the New Theologian wrote in the tenth century a deeply
touching hymn to our bodily unity with Christ:

> We awaken in Christ's body
> As Christ awakens our bodies,
> And my poor hand is Christ, He enters
> My foot, and is infinitely me.
>
> I move my hand, and wonderfully
> My hand becomes Christ, becomes all of Him
> (for God is indivisibly
> Whole, seamless in His Godhood).
>
> I move my foot, and at once
> He appears like a flash of lightening.
> Do my words seem blasphemous? – Then
> Open your heart to Him
>
> And let yourself receive the one
> Who is opening to you so deeply.
> For if we genuinely love Him,
> We wake up inside Christ's body

---

[14] De Resurrectione carnis liber viii.2.

Where all our body, all over,
Every most hidden part of it,
Is realised in joy as Him,
And He makes us, utterly, real,

And everything that is hurt, everything
That seemed to us dark, harsh, shameful,
Maimed, ugly, irreparably
Damaged, is in Him transformed

And recognised as whole, as lovely,
And radiant in His light
We awaken as the Beloved
In every last part of our body.[15]

St Augustine liked to say: 'He touches Christ who believes in Christ'.[16] We are stripped so as to be vulnerable to Christ as he comes to us in those whom we love, but also in the poor, the oppressed, the imprisoned, the needy. 'Whatever you did to the least of these, you did to me' (Matt. 25.40). We strip off whatever makes us insensitive to them. We remove the armour, the hard carapace, the iron glove that would prevent our humanity being touched.

Touch, Aquinas says, is the most basic of all senses. It is the root and foundation of all our senses. It is the fine point of our life as physical, embodied beings. Eagles see better than we do; compared with dogs we have not got noses worth speaking of. Bats can hear more than we do. When I said this in Brisbane Cathedral, the congregation applauded. I had not realized that 'Bats' was the nickname

[15] Ed Stephen Mitchell, *The Enlightened Heart: An Anthology of Sacred Poetry* (London, 1993). I suspect that this is a very free translation but wonderful.
[16] Quoted by Raniero Cantalamessa in 'Let your love be active and genuine', 60th General Assembly of Caritas Internationalis, 23 May 2010, www.caritas.org

of their wonderful archbishop, John Battersby. Humans excel at touching.

Touch is the most mutual of all senses. It can be invasive or rapacious or greedy, but, when it is gentle, it is reciprocal. You can see and not be seen, or hear and not be heard, smell and not be smelt, but you cannot touch well without being touched. It is expressive of the mutuality of love. It is the most physical of senses, and yet opens us to love and understanding. Kenelm Foster OP writes of the centrality of touch for Aquinas:

> It is the whole body which touches, touch or *tactus* most properly bespeaks the embodied condition of man; whilst, on the other hand, since touch is at its most perfect in man, of all animals, it connotes in us, where it is most truly itself, the human soul, intellectual yet essentially embodied, with its balancing of contrasts, its discernment, its submission to, and its gradual penetration of, the order of the world.[17]

When we love we need to reach out to touch, to pierce the space between us, to break down our isolation and solitude. Bernard O'Donoghue wrote:

> It's strange, considering how many lines
> Have been written on it, that no one's said
> Where love most holds sway: neither at sex
> Nor in wishing someone else's welfare,
> But in spending the whole time over dinner
> Apparently absorbed in conversation,
> While really trying to make your hand take courage

---

[17] Kenelm Foster, *God's Tree: Essays on Dante and other Matters* (London, 1957), p. 149.

To cross the invisible sword on the table cloth
And touch a finger balanced on the linen.[18]

To be fully alive is to touch and be touchable. Gandhi refused to let the lowest caste in Hinduism be called the 'untouchables'. It meant that they were excluded from the mutuality of human life. Hitler did not like to be touched. Recently the Dalai Lama came to visit my community of Blackfriars, to take part in a discussion about contemplation in our different traditions. But what leapt across the divisions was not so much what the Dalai Lama said but what he did. A friend of the community was there who had been disabled by a stroke. And when the Dalai Lama came in he paused by her wheelchair, and rested his cheek on hers in silence. He spent longer with her than anyone else. It was the embodiment of compassion.

When I became involved a little bit in work with people with Aids in the early eighties, I discovered the importance of touch. My community organized a conference on the Church and Aids, and we were overwhelmed by the response. Doctors, nurses, chaplains, people with Aids and their friends all wanted to come. It was early days. Most of us had never met anyone with Aids. We were a little nervous. But at the final Mass, a young man called Benedict who had Aids came up to me for the kiss of peace. And when I hugged him I thought, 'this is the body of Christ'. And Christ in him hugged me. In Christ, God came and touched us. God is in touch with us even to this day. We must share that touch.

My parents were wonderful, but we hardly ever touched, except a shake of the hand or a peck on the cheek. I remember my surprise and delight when I arrived at Blackfriars, and was enfolded in a great bear hug by the Master of Students, Geoffrey Preston. Because our

---

[18] Bernard O'Donoghue, 'The Definition of Love', in *Selected Poems* (London, 2008), p. 70.

society is so worried, rightly, about the risk of sexual abuse, we have become nervous about touch. The worries are certainly justified. There has been much abusive and destructive touching. But we must recover this most human and most Christian way of being the Body of Christ. We shall be deeply deprived and seem to undo the Incarnation if we keep our distance all the time when God has drawn near. How can we embody Christ's embrace of others? How can the Word become again flesh in us?

11

Take the plunge

We come now to the pivot of baptism, as the name of the Trinity is invoked and water is poured. Everything has been building up to this moment: the naming, the litany, the exorcism, blessing of the water. But it might seem rather a letdown. How can such a simple daily act as being washed by water be symbolic of so much? This was the reaction of Naaman, the great general of the King of Aram, who made a long trek across the desert to find Elisha and ask to be healed of leprosy. When Elisha just asked him to go and bathe in the Jordan, he was angry: 'Are not Abana and Pharpar, the rivers of Damascus, better than all the waters of Israel? Could I not wash in them and be clean?' (2 Kgs 5.12). Why are we not given a more dramatic sign of the conquest of death and sin than just being splashed with a bit of water? Is this all? In the words of Peggy Lee's famous song we might ask: 'Is that all there is, my friend? Then, let's keep dancing'.

St Ambrose of Milan, anticipating Peggy Lee by a millennium and a half, said: 'If anyone should perhaps be thinking of saying: "Is this all?", I say, indeed it is all. There truly is all, where there is all innocence, all devotion, all grace, all sanctification'.[1] It is somehow

---

[1] 'Sermons of the Sacraments', in Yarnold, *Awe-Inspiring Rites*, p. 103.

fitting that our God, who drew near to us as a child born in obscurity, should touch our lives with such an everyday act as being washed. We are stripped of all pretension in preparation for a modest, humble sign of our sharing in the death and resurrection of our self-effacing God.

In baptism we share Christ's death so as to share his resurrection. This sounds odd. Most baptisms are of babies. They are hardly born when we ceremonially pre-enact their death. That seems morbid. When Clare Watkins told her eight year old daughter that baptism was being buried with Jesus, 'she looked at me, with a penetrating, slightly disgusted look – "Well! That's not very nice".'[2] Why can't we let a child enjoy life for a while before we think of its death? For our ancestors birth and death were closely associated. Many children did not survive, and their birth often caused the death of their mothers. In many parts of Africa, the death rate of babies remains high. In Sierra Leone, for example, 16 per cent of babies die within their first and only year of life. 27 per cent die before the age of five. Birth and death still go together for many people.

More fundamentally, to be born at all is to be destined to die. Charles Dickens calls the newborn Oliver Twist, this 'item of mortality'.[3] The only certain thing we know is that we shall die, and yet we have no idea what it means to be dead. So death is both our surest knowledge and our deepest ignorance. Every year we celebrate our birthday. We also have a deathday, but we do not know which it is. Awareness of our mortality is intrinsic to understanding what it means to be alive. After years of being blinded by Cartesian ideas of animals as machines, we are rediscovering that they are more intelligent than we had presumed in recent centuries. Sheep turn out to

---

[2] Watkins, *Living Baptism*, p. 58.
[3] Charles Dickens, *Oliver Twist*, chapter 1.

be surprisingly bright according to recent research, and even flies are not completely dumb. But do they know that they must die? I don't know, but facing our death squarely is central to human maturity. It belongs to wisdom in the Old Testament: 'Make us know the shortness of our life that we may gain wisdom of heart' (Ps. 90.12). Martin Heidegger, the German philosopher, defined being human as 'being-towards-death' (*Sein zum Tode*).

This sounds macabre, not to say depressing. This is not so, as we shall see. Laying hold of one's death is necessary if one is to know the joy of being alive. People who run away from mortality are only half alive. One reason why our society sometimes is tinged with the gloom of pagan Rome is because we flee awareness of our death. Saul Bellow, the American novelist, claimed that 'ignorance of death is destroying us'.[4] Death is the dark backing a mirror needs before anything is seen. We are like the man who fell off the 50th floor of a skyscraper. As he passed the 15th floor, some friends shouted out, 'How are things?' 'Alright so far!' Someone told a friend that a mutual acquaintance had died. "How old was he?" '94'. 'A good age to die'. 'Not if you are 93'.

This suppression of the public acknowledgement of death is rooted, it has been argued, in two world wars, during which public displays of any grief were discouraged lest they undermine morale.[5] Some doctors also see death as the ultimate failure and so fear to face it with their patients. In one of the greatest accounts of death, 'The Death of Ivan Ilyich' by Leo Tolstoy, a famous doctor refuses to see that what is at issue for the sick man is whether he will live or die. It

---

[4] Gloria Cronin and Ben Siegel (eds), *Conversations with Saul Bellow* (Jackson, MI, 1994), p. 228.
[5] Pat Jalland, *Death in War and Peace: A History of Loss and Grief in England, 1914–1970* (Oxford, 2011).

is just a mechanical question, a matter of organs and not the life of a human being: 'It was not a question of the life of Ivan Ilyich, but the question between the loose kidney and the intestinal appendix'.[6]

We believe that death no longer has dominion. Does that mean that it no longer really matters? No. We should not think of it just as slipping effortlessly into another life, as if going to heaven were like moving from Birmingham to Oxford. For most of us death remains menacing, and rightly so. Newman, in *The Dream of Gerontius*, describes it as 'the masterful negation and collapse of all that makes me man'. Perhaps the most closely followed illness and death in the history of humanity was that of Pope John Paul II. He gave living witness to his hope in the face of illness and death, and yet he too recognized that there is something terrible about death: 'Death primarily involves the dissolution of the entire psychophysical personality of man…the evil which the human being experiences in death has a definitive and total character'.[7]

For me, even as a Christian, death is the end of my individual story. When I die, I will be buried, I hope, and a date put on my grave-stone. I have no idea how near I am to that date, but it will come, and then it will be possible to tell the story of my life, of what I became. Blaise Pascal, the philosopher and devout Christian, wrote: 'The last act is bloody, no matter how fine the rest of the play. They throw earth over your head and it is finished forever'.[8] God says to Adam: 'you are dust and unto to dust you shall return' (Gen. 3.19). We shall be done and dusted!

But in another sense, my death will not be the end of my story, because to be baptized is to be taken up into a larger and longer story,

---

[6] Leo Tolstoy, *The Death of Ivan Ilyich and Other Stories* (London, 2004), p. 101.

[7] Apostolic Letter *Salvifici Doloris* 1984, quoted by Watkins, *Living Baptism*, p. 65.

[8] Blaise Pascal, *Pensées*, trans A. J. Krailsheimer (London, 1966), p. 165.

which is that of God's love for humanity, consummated in the death and resurrection of his Son, Jesus. This, we have seen, is the story of the Creed. My private story will be extinguished, but we believe that in God no one's private story is ever the truest story that can be told of them. Who I am is only known in the shared story of the sons and daughters of God.

Paul writes to the Colossians: 'Do not lie to one another, seeing that you have stripped off the old self with its practices and have clothed yourself with the new self, which is being renewed in knowledge according to the image of its creator. In that renewal there is no longer Greek and Jew, circumcised and uncircumcised, barbarian, Scythian, slave and free, but Christ is all and in all' (Col. 3.9-11). The 'old self', which is consigned to death at the font, is a purely private self. It is Timothy as the centre of his world, his desires, his projects and, indeed, his story. In that story, everyone else has a walk on part as supporting cast. In that private and illusory story, I am Hamlet, Othello, Romeo and Juliet, King Lear, always the centre of the stage. Living my baptism is letting go of that narrow and boring little story so that I can flourish with my brothers and sisters in the spacious love of the Father, the Son and the Holy Spirit. This is the new self in which there is neither Greek nor Jew, slave or free for Christ is all and in all.

So the life of the resurrection is not what awaits us on the other side of death, another sort of life as if, in the image of Ludwig Feuerbach, we just changed horses and went galloping onwards. Eternal life begins whenever I love and so am taken up into the eternal love of the Father and the Son, which is the Holy Spirit. We are baptized into that threefold name. When I come to die, then the pretence that I have a purely private life will be shattered, like the collapse of an unconvincing stage set, a pretend castle, a make-believe house, and I shall be liberated into the real story of any human life, the wide-open love which is God, which preceded my birth and in which I shall flourish for eternity. Then I shall have, as the Irish say, 'completed my baptism'.

So when we come to die it both is and is not our end. Because both are true, then death is both a moment of joy and hope and also of sorrow and maybe even of fear. I have been with so many brethren when they have died. It has always, so far, been a beautiful moment, their final preaching of the gospel. But there is often a brief time of struggle. The desire for survival is a profound and good human instinct. It would be odd to die too easily. There is usually a moment when death sits up and tries to frighten us with the horror of extinction. We are bodily beings, and not souls trying to escape and so it would be bizarre, almost unnatural, if there were not a struggle with 'the strong man' (Mk 3.27), tempting us to think that this is indeed *only* the end, and that God's love cannot reach thus far, or that our sins are beyond forgiveness, or that our faith has been an illusion. But Christ is in the waters with us, having gone in with all the sinners at his baptism, and fights beside us against the beast of the waters that threatens to overwhelm us.

Death undoes the small private story of my life and reveals the only story that really matters, that I am even now embraced by the infinite love which is God. But whatever I make of my life, however good and loving a spouse, parent, friend, neighbour or citizen I may have been, I must acknowledge that I have not loved infinitely. Even saints, especially the saints, know that they are just at the beginning of learning to love. St Paul prays that 'you may have the power to comprehend, with all the saints, what is the breadth and length and height and depth, and to know the love of Christ which surpasses knowledge, so that you may be filled with all the fullness of God' (Eph. 3.18-19). But every one of us dies without having grasped the breadth and length and height and depth of love. It is always more. Indeed it is only in death that our tiny world, with our little fumbling egotistical loves, crashes so that we may enter the mystery of a love beyond all words.

An English oak grows for three hundred years, rests for three hundred years and then takes three hundred years to die. It then has run its natural course and been all that an oak is made to be. I am very fond of dogs, and sorrow when a beloved dog dies. But I have the impression that if its life has been happy, then it has fulfilled its nature and run its course. Because we are made for what is more than natural to us, then every life is, in a sense, a failure. This is why we always face death by asking for forgiveness. It is not that God is so hard-hearted that he will not admit us to heaven unless we grovel. It is not because God is poised to send us to eternal damnation and might just be persuaded to relent if we say that we are very, very sorry. Rather we are made for an infinite love, and can be satisfied with nothing less. We are, as the medievals said, *capax Dei*, open to God. But this can only be given to us as a gift. Forgiveness is the fore-giving, the giving in advance of any merit.

As Ivan Ilyich, in Tolstoy's short story, draws near to death, he is tormented by the question: 'Did I live a good life?' He has a vision of a black hole into which he fears and longs to disappear. 'What hindered him from getting in to it [the black hole, death] was the claim that his life had been good. That justification of his life held him fast and would not let him get forward, and it caused him more agony than all'. And then he accepts and wants forgiveness but cannot ask for it but does not worry 'knowing that He would understand whose understanding mattered'. Then he can die, and death is no more. '"Death is over," he said to himself. "It is no more." He drew in a breath, stopped midway in the breath, stretched and died'.[9] The

---

[9] Tolstoy, *Ivan Ilych*, p. 130.

dominion of death is defeated when he accepts the gift of being loved, whatever he has done and been.

So in baptism our dying with Christ and the forgiveness of our sins are profoundly linked, because to die well is to open oneself to an infinity of love which none of us can have achieved and which is always fore-given. We ask for forgiveness not because we are all wretched worms and extremely bad and depraved, but because we are made for what is beyond our grasp.

When we face death, then, we may do so with a natural sense of foreboding, for it is indeed the end of my private story. So however peaceful a death may be, there is something awesome about it. Tolstoy wrote with an extraordinary clarity about death, but when his own death came his wife wrote in her diary: 'Something terrible is approaching, and although everyone expects it, it is still completely unexpected when it is truly about to happen: the end of life'. We never can get our minds around it. And yet we can face death with hope and even confidence and joy. We need forgiveness but we know that it is given and indeed always has been given, long before we ever sinned; we just have to accept it. And so we can also face death with joy.

Brother Luke, one of the Cistercian monks martyred in Algeria,[10] seems to have been a wonderful humane person, much beloved of their Muslim neighbours. In the diary kept by one of his brethren it is noted: 'On January 1, 1994, the beginning of the year and month of Luke's eightieth birthday, we listened in the refectory to the cassette he was keeping to be used the day of his burial. It was Edith Piaf singing: "No, I have no regrets."'[11] '*Je ne regrette rien*'. With God's grace, even our failures become, somehow, fertile and fruitful. There is nothing to regret.

---

[10] Cf. Chapter 4.
[11] Olivera, *How Far to Follow?* p. 61.

Serge de Beaurecueil, a French Dominican who spent most of his life in Egypt and Afghanistan, asked for the words of Abdullah Anārī of Herāt, an eleventh-century Sunni poet, to be inscribed on his own tomb: 'If you come to visit my tomb, do not be surprised to see the monument dance. Bring your tambourine, for sadness is not appropriate for God's banquet'.[12]

Living as those who have died and risen with Christ

How then are we to live day by day as those who are no longer under death's dominion? As I grow older, I must face the ageing of my body. When I shave in the morning I must confront the signs that not only has youth passed, but that middle age is now saying 'goodbye'. I fully identify with the temptation of this poem by Nanao Sakaki.

In the morning
After taking a cold shower
---what a mistake ---
I look at the mirror.

There, a funny guy,
Grey hair, white beard, wrinkled skin
--- what a pity ---
Poor, dirty, old man!
He is not me, absolutely not!…

---

[12] 'Si tu viens visiter ma tombe, ne t'étonne pas de voir le monument danser. Prends ton tambourin, car la tristesse ne convient pas au banquet de Dieu'. I thank Jean-Jacques Perénnès OP for this wonderful quote. I hope that we shall not have to wait long for his biography of this remarkable French brother.

Land and life
Fishing in the oceans
Sleeping in the desert with stars
Building a shelter in the mountains
Farming the ancient way
Singing with coyotes
Singing against nuclear war –
I'll never be tired of life.
Now I'm seventeen years old,
Very charming young man.

I sit down quietly in lotus position,
Meditating, meditating for nothing.
Suddenly a voice comes to me:
'To stay young,
To save the world,
Break the mirror'.[13]

I admire the actress who said to the photographer: 'Don't airbrush out my wrinkles. I have worked hard for them'. I find myself hoping that maybe a good night's sleep will restore the sagging face and make the wrinkles disappear. There must surely be a patron saint for regrowing lost hair! A religious ought to be beyond that by my age! But to be alive, sparkling and vibrantly alive now, means surely being unafraid to let go of what is passing and live as one is. If we flee from the signs of age, then we let mortality call the shots, and are caught in a defensive reaction to life's passing, passively resisting what cannot be beaten, a victim of the years.

---

[13] Nanao Sakaki, 'Break the Mirror', in *Break the Mirror*, trans. Gary Snyder (Nobleboro, *ME* 1996).

More positively, we show Christ's victory over death by loving, for 'love is stronger than death' (Song of Songs 8.6). We refuse to accept death's isolation. When Ivan Ilyich is dying, he is overwhelmed by loneliness: 'Of late, in the loneliness in which he found himself, lying with his face to the back of the sofa, a loneliness in the middle of a populous town and of his numerous acquaintance and his family, a loneliness than which none more complete could be found anywhere – not at the bottom of the sea, not deep down in the earth; of late in this fearful loneliness Ivan Ilyich had lived only in imagination in the past'.[14]

Every death is a confrontation with loneliness. In November 2010, our brother Austin died after a short illness, an aggressive form of leukaemia. He was surrounded by the community, who cared for him lovingly and who were with him when he died, as is our tradition, to sing the *Salve Regina*. He was never left alone. For all of Austin's joy in his brethren and Christian hope, there must have been that lonely knowledge of approaching death. But just before his death, after he renewed his baptismal promises he invited all of the brethren to have a good drink. We could be joyful because in death we are not alone. We die with Christ who shared our solitude on the utter isolation of the cross.

Our mutual love confronts death's terrifying solitude and refuses it. The Abbot General of the Trappist monks killed in Algeria wrote that 'they lived together, died together and went together into eternal life'.[15] They refused to let the terrorist violence destroy their love for the people of Algeria. Their Prior, Brother Christian, wrote in a circular letter: 'I am certain that God loves the Algerians, and that he has chosen to prove it by giving them our lives. So then, do we truly

---

[14] Tolstoy, *Ivan Ilych*, p. 125.
[15] Olivera, *How Far to Follow?* p. 47.

love them? Do we love them enough? This is a moment of truth for each one of us and a heavy responsibility in these times when our friends feel so little loved'.[16] Any love in the face of our mortality is a refusal of the solitude of the grave.

The love of a married couple facing a terminal illness together is already sharing in the eternal life of God and refusing death's dominion. In *The Finkler Question* by Howard Jacobson we come across a Jewish couple who do not believe in eternal life, but whose love speaks powerfully, at least to me, of a hope which they do not hold:

> She wanted laughter to be her final gift to him. In the stealthy alternations of rudery and sweetness, somewhere between waking and sleep, light and darkness, they found – she found, she found – a *modus mortis*. It was bearable, then. Not a peace or a resignation, but an engagement of the fact of death with the fact of life. Though she was dying they were still living, together. He would turn the lights out and return to her side and listen to her going off and know that she was living with dying. But in the morning the horror of it returned. Not only the horror of the pain and what she knew she must look like, but the horror of the knowledge. If Libor could have spared her that knowledge! He would have died for her to spare her that knowledge, only that would have been to burden her with another, and she assured him, greater loss.[17]

They do not believe, and yet I find in this love in the face of death something heroic, a defiance of death even, which speaks to me of love's final victory. His willingness even to die to spare her from the knowledge of that death speaks of love which will not be defeated.

---

[16] Ibid., p. 99.
[17] Howard Jacobson, *The Finkler Question* (London, 2010), p. 244.

Another way in which we live our baptismal hope is by living fully *now*. Michael Caine, the actor, said: 'When people ask what I feel about getting old, I reply, "Compared with the alternative, it's fantastic."' If eternal life is the fullness of life, then we accept its gift by grasping our present life with enthusiasm. Irenaeus of Lyon famously wrote that the glory of God is a human being fully alive. If we are to be fully alive for all eternity, then we had better start now. God 'loves the living' (Wis. 11.26). Moping in the present, as if it were just an antechamber to real life, is no preparation for eternity. All life is a gift, and we prepare for the joy of eternal life by savouring our present lives. When people have faced their own mortality, then, paradoxically, they often begin to enjoy life as never before. Each day is a gift but the dying know this acutely. My mother died slowly of multiple little strokes. But every day, when she was installed in her chair by the window, able to see the garden she had spent years cultivating, she seemed to grow in her happiness at the gift of the new day.

Dennis Potter, an English playwright who died in 1994, gave a last interview shortly before his death, in which he shared his intense joy of seeing things as if never before: 'Instead of saying "Oh that's nice blossom"…last week looking at it through the window when I'm writing, I *see* it is the whitest, frothiest, blossomest blossom that ever could be… The newness of everything is absolutely wondrous, and if people could *see* that, you know. There's no way of telling you, you have to experience it, but the glory of it, if you like, the comfort of it, the reassurance.'[18] If we face our mortality with open eyes, but have confidence that death has no final dominion, then we would glory in the utter gratuity of each day.

Death is feared in our 'culture of control' because it shows that there are limits to our mastery of our lives. In the end, we are not in

---

[18] Dennis Potter, *Seeing the Blossom* (London and Boston, 1994), p. 5.

charge. We cannot determine when and how we shall die. The unpre-dictability of death makes mockery of our claims to be the masters of the universe. This must surely be part of the appeal of euthanasia and the movement for assisted suicide. It expresses a desire to remain in charge. That belongs to our dignity, the name of the Swiss clinic where many people go to take their own lives.

Before Christians rush to condemn, we must always first under-stand. However much we may reject and oppose any act which colludes with the taking of life, we must try to understand how there may be some good and healthy desire being expressed by those whose opinions we oppose. We must burrow down with every ounce of our intelligence and imagination to discover how some good impulse is trying to find expression to which we can say 'Yes'. Otherwise we shall fall back into a simplistic world of 'goodies' and 'baddies', in which we side with Satan in hurling accusation and claiming the moral high ground.

The one whose death we share at baptism *did* keep his hands on his own death. Jesus said: 'For this reason the Father loves me, because I lay down my life in order to take it up again. No one takes it from me, but I lay it down of my own accord' (Jn 10.17-18). Death was not something that just happened to Jesus. It was not an accident. He laid down his life, but not by committing suicide. Martyrdom and suicide may look very similar but they are as different as can be. Martyrs so love life that they refuse to collude with anything that smacks of death. They so reject violence that they would rather suffer it than transmit it, and so there can be no such thing as a martyr who is a suicide bomber.

Jesus lays down his life not by taking it but by giving it away. His enemies would violently rob him of his life, but he makes it a gift: 'This is my body, given for you'. When the monks of Atlas chose to stay, after they had received warnings that it might cost them their lives, it was so that they might give themselves to the Algerian people, and even to those terrorists whom they called their 'brothers from the mountain'. They shared their lives right to the end. They were free because they believed that death had no dominion. In the film, Brother Luke says to the Prior, 'I am not afraid of death; I am a free man'. In *A Man for All Seasons*, when the Duke of Norfolk told St Thomas More that he must be careful in his response to Henry VIII, 'for Master More, the wrath of the prince is death', St Thomas replied: 'Is that all, my Lord? Then in good faith, is there no more difference between your grace and me, but that I shall die today, and you tomorrow'.[19]

Few of us are called to be martyrs, but we have to spend our lives, give them away, lay them down. Death comes for us like a thief in the night (Lk. 12.39; 1 Thess. 5.2 etc.), but if we give away our lives there is nothing to be stolen. If we hug our lives to ourselves, like Gollum in *The Lord of the Rings* hanging on to his ring, 'My precious, my precious', then the Lord will have to prise open our reluctant hands to take our lives. If our lives are already given, then we may go 'gently into that good night'.[20]

We may do this as parents raising children, getting up in the middle of the night to feed and quieten them and change their nappies; suffering their teenage tragedies and dramas, not demanding gratitude then if ever. Flying back from the Sudan recently, in fact the very night of Austin's death, I found myself on a plane sitting by a screaming child. At first, like a grumpy old celibate, I cursed my bad luck at having to endure nine hours of infantile rage, and then I tried to grasp the martyrdom of the parents who bear this every day

[19] John Guy, *A Daughter's Love: Thomas and Margaret More* (London, 2009), p. 227.
[20] Dylan Thomas, 'Do not go gently into that good night', in *The Oxford Book of Twentieth Century Verse* (Oxford, 1973), p. 474.

so that humanity can have a future. Or think of those who spend their lives for their sick spouses, giving away their strength, caring for someone who may even have forgotten their name. One can live this as a violent robbery of one's life. But if we make it a giving of ourselves then when death takes our life away, we will find that it is not so hard, since we have already let it go. Karl Rahner wrote: 'Because we die our death in this life, because we are permanently taking leave, permanently parting, looking towards the end...we die throughout life, therefore what we call death really is the end of death, the death of death'.[21]

Many cultures recognize that a moment may come when one lets go of life, because the time has come to die. *I Heard the Owl Call my Name*[22] is a moving novel about an Anglican priest who is taught by Native Americans to recognize the summons and embrace it. I flew home to be with my mother when she died. She had clung on to life until I was back, and I was able to tell her that now she could let go. Often people, especially loyal and dutiful people, feel that they need permission to die. Then we share Christ's last moment when he entrusted himself to his Father and ours: 'Into your hands I commit my spirit' (Lk. 23.46). He yields his life. This is not suicide. We cherish the gift of life by giving it back when the time is due.

Then our dying will be, as it was for our ancestors, something that we do rather than something that is done to us. They celebrated their deaths with the rituals of the Church, surrounded by their families and neighbours, playing the central part in their last drama on this

---

[21] *On the Theology of Death*, Quaestiones Disputatae 2 (New York, 1961), p. 85. Quoted in David Albert Jones, *Approaching the End: A Theological Exploration of Death and Dying* (Oxford, 2007), p. 162.

[22] Margaret Craven, *I Heard the Owl Call My Name* (Toronto, 1967).

earth, instead of passing away alone and invisible behind curtains in a hospital ward.

A young seminarian in his twenties, Andrew Robinson, found that he was dying of cancer shortly before he was due to be ordained. His Archbishop of Birmingham, Vincent Nichols, had the good idea of asking him to keep a diary so that he could share his living and dying with his friends. This is what he wrote a few days before his death: 'My illness has played a substantial part in my journey to God, to peace and to freedom. The journey is by no means easy, but when you come towards the light at the end of the tunnel, and you feel its warmth, you taste its peace and freedom, you hear the noise of the crowds of angels cheering you on in praise of God who draws us to the light'.[23]

Brother Christian, the Prior of the Atlas monks, composed a poem which he called 'Testament', his last testament to his brethren. He was already aware that his death would probably come violently, but, in this moment, he hands it over willingly and with gratitude.

My body is for the earth
So please
No preservatives, just earth and me

My heart was made for life
So please
No affectation
Just life and me

My hands were made for work
They fold
Quite simply

---

[23] Vincent Nichols, *Tears at Night Joy at Dawn: Journal of a Dying Seminarian* (Stoke on Trent, 2003), p. 73.

As for my face
Uncover it
For an easier kiss

And for my gaze
Let it SEE
PS thank you[24]

---

[24] Olivera, *How Far to Follow?* p. 41.

12

God's anointed

Everything that led up to our baptism with water expressed what it means for us to be caught up in God's transforming love. Everything after that pivotal moment brings to light how the baptized are to live their new identity in the life of Church and share its mission to the world. We begin with the anointing as priests, prophets and kings.

Unless the baptized are going to be confirmed immediately, the minister now says: 'As Christ was anointed Priest, Prophet and King, so may you live always as a member of his body, sharing everlasting life'. The baptized are then anointed with chrism on their foreheads. We are, in the words of an early address to the baptized, 'a chosen race, a royal priesthood, a holy nation, God's own people, in order that you may proclaim the mighty acts of him who called you out of darkness into his marvellous light' (1 Pet. 2.9).

That sounds wonderful but isn't the language rather inflated? Most Christians do not feel themselves to be priests, let alone prophets or kings. We talk about 'the priesthood of all believers', which is the participation of the baptized in the priesthood of Christ, but this seems rather vacuous, given that most lay people are rather passive in the life of the Church. Why is there such an apparent gap between what we celebrate in baptism and the life of the Church, which is often dismally clerical? A former Irish bishop is supposed to have said: 'Everyone in this diocese is equal, from me downwards!'

If I may respond to this question as a Catholic, this is a paradoxical moment in the life of the Church. On the one hand lay leadership has expanded enormously since the Second Vatican Council, and yet some bishops and priests react nervously and uncertainly to this new phenomenon and are tempted to tighten the clerical ranks.

Before the Second Vatican Council, many lay people were involved in the mission of the Church, as catechists, volunteers for the St Vincent de Paul movement working with the poor and so on. But since the Council there has been an explosion in the number of lay 'ministers'. In the United States, by 1990, there were 22,000. Today there are some 31,000.[1] The number of priests and religious has been declining with equal rapidity. One might think that the former is a response to the latter, but it is not so simple. The flood of lay people seeking a role in the Church predates the fall in the number of vocations to the ordained priesthood and religious life by about ten years.[2] In Germany, there is also a vast expansion of lay involvement. In France, Spain and Italy, there has been a surge in the number of lay movements, which often demand a life-long commitment, and which frequently have members who are priests and religious, but not necessarily in the positions of leadership: L'Arche, the Focolari, Communion and Liberation, the community of Sant'Egidio, the Beatitudes, the Emmanuel community, Opus Dei, the neo-catechumenate, the Chemin Neuve, and so on and on. And in other continents, this explosion takes different forms. In Vietnam,

---

[1] Allen, *The Future Church*, p. 192.
[2] Thomas O'Meara OP in Richard W. Miller II (ed.), *Lay Ministry in the Catholic Church: Visioning Church Ministry through the Wisdom of the Past* (Kansas City, 2005), p. 92.

for example, there are now almost 100,000 lay Dominicans, who are often, for all intents and purposes, the Church in remote regions of the country where priests are forbidden access by the government. Never have such vast numbers of lay men and women been actively committed to the life and ministry of the Church. This is a time of immense vitality for lay leadership in the Catholic Church.

At the same time, our people often complain of a growing clericalism, a failure for the Church to acknowledge the dignity and wisdom of lay people, to care for their rights and to use their talents. We are offered this vast gift of the people of God who are, as never before, educated and prepared for a role in the Church's life and mission, and yet the Church seems uncertain how to welcome this new moment, even fearful at times.

We are the community of Christ's body. To be a Christian is to be alive in God, now and for ever. But ever since the conversion of the Emperor Constantine, the Church has struggled to preserve her freedom to be such a community from the powers of this world: Roman Emperors, Arian Kings, the Holy Roman Emperor, absolute monarchs, centralized State power, nineteenth-century Empires, twentieth-century Communism and Fascism. These battles were necessary and unavoidable if the Church were to remain free to be herself, but in fighting against these powers, it was tempted sometimes to think of itself more as a power structure rather than a communion. After centuries of resistance, it is not surprising that the Church ended up by often looking rather like the powers whose control it sought to evade. Paradoxically, it had to fight to remain itself, but, in the struggle, sometimes weakened its identity as the communion of the baptized.

This is not to suggest for one moment that a church hierarchy is an alien imposition on an original egalitarian community. Not at all! From the moment that Jesus chose the twelve apostles, some such institution has been a part of the Church's life in Christ: 'You are part of a building that has the apostles and prophets for its foundation, and Christ Jesus himself for its main cornerstone' (Eph. 2.19-20). The Church is given to us by Christ, given in the Eucharist, given at Pentecost. And part of this gift of communion is that mutual belonging to each other, transcending every nation, and even death, which is expressed by the communion of churches, each in the care of a successor of the apostles, the bishop. So the hierarchy as such is part of the good news! But the pressure of two thousand years of history, an unending struggle for the freedom to be such a community of God's love, has sometimes left the hierarchical structure of the Church looking more like a power structure than a communion of life. It had to be militant to survive but in the process tended to become rather too military.

The temptation for the Church to think of itself as primarily a power structure is exacerbated by the fact that this is how it is only seen in the media. All our churches are reported as if they were political parties, whose leaders take policy decisions just like their political counterparts, or NGOs pushing an agenda. There is no understanding that Christianity is above all a life to be lived. And so the bishops are regarded as cabinet ministers in the Church, the ordinary clergy as backbenchers, and the laity as party members whose only role is 'to pray, pay and obey'. They are not seen by the media to count for much.

John Allen, a well-known reporter on Church matters, was approached by the BBC which was preparing a documentary on women in the Church and wanted suggestions as to who from the Church they could speak with. He suggested Mary Ann Glendon, the Head of the Pontifical Academy of Social Scientists and a frequent representative of the Holy See. The producer replied, 'I must not have

made myself clear. I meant someone from the Church'.[3] We all read
the newspapers, scan blogs and watch TV – bishops, clergy and laity
– and our understanding of who we are is moulded almost as much
by the media as by the Church's own tradition. When people ask me
when I 'joined the Church', they are surprised when I say that I was
three days old at the time.

But this is a new time. The challenges that the Church faces, at
least in the West today, are not so much direct State interference,
as secularism, relativism and indifference. We will only be able to
respond effectively to these if we release the creativity of the whole
People of God. We cannot remain imprisoned by past struggles.
Otherwise we shall be like the French knights at Agincourt, weighed
down by armour designed for earlier battles and unable to cope with
the nimble English archers with their new longbows!

Forgive this extended plea. It is necessary to grasp why so much
hangs on our understanding of this moment of baptism, when all the
faithful are anointed as priests, prophets and kings. This anointing,
with confirmation, grounds the participation of all the baptized in the
Church's ministry. The flourishing of all our Churches depends upon
getting this right. If we do, the energy of the whole Body of Christ will
be unlocked. If we do not, many people may either fall into passivity,
walk away, or just become angry and frustrated. Thomas O'Meara OP
warns us: 'To repress life's activities is dangerous. When human life
is repressed, suppressed, the person becomes sick, becomes neurotic,
becomes moribund'.[4] This is what happens when life in the Spirit is
repressed. 'Do not quench the Spirit' (1 Thess. 5.19).

Being priest, prophet and king all flow from being alive in God.
We are alive, rather than just ticking over, because we are able to

---

[3] Allen, *The Future Church*, p. 213.
[4] Miller, *Lay Ministry*, p. 71.

love, and to mediate God's love for humanity, and humanity's love for God. That is the fundamental way in which the baptized share in Christ's priesthood. We are prophets in so far as it is given to us to speak words that give life and truth, God's own word. To be a mature human being also means that we bear responsibility in the life of society and the Church. Sharing Christ's kingship, we are all called to exercise our proper role in the community.

We shall glance at each of these three aspects of our Christian life. It will be impossible to separate them completely, for they are all aspects of being fully alive.

Priests

When the early Christians were baptized, sometimes they were vested with the clothes of ordained priests, stoles and chasubles, as a sign that they now share Christ's priesthood. They were members of the 'laity' but that means literally 'the people' of God, God's holy people. And so bishops and clergy are also members of the laity, in this sense. 'Laity is a priestly name for a priestly people'.[5]

What does it mean for us to share Christ's priesthood? Priests are usually thought of as people who do religious things, usually in old buildings. When I told a friend that I was going to be ordained, he replied: 'I also like Gothic architecture'. In the time of Jesus there was an enormous army of priests who took their turn at running the Temple and offering sacrifices. It was like an enormous abattoir, with the daily slaughter of innumerable animals. The noise must have been terrible. You would have smelt the Temple before you saw it.

---

[5] Aidan Kavanagh, 'Unfinished and Unbegun Revisited', in Maxwell Johnson ed., *Living Water, Sealing Spirit: Readings on Christian Initiation* (Collegeville, MN 1995), p. 269.

But Jesus was not one of these priests. He was a lay man, who took his part in the annual sacrifices and feasts like other lay people. His priesthood is to be the mediator between God and humanity. He embodied God's love for us, and our love of God. His only sacrifice was his self-offering.

The baptized share in his priesthood by embodying God's love for humanity, and humanity's worshipful love of God. We do this in all the ways in which we love other people with God's own love: the love of spouses for each other, of parents for their children, the love that we offer our friends. Nurses and teachers are priestly when they offer God's love for those in their care. I was shown around the southern Sudan by a young man who co-ordinated CAFOD's aid in the region. He helped to establish the Aids centres, the food distribution points, training people to sow new crops and so on. All this is an expression of his baptismal priesthood.

The baptized is anointed at this point with chrism, perfumed olive oil, and so also associated with gladness. Cyril of Jerusalem said, 'Christ was anointed with the spiritual oil of gladness because he is the author of spiritual joy; and you have been anointed with chrism because you have become fellows and sharers with Christ'.[6] Jesus embodied the Father's joy in all of humanity. So it belongs to the priesthood of the faithful to take pleasure in people, whether it is a grandmother rejoicing in her latest descendant or an aid worker delighting in the refugees for whom she is caring. We have a priesthood of joy.

When Etty Hilesum left the camp to take the train to Auschwitz, to go to her death, she went with joy: 'Talking gaily, smiling, a kind word for everyone she met on the way, full of sparkling good humour, perhaps just a touch of sadness, but every inch our Etty, the way you

---

[6] Yarnold, *Awe-Inspiring Rites*, p. 80.

all know her… And the way they [the inmates] felt about her leaving spoke volumes for the love and dedication she had given them all'.[7]

The chrism is also called 'the oil of thanksgiving'.[8] That is the other direction in which we exercise our priesthood, offering thanks to God. This is the 'Eucharist', literally 'the thanksgiving', that we offer for everything that we have received, and for all the unacknowledged gifts that God showers on everyone. Parents and grandparents fret sometimes that their offspring do not believe and pray, but they have the priestly service of offering thanks on their behalf.

All the baptized exercise Christ's priesthood when they take part in the great thanksgiving of the Eucharist. For the first twelve hundred years of the Church's existence, there was a strong sense that the baptized concelebrated with the ordained priest. He did not offer the Eucharist for them so much as *with* them. According to Cardinal Congar the little dialogue that precedes the preface – 'The Lord be with you', 'And with your spirit'[9]; 'Lift up your hearts', 'We lift them up to the Lord'; 'Let us give thanks to the Lord our God', 'It is right and just' – was when the congregation gave the priest permission to celebrate the Eucharist on their behalf.[10] This is their consent to his enacting of their common priesthood. 'By their baptismal

---

[7] Hilesum, *An Interrupted Life*, pp. 667-68.

[8] Kenan B. Osborne OFM, *The Christian Sacraments of Initiation: Baptism, Confirmation, Eucharist* (New York and Mahwah, NJ 1987), p. 67.

[9] The new English translation of the missal has recently changed the response to 'The Lord be with you' to 'with your spirit'. This has provoked irritation and incomprehension but this is what Catholics say in almost every language and so we are rejoining the wider tradition. It is also a Biblical expression. A Jesuit friend of mine, John Moffat, argues that it is an adaptation quotation of 2 Tim. 4.22, which refers us back to the exhortation at the beginning of the letter: 'I remind you to rekindle the gift of God that is within you through the laying on of my hands; for God did not give us a spirit of cowardice, but rather a spirit of power and of love and of self-discipline' (1.6-7). So this greeting is an invitation to use the charismatic power given to him on behalf of the community.

[10] Paul Philibert OP (trans. and ed.), *At the Heart of Christian Worship: Liturgical Essays of Yves Congar* (Collegeville, 2010), p. 61.

consecration, the faithful are constituted as legitimate co-celebrants in this sacrifice'.[11] Guerric of Igny wrote: 'The priest does not sacrifice alone, he does not consecrate alone; rather the whole assembly of the faithful who are present consecrate with him and sacrifice with him'.[12] And when the congregation says 'the Great Amen' at the end of the Eucharist prayer, then this is their consent to the consecration. Augustine says: 'Your Amen is your signature'.[13] This is our ratification of the event.

So why do we need ordained ministers? Why cannot any lay person preside at the Eucharist if we all share in Christ's priesthood? There is no sacrament of priesthood. It is 'the sacrament of orders'. This is not, you may be surprised to hear, because the ordained are supposed to give orders to the laity but because we share in Christ's priesthood by being ordered – orientated – towards each other. We are priests as members of a community, the people of God, and not as isolated individuals. We have an organic relationship, we are one body. The ordained have care for how we belong together, and for how each community belongs to the universal Church. They are ordained so that every Eucharist is in communion with the whole Church. Their priesthood is at the service of the one priesthood of Christ, which we share as members of his body. They do this also by cherishing the faithful, delighting in them, giving them strength and building communion. Peter was told by the Lord that he must strengthen his brethren. The day that John XXIII died, a ticket collector on a Roman bus said: 'He was a pope who made you feel like a person'.[14]

---

[11] Ibid., p. 105.

[12] Ibid., p. 28.

[13] Sermon 272, quoted in Philibert, p. 61.

[14] 'Era un papa che ti ha fatto sentire come una persona', quoted in Ladislas Orsy, *Receiving the Council: Theological and Canonical Insights and Debates* (Collegeville 2009), frontispiece.

The ordained priests should cultivate the priestly gifts that each of us brings to the community. Vincent Donovan was a missionary priest who worked with the Masai in East Africa. For years he quietly served them but was reluctant to impose his faith. When finally he talked about his beliefs, they said: 'We always wondered why you were here, and now at last we know. Why did you not tell us before?' And so he prepared them for baptism. When the time drew near, he wondered what his role as their priest would be. He discovered that:

> He would not be the one in the community who knew the most theology, the theologian. He would not be the preacher or the evangelist of the community. He would not be the prophet. He would not be the most important member in the community, in the sense of being the one who was to make the most important contribution, of which the community might someday be capable. But he would be the focal point of the whole community, the one who would enable the community to act, whether in worship or in service. He would be the animator of the individual members of the community, enabling them to make their various contributions, enabling the preacher to preach and the teacher to teach and the pray-er to pray and the prophet to prophesy. He would be the necessary sign of the power that is in all of them. He would be the sign of unity that exists among them. He would be their link with the outside, the sign of their union with the outside, the universal church. He would be their priest.[15]

---

[15] Vincent J. Donovan, *Christianity Rediscovered: An Epistle from the Masai* (London, 1978), pp. 144–45.

Prophets

At Pentecost, Peter quotes the prophet Joel: 'In the last days, it will be, God declares, that I will pour my Spirit upon all flesh, and your sons and your daughters shall prophesy, and your young men shall see visions, and your old men shall dream dreams. Even on my slaves, both men and women, in those days I will pour out my Spirit' (Acts 2.17-18). All the baptized are called to be prophets.

Prophecy is not foretelling the future. The prophet speaks God's word – the word, as we have seen in chapter 8, that enlivens and makes people flourish. The vocation of every human being is prophetic, to speak fertile words that nourish people and make them strong: 'Let no evil talk come out of your mouths, but only what is useful for building up, as there is need, so that your words may give grace to those who hear' (Eph. 4.29). We exercise our prophetic ministry a hundred times a day, in how we speak to and about each other, how we gossip, joke and comment, bless or curse, praise or accuse. Everyone whose life is especially bound up with words has an obviously prophetic vocation: teachers, writers, poets, journalists, playwrights, campaigners and politicians. Prophesy is inseparable from speaking words that are true, that reverence the dignity of others, that uncover their goodness. Of course prophets also denounce and challenge, but always in the context of God's delight in his sons and daughters, never with contempt.

Think of the role of Christians in the media. The media have a power in our society beyond even that of politicians, a power that is largely unaccountable. Our perception of the world, and even of the Church, is shaped by what we see on the television, read in the papers and discover on the Internet. We are informed, protected from tyranny, share in the community of our planetary village, and are entertained. One of the first things that I do every day is read the papers and before I sleep I listen to the news.

But the media also have a potentially destructive power, through lies, oversimplification, and poisonous innuendo. Reputations are created and then are destroyed without a thought. Britain has been shaken by the revelation that reporters have hacked into people's phones. Christian journalists have a prophetic role in speaking the truth, holding back from destroying people, challenging stereotypes. Above all, they are called upon to resist the simplistic categories that blind us to subtlety and nuance. It is extremely difficult to be a Christian journalist, to deliver the stories that the media want and resist the seduction of sensationalism. Do we give enough support to Christians who have the courage to immerse themselves in this fascinating, wonderful and terrible world?

Think of a more obvious prophetic role, of those who struggle for a more just world, and who risk imprisonment and even death. Think of Sister Dorothy Stang, the Notre Dame Sister who was murdered in the Amazon for her defence of indigenous people from the predations of the loggers and great landowners. Or Henri Burin des Rosiers, a French Dominican lawyer who has a price on his head because of his fight against the enslavement of poor people on these vast Amazonian estates. He jokes that because he is getting old, the price on his head has been reduced from $30,000 to a mere $20,000. 'I have been devalued!'

Think of the prophetic role of poets and novelists and all who have a creative care for our language. When our words become tired and cheap, they refresh and renew our language so that we can speak words that open up the beauty of God's creation. So we need poets and song writers to uncover the joy of each thing's existence. Gerard Manley Hopkins sought to reveal what he called 'the inscape' of

things, their intrinsic unity, their 'thisness', the inexhaustible variety
of creation:

> Glory be to God for dappled things –
> For skies of couple-colour as a brinded cow;
> For rose-moles in all stipple upon trout that swim;
> Fresh-firecoal chestnut-falls; finches' wings;
> Landscape plotted and pieced – fold, fallow, and plough;
> And áll trádes, their gear and tackle and trim.
>
> All things counter, original, spare, strange;
> Whatever is fickle, freckled (who knows how?)
> With swift, slow; sweet, sour; adazzle, dim;
> He fathers-forth whose beauty is past change:
> Praise him.[16]

The baptized also have a prophetic role within the Church. Our
baptism gives us the authority, indeed the duty, to speak openly when
the Church commits injustice or lies or fails to live as the community
of God's people. This is even recognized by Canon Law![17] This is the
most painful, costly and delicate prophetic role of all. Here many feel
the pain of being the prophet not recognized in their own land, the
Church. Speaking as a Catholic, we treasure the unity of the Church
supremely for it is the unity of the Body of Christ. It is hard to find
words on some contentious issue that are clear and unambiguous
and yet which do not trouble the unity of the Church. It is easy to
be seduced by models of protest taken from political life that are
neither effective nor appropriate, sign resolutions, organize protests,

---

[16] Gerard Manley Hopkins, *Poems and Prose*, ed. W. H. Gardner (London, 1985),
pp. 30–31.
[17] Code of Canon Law 212.3.

to denounce and accuse. This, again, is to treat the Church as if it were primarily a power structure rather than a living communion.

The challenge is to be truthful and humble, truthful and gentle, truthful and patient, courageous without aggressivity. One must resist the temptation to claim the prophet's role, for true prophets never claim that honour for themselves. It is tempting to become a celebrity in the media, and succumb to the media's oversimplifications and compromises with the truth.

Yves Congar OP offers us the example of man who found a way, with great pain and sorrow, to remain both truthful and also, in the best sense, loyal. His early books on the laity and on ecumenism led to his being silenced by the Vatican. He was furious, hurt, at times depressed, but he remained true. He wrote in 1954, in the middle of the crisis: 'To speak the truth. Prudently, without useless or provocative scandal. But remain – and become more and more – an authentic and pure witness of what is true'.[18] This requires the humility to recognize that one's answers might not be true, but one has the duty to contribute to the search. When someone asked whether he thought that he had the right answers, he replied: 'Maybe the answers I give are incorrect, but the questions are real!'[19] He went on asking them.

He was sustained by the conviction that the truth triumphs in the end, even if one has to wait a long time, even if one does not see its victory. He was astonished when he was invited to attend the Second Vatican Council as an expert, whose opinions were sought at the highest level, and he was even, not long before his death, created a

---

[18] *Journal d'un théologien 1946–1956*, ed É. Fouilloux (Paris, 2000), p. 271.
[19] Wojciech Giertych OP, 'The Importance of the Study of Theology in the Dominican Tradition', in Dominican Sisters International *et al.*, *Building Bridges: Dominicans Doing Theology Together* (Dublin and Manila, 2005), p. 44.

Cardinal. The prophet offers a word that is true, effective, bringing about God's purpose. But we are most prophetic in letting that word take its time, trusting that if it is indeed the Lord's word, then it will bear fruit, maybe long after the speaker has died. 'So shall my word be that goes forth from my mouth; it shall not return to me empty, but it shall accomplish that which I purpose, and succeed in the thing for which I sent it' (Isa. 55.11). And if it is not the word of the Lord, it will disappear.

Christ's Kingship

We are also anointed to share Christ's kingship. This may seem odd, despite popular obsession with the British Royal Family. But Jesus was an unusual king, who ruled from a cross, and who died with a sign over his head saying 'The King of the Jews' in Hebrew, Greek and Latin (Jn 19.20). It is a kingship that 'was not of this world' and that he exercised by refusing violence. We share his kingship in the non-violent ways in which we share in decision-making in our society and Church. We have a ministry of gentle government within our families, taking decisions about the raising of our children and the building of the home, our domestic economy. It is also the special ministry of Christians involved in any form of government, whether in Parliament, businesses or trade unions. Administrators, managers, economists, bankers, for example, are all called to exercise just responsibility. It belongs to our stewardship of the common good.

A fine example of Christian kingship would be Shahbaz Bhatti, the only Christian minister in the government of Pakistan. He was murdered on 2 March 2011, as he left his mother's home in Islamabad, for his opposition to the blasphemy laws, which are often used to persecute Christians. A month before his death, he said: 'I have been told by pro-Taleban religious extremists that if I continue to speak against the blasphemy law, I will be beheaded. As a Christian, I believe Jesus is my strength. He has given me a power and wisdom and motivation to serve suffering humanity. I follow the principles of my conscience, and I am ready to die and sacrifice my life for the principles I believe.'[20]

The baptized also should exercise their 'kingship' within the Church. Pope Paul VI wrote, 'It belongs to the laity, without waiting passively for orders and directives, to take the initiative freely and to infuse a Christian Spirit into the mentality, custom, laws and structures of the community in which they live.'[21] How can the laity exercise their proper 'kingship' within the life of the Church? Mgr Talbot, a nineteenth-century Vatican official and my great, great uncle, believed that they should stick to hunting, shooting and entertaining. He was strongly opposed by Blessed John Henry Newman who replied that without the laity the Church would look rather foolish!

There is a deep desire by many people for their voice to be heard in the Church. This is their right, as those anointed with Christ's kingship. If this is not given a healthy outlet, recognized by the Church, then it will find perverse expression. There are innumerable blogs, both liberal and conservative, which are often a positive contribution to the life of the Church but sometimes are vicious, spreading untrue allegations, failing to respect the right of every person to preserve their good name, and are profoundly damaging. Yet these blogs are often influential. Rather than simply condemning them, we should see them as an unhelpful expression of a legitimate desire, for the baptized people of God to exercise their participation in Christ's kingship. How can this be achieved?

---

[20] http://www.zenit.org/rssenglish-31937
[21] Paul VI, Octagesima Adveniens, 1971, paragraph 48:1.

Newman believed that in the Church we must recognize three authorities, or offices.[22] There is the authority of 'devotion', of the experience of God, which is shared by the whole people of God. We all have authority because of our encounter with the Lord in prayer. We have all received the Spirit, who animates our hearts and our minds. There is also the authority of truth, cultivated by reason. Pope Paul VI said: 'The world is in trouble because of a lack of thinking'.[23] Alas, the Church is often in trouble too because faced with divisive issues we do not think! Again this belongs to us all in so far as we bring our minds to bear upon our faith but it is an especial responsibility of theologians and philosophers. Our faith cannot be contrary to reason, and so the Church needs people who wrestle with difficult issues, puzzle, pose hard questions, and doggedly go on thinking. The Church must make sure that they are free to do so. Finally, there is also the authority of government. This is especially invested in the hierarchy of the Church, but we all share in responsibility for the Church's life.

Newman believed that the authentic authority of the Church depended upon the respect for each of these 'authorities' or offices. If the hierarchy charged with government, or theologians and their responsibility to reason, or the whole people of God with their experience, are disregarded then the authority of the Church is weakened. Each can go wrong if it excludes or undermines the other. In the history of the Church they are always mutually corrective. If reason became the absolute authority, then one would end up with an arid rationalism; if religious experience became the only authority, then Newman thought that one might fall into superstition. And if

---

[22] Preface to the 3rd edition of *Lectures on the Prophetical Office of the Church* (London, 1874) and the 3rd edition of the *Via Media* (London, 1877).

[23] *Populorum Progressio*, quoted by Pope Benedict, *Caritas in Veritate*, para. 53.

the authority of the Church's government became too strong then, Newman said, the danger was 'ambition and tyranny'.[24]

So good governance in the Church requires the voices of reason and of experience to be heard. This is because the government of the Church, her kingly office, is at the service of her prayer and preaching. Nicholas Lash wrote: 'All Christian governance is at the service of the twofold pedagogy of discipleship, of apprenticeship in holiness and understanding, the exercise of the priestly and prophetic offices'.[25] If it ceases to serve these, then it will be just the assertion of what Augustine calls the *libido dominandi*, the lust to dominate.

What would this renewed Church look like? It cannot be simply a question of democracy: one baptized one vote. The Church is the communion of the living and the dead, and most of the baptized are dead! We have to attend to their voice, recorded in the past councils and teaching of the Church and writings of the saints. We cannot just reinvent Christianity as we go along, like a political party rebranding its policies. But the voice of those now living must also be heard. Congar reminds us that 'the Church's concrete regime is traditionally one of councils, not of solitary personal decisions'.[26] The voice of the laity must count in the councils of the Church, for we all share in Christ's kingship.

---

[24] *Via Media*, quoted by Nicholas Lash, 'Authors, Authority and Authorization', in Bernhard Hoose (ed.), *Authority in the Roman Catholic Church: Theory and Practice* (London, 2002), p. 62.

[25] Ibid., p. 63.

[26] Yves Congar, *Lay People in the Church*, trans. Donald Attwater (Westminster, 1985), p. 237. Quoted by Anthony Oelrich, *A Church Fully Engaged: Yves Congar's Vision of Ecclesial Authority* (Collegeville, MN, 2011), p. 64.

13

God's holy people

The newly baptized are now clothed in white garments, and the minister says: 'You have become a new creation, and have clothed yourself in Christ. See in this white garment the outward sign of your Christian dignity. With your family and friends to help you by word and example, bring that dignity unstained into the everlasting life of heaven'.

For the early Christians, these white garments proclaimed that they now shared in Christ's own holiness and were his brothers and sisters. In the words of a third-century sermon: 'Whoever goes down into these waters of rebirth is raised to filial status. He comes up from baptism resplendent as the sun, radiant in his purity, but above all he comes as a child of God, and a coheir with Christ'.[1] In some places the newly baptized paraded around dressed in white for a week after baptism at the Easter Vigil. It was known as 'shining week'.[2] In Burundi, I have seen crowds of Christians walking over the hills on a Sunday morning, going to Church dressed in white, just like our forebears two thousand years ago.

---

[1] Attributed to St Hippolytus of Rome, '*On the Epiphany*', *Patrologia Graeca* 10.859.
[2] Yarnold, *Awe-Inspiring Rites*, p. 29.

Often today this part of the ritual of baptism is hardly noticed. A baby has a white shawl hastily wrapped around its shoulders, perhaps to be removed as quickly as possible before it can be sick over it. In the West we have virtually ceased to see clothes as ceremonial expressions of identity. In most societies, and our own until recently, what you wore proclaimed who you were. Clothes declared your sexual identity. When I was a child, the clothes worn by boys and girls were different in every detail, even down to the direction in which their belts fastened. There must be no confusion of the sexes! Clothes declared your age. I remember the glory of putting away the shorts of childhood when I proudly wore my first long trousers, a sign that I was on my way to being a grown up. Clothes proclaimed your status as married or single or widowed, your social class and your wealth. Your clothes stated what relationships you had with other people, to whom you might speak and where you were in the pecking order, by which door you might enter a house, and where and with whom you ate. To change your clothes was to become a new person.

Our democratic spirit rebels against such sartorial stratifications. Ceremonial clothing is experienced as a straightjacket or else as absurd. Of course our clothes still give signals as to wealth and identity. I am told that what appear to me to be identical pairs of jeans make vastly different fashion statements, but then I am sartorially blind. Designer labels are treasured and pirated. But our clothes rarely have the same formal, prescribed role in identifying who we are.

But for our ancestors, these white garments made a bold statement about who they had become in Christ. They made visible the extraordinary claim that social status is, at least within the Church, abolished. We are all brothers and sisters. Senators and slaves were equally children of God. Margaret of Antioch was a popular fourth-century saint who, if she existed at all, was supposed to have survived being swallowed by a dragon. She said: 'Servitude has nothing to do with me because I am a Christian'.[3] We share in the glory of the Risen One. True glory does not belong to the great generals, the rulers and the wealthy, who wore togas and who were honoured with statues in the public squares. It belongs to the least of Christ's brothers and sisters who share his holiness. The baptized belong to God's holy people. In the New Testament, Christians are quite simply 'the saints' (Rom. 1.7; 1 Cor. 1.2; 2 Cor. 1.8 etc.).

I argued in the last chapter that the Church will only flourish as Christ's Body, if we renew the vocation of all the baptized to be priests, prophets and kings. If not, the Church will be seen as a clerical institution in which the laity is just about tolerated. But the *soul* of the Body of Christ is surely holiness. So these white garments are indeed good news. They speak of the radical equality of the baptized in the Church, and our shared vocation to be saints. We might not want to wear them the whole of Easter week, but they are a small gesture that challenges the world. We may even sympathize with the claim of the exuberant pop star Lady Gaga that she was going to change the world, 'sequin by sequin'!

But in what sense are we a holy people? By what right do we wear white? Our Churches are not obviously communities of saints. The founding disciples were hardly heroes, with Judas betraying Christ and Peter denying him, and Paul, the apostle to the Gentiles, murdering the first Christians. The early community squabbled over the distribution of the common bread, and Ananias and his wife Sapphira tried to cheat the community (Acts 5). The histories of all our Churches are marked by sin, from the Borgia Popes to the scandals of sexual abuse today.

---

[3] Brown, *Discipleship and Imagination*, p. 92.

We must distinguish between a biblical understanding of holiness, and another subsequent meaning of the word which evolved as the Church struggled to make sense of its experience of failure. Both senses of 'holiness' are important for the baptized. We shall consider the first in this chapter and the second in the next.

We are holy now, in the Biblical sense, because we share the life of the Most Holy God. However sinful and unworthy the Church may be, we are God's people and he is our God. Israel was called out of Egypt because God chose her. This was not because there was anything special about Israel. She was not greater or better than any other nation. God chose her because he loved her. 'It was not because you were more numerous than any other people that the Lord set his heart on you and chose you – for you were the fewest of all peoples. It was because the Lord loved you and kept the oath that he swore to your ancestors, that the Lord has brought you out with a mighty hand, and redeemed you from the hand of Pharaoh, king of Egypt' (Deut. 7.7-8).

In fact God tended to choose people to guide Israel who were spectacularly unholy in the modern sense of the word. Abraham, our father in faith, was a shifty character who tried to pass off his wife as his sister when the Pharaoh set his eyes on her. Jacob, the father of the twelve tribes of Israel, was a trickster who cheated Esau of his inheritance. Moses was a murderer, and his brother Aaron, the first high priest, was an idolater who made the golden calf the moment that Moses' back was turned. David, the one whom God loved and chose as king, was an adulterer with Bathsheba, and then murdered her husband Uriah the Hittite. God seemed to have a fondness for ruffians. In the New Testament, we find this same choice of sinners, with Jesus eating and drinking with prostitutes and tax collectors, and gathering around him disciples who were not particularly edifying. We believe that in Christ we too are chosen to share God's life for no other reason than that we are chosen. Being holy, in this sense, is rather like being a celebrity who is famous only for being famous. There is no merit in it.

So, in the New Testament, 'the saints' usually refers simply to the Church. Maureen Tilley, Professor at Fordham University, wrote that

> for the early Church holiness was not so much a personal attribute as it was an institutionally based characteristic. It was intimately related to being in the holy Church that was one and catholic... In the New Testament holiness is a function of the group. The predominant use of 'holy' concerns the Holy Spirit active in the united Christian community. The Spirit is the source of unity. So holiness is not an individual project but a communal one. It is the church and not individuals who are called holy in the New Testament. One is holy not by individual effort but by belonging to and being the holy group and thus participating in its Spirit.[4]

The newly baptized are not clothed with the garments of holiness because they have suddenly become very good. The early Church painfully learned that this was not the case. Most went on sinning much as before. We are indeed a holy nation, not because we love God but because we accept that God loves us, despite all our endless failures. Our holiness lies in the acceptance of forgiveness again and again. Rowan Williams wrote: 'Humanly speaking, holiness is always this: God's endurance in the middle of our refusal of him, his capacity to meet every refusal with the gift of himself'.[5]

---

[4] Maureen Tilley, 'One Wholly Catholic: Saints and Sanctity in the Post-Apostolic Church', Catholic Theological Society Annual Meeting, 9 June 2011, to be published.
[5] Rowan Williams, *Open to Judgment: Sermons and Addresses* (London, 1994), p. 136.

So we build God's holy people by welcoming everyone, especially the despised, into the community of God's delight. We wear white because, mysteriously and beyond all comprehension, God takes pleasure in us just as we are, warts and all. This is what Father Gregory Boyle tries to show his beloved gang members in Los Angeles, that they are utterly accepted: 'Behold the One who can't take His eyes off you.'[6] When he calls young Lula by his name, 'you would have thought that I had electrocuted him. His whole body spasms with delight to be known, to be called, to hear his name uttered out loud. For his entire trip through the crosswalk, Lula kept turning back and looking at me, smiling.'[7] This is the delight that we proudly show when we are clothed in white, the dazzling glory of God's pleasure in us.

This is not a holiness that puts us above anyone else, or that embodies any claim to superiority. It is a sign of the holiness of every human being who, whatever they may wear in public – old jeans or smart suits – are clothed in God's glory for those who have eyes to see. The Church is rather like the community of Cannery Row, in John Steinbeck's novel of that name: 'Its inhabitants are, as the man once said, "whores, pimps, gamblers, and sons of bitches," by which he meant Everybody. Had the man looked through another peephole he might have said, "Saints and angels, and martyrs and holy people," and he would have meant the same thing.'[8]

The white garments proclaim what the French novelist Romain Gary calls 'l'honneur d'être un homme', the honour of being a human being.[9] A friend wrote to Thomas Merton: 'When people ask me

---

[6] Boyle, *Tattoos on the Heart*, p. 39.

[7] Ibid., p. 47.

[8] (London, 1992), p. 1.

[9] In *La Promesse de l'aube*. Quoted by Jérôme Cordelier, *Rebelles de Dieu* (Paris, 2011), p. 7.

what I *do*, I simply tell them that I am a human *being*.[10] A turning point in Merton's life was when he discovered that his monastic vocation did not make him superior to anyone else. Indeed the life of a monk or nun opens one's eyes to the beauty of just being a human being. In 1958 he wrote: 'I am still a member of the human race – and what more glorious destiny is there for man, since the Word was made flesh and became, too, a member of the Human Race! Thank God! Thank God! I am only another member of the human race like all the rest of them. I have the immense joy of being a man!'[11] That is the glory which we show when we put on our baptismal clothes.

Paul Murray, the Irish Dominican, wrote a lovely poem about coming into the presence of his father after his bath, probably wrapped in a white bath towel, like a newly washed Christian, filled with the delight of his father's pleasure in him, who lays his hands on his head, as if in ordination.

> I was five or at most six years old,
> the second-youngest. But once
> I had braved the darkness of the stairs
> alone, my trial was over.
> From shadows into light
> the door opened, and I stepped
> into the hush of the room.
>
> So vivid, I remember, that bright
> threshold!
> But real illumination

---

[10] William H. Shannon, *Seeds of Peace: Contemplation and Non-Violence* (New York, 1996), p. 55.

[11] Quoted in Paul Elie, *The Life You Save May Be Your Own* (New York, 2003), p. 254.

came, moments later, when I
knelt down next to the fire, as near
as I could to my father's chair
and bowed my head.

I remember, as soon as he began
to dry my hair with the towel
and warm my hair with
his hands
lifting his two palms to the fire
and letting them rest on my head

I thought I was the son of a god.[12]

So we are a holy people because we are given God's Spirit which gathers us into one. And so our first duty is to care for the unity of the communion of 'the saints'. At his last prayer before his death, Jesus prays to the Father: 'The glory that you have given me I have given them, so that they may be one even as we are one, I in them and you in me, that they may become completely one, so that the world may know that you have sent me and loved them even as you have loved me' (Jn 17.22-23). Our holiness is in belonging to the unity of the Church which is a sign of the unity of the Father and the Son, the Spirit of love. This is why St Paul tells Christians to greet each other with 'a holy kiss' (2 Cor. 13.12). This is not a chaste kiss as opposed to a sexy kiss, though some pagans did wonder what these Christian men and women were up to kissing each other so much. It was a kiss that embodied holy unity. The kiss of peace, rather than a mere embarrassed handshake, is an expression of how we are a holy people, because we are one.

---

[12] 'The Second Youngest', in *These Black Stars* (Dublin, 2003), pp. 45–46.

So we are bound to heal divisions within our Churches and between our Churches. In the breviary reading for Pentecost, St. Irenaeus, the second-century bishop, says that at the descent of the Spirit, the new covenant is opened to all nations: 'In every language they sang a hymn to God in unison; for the Spirit brought the scattered races together into unity and offered to the Father the first fruits of all the nations'.[13]

Every year we celebrate the Week of Christian Unity. Of recent years, this has become a slightly flat event. The great dreams of forty years ago, of bringing all Christians into full unity, have faded. We have lost that earlier dynamism and some Churches have enough difficulty preserving their own unity without dreaming of becoming one with other Christian churches. But I believe that Christian unity is not an option to which we may or may not be committed. We are impelled by our baptism to seek it. We cannot impose it. It is God's gift, given in the Spirit of his love. But we must hunger for it, pray for it, work for it, for unity is our holiness in the Holy Spirit.

In the Old Testament, it is dangerous to share the life of the holy God. When Jacob dreams at Bethel of the angels ascending and descending from heaven, then he declares: 'terrible is this place' (Gen. 28.17). When Aaron's sons offer the wrong sort of incense, they are burnt up on the spot (Lev. 10). When Isaiah sees a vision of the Lord, and hears the seraphim calling out 'Holy, holy, holy is the Lord of hosts' he is terrified: 'Woe is me. I am lost, for I am a man of unclean lips, and I live among a people of unclean lips; yet my eyes have seen the King, the Lord of hosts' (Isa. 6.5) One cannot see God and live.

In the Old Testament, God's holiness is mortally dangerous because God is utterly alive. His holy name, revealed to Moses, is 'I AM'. God utterly *is*. God is so intensely alive, he exists so boundlessly,

---

[13] *Against the Heresies* Bk 3, 17. The breviary translation.

that those who are only half alive are liable to be burnt to a cinder. I watched a rather portly friend of mine, of my age, dancing with his exuberant two-year-old grandson, and feared he might have a heart attack. God lives exuberantly like a child. Augustine said 'God is younger than all else'.[14] God's sheer energy and vitality was in danger of burning people up.

So the Israelites could only come into God's presence if they were cleansed of any hint of death or illness, of anything that weakened their vitality. Otherwise it would be like going into a nuclear reactor without wearing the necessary protective clothing. The endless ritual of purification, of washing and offering sacrifices, was a ritual washing machine, ridding them of any contagion of death or sickness so that they could be in the presence of God and not be burnt to ashes. Then they could be like the burning bush which puzzled Moses, on fire and yet unconsumed, or like the three young men in the fiery furnace who were not harmed (Daniel 3).

In the New Testament, John the Baptist warns of the one who would come and baptize with fire. But the danger no longer lies in our impurity and sinfulness. Jesus turns the Old Testament understanding of holiness on its head, and touches the sick and the lepers and even the dead. He reaches out across the boundaries of the pure and the impure, and finally dies that most unholy death, on a cross cast out of the city. In Jesus, God claims all that is unholy, half dead, cursed and makes it his own. God's holiness is revealed not in separation from death but in embracing it. This is why our Christian communities, with all our sinfulness, hypocrisy and moral failure, are God's holy people. And if we have a place in the Kingdom, then who does not?

In this new dispensation it is still dangerous to share God's holy life, but not because he might burn us up, but because if we love like

---

[14] De Genesi 8,26,48.

that, then we may share the fate of his Son. Such unconditional love is hard for humans to tolerate. Herbert McCabe claims that

> there is a twist or a contradiction in our human life that means we build a world unfit for humans. The only way to get by is to restrict your humanity rather carefully, otherwise you will get hurt. The world is not totally unfit for human habitation, but it can take just so much of it. You have to ration your love, keep a wary eye out for enemies if you want to survive. Jesus did not ration his love, so naturally he didn't last.

McCabe often said that if you love you are likely to be killed, and if you do not love you are dead already.

Leo the Great, the fifth-century Pope, wrote: 'For if God is love, charity must have no limit because God cannot be confined within any bounds'.[15] This conflicts with the wisdom of this world which tells us that we will not survive if we love too much. *The Other Hand*, by Chris Cleave, is a novel about a woman who dares to love too much and takes an illegal immigrant from Nigeria into her house. A friend who is a civil servant in the Home Office warns her: 'You are going to have to choose between your life and her life... Charity is lovely, Sarah, but there has to be some logical point where it stops'.[16] But which logic do we follow? Is it the logic of this world which says that we must preserve our lives, or the logic of the Logos, which says that we shall only really be alive if we give away our lives and that mere survival is no life at all. This is the wisdom that looks like folly.

Sharing the life of the God who is revealed in Jesus Christ is indeed dangerous, but not so much because God will destroy

---

15 Sermon 10 on Lent; breviary reading for Tuesday, 4th week of Lent.
16 Chris Cleave, *The Other Hand* (London, 2009), p. 247.

us as because if we too love outrageously, then we may well get hurt. Those who dare boldly to take that risk are the saints in the second sense of the word, whom we shall consider in the next chapter.

14

The paradoxes of sanctity

At baptism, we put on white garments because, as St John Chrysostom said, we are publically enrolled among God's friends.[1] This is a sign of God's delight in all human beings. Dominicans wear white garments all the time, despite having the nickname 'black friars'.[2] This is not because we are especially holy but possibly because undyed sheep's wool was cheapest. Masters of the Order enjoy reminding Popes that they wear white because St Pius V refused to stop wearing his Dominican habit when he was elected Pope. That at least is the story.

In the New Testament, as we saw, 'the saints' were simply members of the Christian community. They were saints because they shared God's life in Christ. Sanctity was linked with unity in the Spirit. But 'saint' acquired another meaning when the community of saints had to face the fact that some of them were unfaithful. Above all, in times of persecution, some witnessed to their faith by dying, whereas others

---

[1] Yarnold, *Awe-Inspiring Rites*, p. 170.
[2] This is because we wear a black cloak over our white habits.

fudged, compromised and even denied the gospel. And so we see the emergence of a new meaning of the word 'saint', someone whose life witnessed heroically to their faith.[3]

We are all members of God's holy people in the first sense, members of God's holy people through baptism. We are also invited to become saints in the second sense, people whose lives witness courageously to God's friendship. The saints are those who 'live as if the truth were true'.[4] Their lives point to God as the secret of their being.

It is hard to describe sanctity because a saint is someone who is on the way to being truly himself or herself. They are becoming the unique persons whom God created them to be. So there are as many ways of being a saint as there are human beings. We sinners are people who have not yet dared to become fully individual but settle for ready-made identities, stereotypical characters, rather than taking the risk of being someone in particular: the rich person, the beautiful person, the scholar, the sexual athlete or whatever. It is the difference between a life like a suit bought off the peg and one that is tailor-made. The hero of Iris Murdoch's *Nuns and Soldiers* says: 'Our vices are general, dull, the ordinary rotten mud of human meanness and cowardice and cruelty and egoism, and even when they're extreme they're all the same. Only in our virtues are we original... Vices are general, virtues are particular'.[5]

If we are to overcome the scepticism of our secular contemporaries, we must witness to the truth of the claim that 'the only tragedy in life is not to be a saint'.[6] Saints are not cardboard figures who

---

[3] Cf. the lecture by Maureen Tilley, referred to in the previous chapter.
[4] I cannot discover the originator of this saying.
[5] Iris Murdoch, *Nuns and Soldiers* (Vintage Digital, 2008), p. 71.
[6] Raïssa Maritain, *Les Grandes Amitiés* (Paris, 1949), p. 117.

live in an ecclesiastical greenhouse. Dorothy Day reacted angrily to people who canonized her: 'Don't call me a saint. I don't want to be dismissed so easily'. But saints, like her, are people who are really alive, friends of the one whose name is 'I AM'. If people see that sanctity is the vocation of every Christian, then our faith will be seen not as an oppressive moral code which stops people having fun, but as the invitation to the fullness of life.

Transfiguration

Because each saint is, by definition, unique there can be no standard way of becoming holy, no adequate 'Teach yourself Holiness'. But there is an incident in three of the gospels which shows Jesus trying to teach his closest friends how to follow him. They have come to recognize that he is indeed the Son of God, but when Jesus says that he must take the road to Jerusalem, to suffer and to die and on the third day rise again, they do not accept it. They cannot understand. And so Jesus brings them up a high mountain and is transfigured in their sight. This text gives us some clues as to what it means for us to be clothed in white garments at baptism and live as God's close friends. Let us look at Mark's version of this incident.

> Six days later, Jesus took with him Peter and James and John, and led them up a mountain apart, by themselves. And he was transfigured before them, and his clothes became dazzling white, such as no one on earth could bleach them. And there appeared to them Elijah with Moses, who were talking with Jesus. Then Peter said to Jesus, 'Rabbi, it is good for us to be here; let us make three dwellings, one for you, one for Moses, and one for Elijah'. He did not know what to say, for they were terrified. Then a cloud

overshadowed them, and from the cloud there came a voice, 'This
is my Son, the beloved; listen to him!' Suddenly when they looked
around, they saw no-one with them anymore, but only Jesus (Mk
9.2-8).

This scene echoes Jesus' baptism. When he emerged from the water,
a voice is heard saying 'You are my Son, the Beloved, with you I am
well pleased' (1.11). It also points forward to when Jesus completes
his baptism and dies on the cross and the veil of the Temple is torn
in two and another voice, the centurion's, is heard saying: 'Truly this
man was God's Son' (15.39). So this story of the Transfiguration helps
us to get from the baptism in the water of the Jordan to the baptism of
Jesus' death on the cross. It is also a story which helps us to get from
our own baptism, perhaps as squealing babies, to the completion of
our baptism when we come to live as truly the friends of God.

This wonderful text brings to light, literally, two related paradoxes
of sanctity, one connected with how we live in time and the other
concerning our identity. Each of us must find our own unique way of
negotiating these paradoxes fruitfully, but they will surely be present
somehow in every holy life.

*And he was transfigured before them, and his clothes became
dazzling white, such as no one on earth could bleach them. Then Peter
said to Jesus, "Rabbi, it is good for us to be here; let us make three
dwellings, one for you, one for Moses, and one for Elijah."*

Jesus takes Peter, James and his brother John up the mountain.
These are his closest friends, the inner circle. These are the only ones
who are allowed to come with him when he raises Jairus's daughter
to life (Mk 5.37); they are with him in the garden of Gethsemane
when he struggles in the face of death. So these are the friends with
whom he shares the most intimate moments of his life and so this
incident tells us something of the nature of friendship with God. As

his closest friends, they struggle hardest to accept his coming death, and so they need this glimpse of the end of the journey, his radiance as God's own Son.

This is a moment which they savour and wish to prolong. Friendship with God means that we delight to spend time in God's company, to taste the sweetness of his presence: 'In your presence there is fullness of joy; at your right hand are pleasures for evermore' (Ps. 16.11). It may not be given to us often. Many of the holiest people, such as Mother Teresa of Calcutta, endure long arid periods when God just seems to be absent. But if we never 'taste and see that the Lord is good' (Ps. 34.8), then religion will become dull duty, hard slog. One element of holiness is surely learning to enjoy lingering with God. We waste time with our friends.

The vast majority of my Dominican brethren are a delight to live with but when I was Prior of Oxford, there was an old friar in his eighties who was as insensitive as a rhinoceros and drove us crazy. Two young friars were determined to soften him with their kindness and tried everything to dislodge him from his self-centredness, even getting him to make tea for the Scottish dancing society! Maybe this kindness began to melt the frozen sea within him. One night I went to see him before he went to sleep, to check if he needed anything, and he told me how that morning he had encountered God. He was in the chapel when he tasted God's beauty for the first time. Four hours passed in a moment. His eyes were opened and he knew himself loved. He began to know happiness. He told me that as an only child, his parents never addressed a word to each other but only communicated through him. He was formed in a loveless home. At last, not long before he died, he was given this experience on the mountain and then he was ready to make his way to his own Jerusalem and die. Just in time he had that glimpse of God and we had a glimpse of this old friar as his child.

Such moments cannot be planned or demanded; they come upon one, often through some experience of beauty, especially of music. They are moments in which the veil between now and eternity is torn open, and we glimpse our final home. They transcend the divisions between religions and we can recognize in the experience of a Sufi mystic or a Hasidic rabbi the same delight in God. Many people may have them without even recognizing explicitly what is happening.

Bede Griffiths, the future Benedictine monk and Christian disciple of Hinduism, described this powerfully in his autobiography. When he was a school boy, he was out walking one evening:

> I came to where the sun was setting over the playing fields. A lark rose suddenly from the ground beside the tree where I was standing and poured out its song above my head, and then sank still singing to rest. Everything then grew still as the sunset faded and the veil of dusk began to cover the earth. I remember now the feeling of awe which came over me. I felt inclined to kneel on the ground, as though I had been standing in the presence of an angel; and I hardly dared to look on the face of the sky, because it seemed as though it was but a veil before the face of God.[7]

In such moments, one somehow breaks through the surface of the world, and sees the Giver in the gift.

Such an experience can throw one to the ground and change one's life, as happened to Paul at Damascus. It might confirm one's faith and keep one going when it is tough. In 1737, Jonathan Edwards, an American Puritan, was out walking in the fields when he had an overwhelming experience of Christ:

---

[7] *The Golden String* (London, 1979), p. 9. Quoted by Taylor, *A Secular Age*, p. 5.

The person of Christ appeared ineffably excellent, with an excellency great enough to swallow all thought and conception. Which continued as near as I can judge, about an hour; which kept me the great part of the time, in a flood of tears, and weeping aloud. I felt withal, an ardency of soul to be, what I knew not otherwise how to express, than to be emptied and annihilated; to lie in the dust, and to be full of Christ alone, to love him with a holy and pure love; to trust in him…and to be perfectly sanctified and made pure, with a divine and heavenly purity.[8]

Friendship with God surely means, among much else, that we want to spend time with God, waiting for such intimations of presence. They may come rarely, not for years, but we await them. They remind us where we are headed. On his death bed, Basil Hume told me that when he first heard that he was dying, he had a vast sense of peace and joy, of God's closeness, and then there was nothing.

When I check in at airports, I am usually asked if London is my 'final destination'. I do not always resist the temptation to say 'No, I hope that it is heaven'. We need moments in the life of the Church of quietness, of attentiveness, when we open ourselves to that joy which may be given, or not, remembering where we are headed. 'Be still and know that I am God' (Ps. 46.10).

Often people are afraid that the young will be bored in church and so we try to find ways to amuse them. Religion must be at least as entertaining as football or TV. But we are doomed to lose that competition. If only we can offer them some hint of that divine beauty. I was rather a bad boy at school, and much inclined to irreverence and found religion boring. But there was a moment of quiet loveliness,

---

[8] Jonathan Edwards, 'A Personal Narrative', in J. E. Smith et al. (eds), *A Jonathan Edwards Reader* (New Haven, CT: 1995), pp. 287, 293.

when I was alone in the Abbey church, when for a few moments the curtain was lifted. It lodged in my subconscious, awaiting the moment when I was ready to attend to its invitation.

We must dare to offer young people a taste of this silence. In the centre of Dublin there is an oasis called Sanctuary. It brings meditation and stillness into the lives of young people. Niamh Bruce wrote: 'The magazines, the music, the mobile phones – it is not the outer noise and chaos we need to be concerned about in terms of our youth. It is the inner stillness and their connection and ability to access it. Inner stillness is where the strength lies; we must allow our children to become strong.'[9] When I was a university chaplain, we used to hold all-night vigils twice a year, with hours of silence punctuated by occasional music. I did not think that any students would be interested, but the church always filled up. They were hungry for silence. Why? Perhaps because in silence we taste both of those dimensions of God's love which I mentioned in Chapter 3, proximity and the gift of space. In silence, we sometimes glimpse the intimacy of God, deep in the core of our being, and yet also enjoy a love that lets us be, and gives love's greatest gift: space to breathe, nothing. In stillness, there is no moral pressure, no manipulation, no demand that one conforms to a group, just the chance to be. There is a Sufi saying: 'Hens do not lay eggs in the market place'.

So we must take time to loiter with God, to rest in his presence, to refuse the busyness of the world. A life that is entirely consumed by frenetic activity destroys us. Thomas Merton wrote:

> The rush and pressure of modern life are a form, perhaps the most common form, of its innate violence. To allow oneself to be

---

[9] Niamh Bruce, *I Can Feel my Toes Breathe: Bringing Meditation and Stillness to Young People*, compiled by the Sanctuary (Dublin, 2010), p. 13.

carried away by a multitude of conflicting concerns, to surrender to too many demands, to commit oneself to too many projects, to want to help everyone in everything is to succumb to violence. More than that, it is cooperation in violence. The frenzy of the activist neutralizes his own inner capacity for peace. It destroys the fruitfulness of his own work, because it kills the roots of the inner wisdom which makes work fruitful.[10]

He did not know what to say, for they were terrified. Then a cloud overshadowed them, and from the cloud there came a voice, 'This is my Son, the beloved; listen to him!'

Peter wants to savour this moment, but this vision of glory has been given so that they will listen to Jesus, descend the mountain and begin the journey to Jerusalem. Moments of sweetness and radiance are wonderful, but you have to walk the walk. Sanctity means the prosaic business of just getting on with what must be done now. The men on the mountain must just get on with being disciples, putting one foot in front of another, walking step by step, day by day to Jerusalem. The final words of Shantaram, that remarkable story of an escaped criminal who learned to be a man of peace, invite us to that endurance: 'For this is what we do. Put one foot forward and then the other. Lift our eyes to the snarl and smile of the world once more... Drag our shadowed crosses into the hope of another night. Push our brave hearts into the promise of a new day... For so long as fate keeps us waiting, we live on. God help us. God forgive us. We live on.'[11]

Meister Eckhart in his *Talks of Instruction* for Dominican novices, who surely were attracted to ecstatic experiences, wrote: 'Even if someone were in rapture like St Paul, and knew a sick person who

---

[10] William H. Shannon, *Seeds of Peace* (New York, 1996), p. 100.
[11] Roberts, *Shantaram*, p. 933.

needed some soup, I think it far better you left the rapture of love and would serve the needy man in greater love'.[12] St. Teresa of Avila liked to say that 'God also walks among the pots and pans'.

Becoming holy sounds a rather ethereal business, involving meditation and introspection and complex spiritual exercises, but holy people know that it is mostly the prosaic challenge of knuckling down to stopping being mean. Rabi'a, a medieval Muslim mystic, said that the only way to become patient was to stop complaining. Thich Nhat Hanh, the Vietnamese Buddhist, said that the first step towards a new way of life was to begin smiling. Most of us go around frowning. Donald Nicholl insists: 'By altering that ingrained habit we are ready to greet our fellow human beings with a smile. Until we can accomplish such small acts as a beginning it is vanity to seek for more heroic tasks'.[13] One has just to get on with it! The first step is the hard one. Young Tolstoy made an elaborate list of good resolutions, but in the end he got it down to one: 'Carry out everything that you resolve must be done'. Then he noted: 'I haven't carried out this rule!' Gandhi said 'If you don't find God in the next person whom you meet, then you are wasting your time'.

For the disciples, coming down the mountain also will mean leaving behind the simplicity of the contemplative life and getting caught up in the complexities of first-century Palestinian power struggles: the tensions between the Roman governors and their Hebrew subjects, between the Sadducean priesthood and the lay Pharisees, between the rebellious Zealots and those who collaborated with Imperial Rome. All of these will try to enlist Jesus on their side or at least catch him out with tricky questions. In the end they will

---

[12] Jeanne Ancelet-Hustache, *Men of Wisdom: Master Eckhart and the Rhineland Mystics* (New York and London, 1957), p. 79.
[13] Donald Nicholl, *Holiness* (London, 1981), p. 26.

find their unity with each other around the cross in opposition to him. The walk to Jerusalem will take Jesus through a minefield, in which he will need practical wisdom.

This is what Moses and Elijah, with Jesus on the mountain, had to do too. Moses talked with God on the mountain as a friend, face to face, and then he had to come down Sinai and get involved with the bickering Israelites, who turned to idolatry the moment he disappeared. Elijah hears God on the mountain of Horeb in 'a sound of sheer silence' (1 Kgs 19.12), but the voice commands him to go down the mountain, get mixed up in the politics of Israel and, once again, tangle with the terrible Ahab and the ghastly Jezebel. A holiness which flees this complexity and takes refuge in pious abstractions is fake. Jesus says to the disciples: 'Behold I send you out as sheep in the midst of wolves, and so be as wise as serpents and as innocent as doves' (Matt. 10.16). On the mountain they may have tasted the innocence of doves, but if they are to get to Jerusalem, then they will need to be as wily as serpents.

Faced with the rise of Nazism, Bonheoffer became thoroughly sceptical about any 'other-worldly' sanctity. This prayerful scholar had to leave the abstractions of the academic world and face complex questions, such as whether he should become involved in a plot to assassinate Hitler. We can only become holy by immersing ourselves in the everyday challenges of what he called 'this-worldiness'. 'By this-worldiness I mean living unreservedly in life's duties, problems, successes and failures, experiences and perplexities. In doing so we throw ourselves completely into the arms of God, taking seriously not our own sufferings but those of God in the world – watching with God in Gethsemane'.[14]

---

[14] D. Bonhoeffer, *Letters and Papers from Prison* (London, 1971), p. 370.

The Trappist monks of Algeria hoped to have a simple life of prayer and adoration. They longed to be on the mountain and glimpse God's beauty. But this contemplative life prepared them to face difficult practical decisions: Should they give medicine to the terrorists, their 'brothers from the mountain', when they came knocking at the monastery door? Should they go to the militants' camp to treat them or ask them to join the villagers waiting to see Brother Luke? Discerning the way to holiness will require discussion, hard thinking as well as prayer. Then they will discover the path that will take them to their Jerusalem, their heads hacked off on a cold Atlas mountain.

In March 2011, protests in London broke out against government spending cuts and the premises of banks were attacked. There was a swell of hatred for bankers, whose vast bonuses seemed to many to be obscene in this time of austerity. At the time of writing, protestors against the terrible inequalities of our society are camped outside St Paul's Cathedral in London. Bankers justify their wealth by pointing to their contribution to the economy and claimed that it would be deeply undermined if they were to move abroad. The papers were filled with denunciation and self-justification. But what might the life of a holy banker look like? Doesn't the Church have an obligation to come down the mountain and help bankers discover how their lives can incarnate holiness?

This may sound absurd. A holy banker! But Stefano Zamagni[15] has shown how the roots of the market economy lie in Medieval Christian Europe. It was the Benedictines with their motto '*ora et labora*' (To pray and to work) who first evolved a definite work ethic, work as a way to holiness. The Franciscans established 'the first true school of economics', and reflected on the ethics of the market place.

---

[15] Stefano Zamagni, 'The Catholic Ethic and the Spirit of Capitalism', in D. Finn ed., *The True Wealth of Nations* (Oxford, 2010), pp. 69–94.

They developed the division of labour, double entry book-keeping, bills of exchange and proper accounting. Zamagni wrote that 'the very same "Minor Friars" who made the vow of poverty their rule of life became the great specialists of wealth – a paradox indeed!' This was not hypocrisy. They rolled up their sleeves and came down the mountain and helped merchants and bankers think about how the production of wealth could contribute to the common good. It was a Florentine Dominican, Remigio dei Girolami, who first struggled with the question of how the new urban civilization could promote the common good. Holiness does not free one from grappling with difficult social and economic questions. The Church must come down the mountain again.

Thomas Aquinas picked up one of the hot potatoes of the thirteenth century, whether the contemplative or active life was better. He concluded that the best of all possible lives is to teach and preach, which combines elements of both. In other words, the best life is that of a Dominican! Perhaps for once he was not being objective. But surely every Christian life must include at least some elements of both the contemplative delight in the Lord, the savouring of God's sweetness, and coming down the mountain to tackle the knotty problems of daily life. The Church will be a school of holiness only if the contemplatives are touched by the questions that most people have to struggle with and if the bankers, journalists, doctors, economists and trade union leaders are invited to find their moments on the mountain.

Perhaps this tension is to be found in all religious traditions. It was probably at about the same time that Mark was writing his account of the Transfiguration that the Bhagavad Gita was assuming its present form. Thousands of miles to the east, religious people were wrestling with similar dilemmas: Should holy people renounce everything and take to the forest for a life of asceticism and contemplation? Or should they fulfil their duties to society, the dharma of their station in life?

Our growth in holiness will involve us, each in our own way, finding times of quiet, hoping to taste the Lord's goodness, and also exposure to the thorny questions of our contemporaries, sharing their perplexity. Our lives may be rooted more in one than the other – there are as many ways to holiness as there are human beings – but at least some minimal experience of both the mountain and the plain must mark every Christian life if we are not to drift into pious platitudes.

The account of the Transfiguration suggests another tension. We must both know and accept who we are, and also neither know nor care very much about our identity because it is beyond our grasp.

Peter did not know what to say, for they were terrified. Then a cloud overshadowed them, and from the cloud there came a voice, 'This is my Son, the beloved; listen to him!'

When Jesus reveals that he must go to Jerusalem to suffer and die, the disciples protest: This cannot be! 'And Peter began to rebuke him'. A new translation has Peter 'scold' him.[16] Peter is like a parent or teacher ticking off a child. Peter has confessed that Jesus is the Messiah and Messiahs have no business getting nailed to a cross. Peter thinks he knows who Jesus is better than Jesus does himself.

When they see Jesus in glory, they are terrified. This is not because they discover he is more powerful than they thought. Quite the opposite, they discover he must endure the weakness of the cross. It is not even that they see that he is the Son of God. This they have already confessed. They are frightened because they do

---

[16] *The New Testament with an Interactive Study Guide*, trans. Nicholas King SJ (Stowmarket, 2004).

not know who he is. Their intimate friend is unknown to them. He shares in the mystery of the hidden, faceless God, who is revealed only in a voice.

They had tried to possess Jesus, to confine him to their perception of his identity. They wished to define him by the categories that they could understand. But on the mountain he is revealed as not belonging to them. He has other friends, long dead, Moses and Elijah, the representatives of the Law and the Prophets. He can only be understood in terms of the longer story of God's relationship with his beloved people. Even more alarmingly, his identity is hidden in the One who acknowledges him as his Son.

If they do not know who Jesus is, then they cannot know who they are either. Their identities are also hidden. Their lives are wrapped in one whom they cannot grasp. St Paul says, 'It is no longer I who live but Christ who lives in me' (Gal. 2.20). 'Set your minds on things that are above, not on the things that are on earth, for you have died and your life is hidden with Christ in God' (Col. 3.3).

If we live 'as if the truth were true', then we cannot fully know who we are. Simon Tugwell wrote:

The essential source of my identity is God. Within my own interiority in myself is God's interiority in me; and according to St Augustine, God is even more intimately within me than I am in myself. There is really only one source of life in us, and that is fully human only in being also divine. God is the heart of our heart. But that means that there is a mystery at the source of ourselves. If God is truly the source of our lives, we cannot expect to grasp or fathom that source. In Thomistic language, we cannot apprehend the essence of our own souls.[17]

---

[17] Tugwell, *Beatitudes*, p. 97.

Our society is obsessed by identity. We are under pressure to create a self-image, to prop up a face, to sell our 'brand'. How we dress and speak, our possessions and our lifestyle, say who we wish to be. But God's friends should be eccentrically unconcerned with identity. The white garment of baptism, undermining all social distinctions, proclaims that we are at home in a friendship beyond our understanding.

If I cannot know who I am, for my life is hidden in Christ, then I should not even bother that much what people think of me. It is all rather irrelevant. In prison Bonhoeffer felt misunderstood by his fellow prisoners, who regarded him more highly than he knew he deserved. After a struggle he was liberated from the torment of needing to know who he was.

> Who am I? This or another?
> Am I one person today, and tomorrow another?
> Am I both at once? A hypocrite before others,
> And before myself a contemptible woebegone weakling?
> Or is something within me still like a beaten army,
> Fleeing in disorder from victory already achieved?
> Who am I? They mock me, these lonely questions of mine.
> Whoever I am, thou knowest, O God, I am thine.[18]

There was a holy Zen master called Hakuin.[19] The daughter of a wealthy fisherman in a neighbouring village became pregnant and blamed it on him. The villagers stormed around and hurled abuse at him, accusing him of being the father. Hakuin just said: 'Is that so?' And he took in the child and cared for it. Eighteen months later, she confessed that he was not after all the father, and the villagers came

---

[18] Bonhoeffer, *Letters and Papers from Prison*, p. 348.
[19] Nicholl, *Holiness*, p. 34.

around to apologize for having destroyed his reputation, and again he just said: 'Is that so?'

Jesus lost his reputation as a healer, a man to be respected, a teacher. He was denigrated as a glutton and a drunkard, the friend of disreputable people, a bad Jew. If we take up our cross, then we must let go any secure self-image. This may be painful but it is, Rowan Williams assures us (and I definitely need reassuring on this point!) ultimately a relief: 'To see – to feel – the cross as a light load is the impossible possibility of faith: letting our best-loved pictures of ourselves and our achievements die, trying to live without the protections we are used to, feels like hell most of the time. But the real hell is never to be able to rest from the labours of self-defence'.[20]

If I think that I am the new St Thomas Aquinas, God's gift to contemporary theology, then it will be desperately important that I am given the time to do research and write books and receive acclaim and applause. But if I do not know who I am, for my life is hidden in Christ, then it ceases to be a matter of life and death what I do. If I am asked to teach, then I can try my best, and if I turn out to be a bad teacher, then it is not the end of the world. What I am to do will be discovered. I will not see rivals for glory all around me, or allies who can help me up the ladder to the success which my identity demands. No one would be a threat because I have not founded my identity on anything that can be threatened.

Suddenly when they looked around, they saw no-one with them anymore, but only Jesus.

But that is only half the story. Finally they are left alone with Jesus, face to face. He is, as it were, given back to them. Elijah and Moses have disappeared. The tension in our lives as God's friends is that we do not know, and should not much care, who we are, and yet, faced

---

[20] Rowan Williams, *Silence and Honey Cakes* (Oxford, 2003), p. 48.

with Jesus, we must accept ourselves as we are. Jesus accepts his vacil-
lating, weak disciples as they are, and we must accept ourselves as we
are, which is true humility.

A saint is someone who is becoming the person whom God
created them to be. This is why no saint is like any other. We are
each unique, but in the saint this individuality becomes visible.
Sin is the flight from the vulnerability and delight of being
someone in particular, taking refuge in ready-made identities,
good or bad, stud, aggressor, rich person, winner, joker, wit,
whatever. You select an identity from the menu offered by your
contemporaries.

Unfortunately most saints' lives make them sound tediously
similar. Often they come from poor but respectable families, live
pious lives, seem to ride high above the struggles and failures
of us ordinary mortals, are cardboard caricatures, thin-blooded
creatures. I long to hear how saints have battled and failed on
their way to becoming someone who is this particular friend
of God. The true story of the saint, surely, is more like the
emergence of a human face from a block of stone, with the bits
that are not face gently and sometimes painfully knocked off. The
strong clear lines and contours surface from the unshaped mass
of stone.

We are all work in progress. There was a notice on the door of the
Dominican Filipino novice master: 'Be patient with me. The Lord
has not finished with me yet'. I have many faces. I hope that I am
not two-faced but I am not *quite* the same person with my brethren,
my family, with different groups of friends. I do not have quite the
same face in England as in France, when I am lecturing as when I
am unobserved, with a benefactor as with a beggar, in the sobriety
of the afternoon as after a couple of glasses of wine, awake as when I
sleep. In India it is said that when we sleep our face 'is the friend of

the world'.[21] None of these, I hope, are masks, but none of them are yet quite my true face. That I hope will emerge with clearer delineation before I die. Often when people die, their faces lose knots and wrinkles and their hidden goodness and beauty shines out. It had been buried by the struggle to keep going, to keep up appearances, to turn a brave face to the world, to hide fear and uncertainty. There is a Nigerian proverb: 'If your face is swollen from the severe beatings of life, smile and pretend to be a fat man'.

The saint is someone with just one face, formed in response to God's loving gaze. Like God's face, it sees through the disguises that we assume and invites us to be ourselves. This can be rather alarming. Graham Greene was a devotee of Padre Pio, the Capuchin who died in 1968 and was canonized in 2002. He attended Padre Pio's Mass with his mistress and was much moved, but when he was offered the chance to meet him face to face Greene turned it down: 'I was invited to see him that night in the monastery, but I made excuses not to go as neither of us wanted our lives changed!'[22] He knew that Padre Pio was a saint, a man of great insight. Maybe Greene did not dare to give up his affair with his lover. He did not want yet to become the good person whom Padre Pio would see concealed in his confused life. It is alarming to meet someone who condemns you. Far more frightening is someone who sees the friend of God whom you are called to be.

And so here is another tension that we must live as God's friends, accepting ourselves as we are, and yet knowing that who we are is hidden in Christ and is not yet known. We accept ourselves with realism, looking at ourselves with a kindly but uncomplacent eye, even being vaguely amused by our own fragile humanity and our silly fears, but in the end not all that bothered with who we are, for

---

[21] Roberts, *Shantaram*, p. 165.

[22] Unpublished letter to Kenneth L. Woodward.

that is to be discovered yet in God. John says in one of my favourite texts: 'Beloved, we are God's children now; what we will be has not yet been revealed. What we know is this: When he is revealed, we will be like him for we will see him as he is' (1 Jn 3.2). How can we live that tension? We draw near to God by discarding false images. We cannot know who God is in this life, just what God is not. And so we follow the *via negativa*, liberating our mind from infantile conceptions of God's identity. If our identity is hidden in Christ, then maybe we follow a similar path, freeing ourselves from false self-images. We cannot know who we are but only who we are not.

15

Seeing in the dark

Each act after our baptism in water unfolds a little more deeply our role in the life and mission of the Church. The culmination is that we are entrusted with the light of Christ. One of the earliest names for baptism is *photismos*, 'illumination'.[1] The baptized are the 'enlightened'. Our eyes are opened to see with the light of Christ. The drama of the Easter Vigil is the victory of light over darkness: 'In him was life and the life was the light of human beings. The life was the light of all people. The light shines in darkness, and the darkness did not overcome it' (Jn 1.4-5).

Faces around the fire

What are our eyes opened to see? When the bonfire is lit at the beginning of the Easter Vigil, the first thing we see are human faces: faces turned towards the light; perhaps the faces of children excited to be up in the middle of the night, amused faces as the priest struggles to light the paschal candle without self-immolation, nervous faces wondering what they are doing here. There are familiar faces and the

---

[1] Johnson, *Rites*, p. 40 and passim.

faces of strangers. It seems obvious that these are the faces of people like us, with the same dignity, subject to the same emotions, touched by the same fears and hopes. But David Bentley Hart argues that one of the extraordinary victories of Christianity, arguably anticipated in the Old Testament, was that it shone a light on the humanity of ordinary people. In the pagan world, most human beings – above all slaves, women and foreigners – were not considered to be fully human. They did not have human faces.

He describes how deeply shocking would have been the description in Luke's gospel of Peter's tears after his betrayal of Christ. How could a Galilean peasant have emotions? He was not an educated Greek or Roman, and so how could he feel like this? The portrayal of Peter's tears is, he writes,

> not merely a violation of good taste; it is an act of rebellion. So we see something beginning to emerge from darkness into full visibility, arguably for the first time in human history: the human person as such, invested with an intrinsic and inviolable dignity, and possessed of infinite value. One could plausibly argue that our very ability to speak of 'persons' as we do is a consequence of the revolution in moral sensibility that Christianity brought about.[2]

This is the light of Christ shining in the darkness.

The awareness of the humanity of others is fragile and easily lost. After the Haitian earthquake, there was a tsunami of sympathy for the vast suffering of the people. Donations poured in. We were touched by the tragedy that had fallen on people just like us. But this was a brief shining of the light. Within days they were being portrayed as dangerous, violent looters. Linda Polman in *The Times* showed how their image was manipulated by the international media

---

[2] Hart, *Atheist Delusions*, p. 167.

which incessantly warned the aid workers and the outside world about the violence of the victims, although it was never nearly as bad as in New Orleans after Hurricane Katrina. She wrote: 'Above all, Haitians are poor and black. In the view of some Americans, those two add up to murderous gangs'.[3] She recalled how after the invasion of Haiti in 1994, the American soldiers saw the wealthy and corrupt drug dealers with expensive cars as the good guys, to be protected from the wicked poor. But, she wrote, 'the good guys in Haiti are the defenceless people in the slums. For Western city dwellers this is the world turned upside down. "Back! Back!" the soldier shouted, aiming his weapon at the good guys'.

Raimund Gaita, the Australian philosopher, reports a conversation with a woman whom he calls M, who had lost a child. She watched a programme about Vietnamese women whose children had been killed during the war. Initially she was shocked and identified with them and then she said, 'It is different for them. They can simply have more'.[4] Gaita remarks that for her these Vietnamese women were incapable of suffering like us. 'They could replace their children more or less as we replace pets'.[5]

It takes time to learn to see other people. When the astronomer William Herschel was congratulated on 'accidentally' spotting his new planet, he replied that it was not by chance. 'Seeing', he said, 'is in some respects an art which must be learnt... Many a night have I been practising to see, and it would be strange if one did not acquire a certain dexterity by such constant practising'.[6] It is even more of an art to learn to see human faces in the light of Christ.

---

[3] 'Fear of the poor is hampering Haiti rescue', *The Times*, 18 January 2010.

[4] Raimund Gaita, *A Common Humanity: Thinking about Love and Truth and Justice* (London, 2002), p. 57.

[5] Ibid.

[6] Quoted in Richard Holmes, *The Age of Wonder: How the Romantic Generation*

When people have their sight restored, often it takes them time to make any sense of what they see. They see patches of colour, bump into them, discover that they are solid and learn to find their way around them. Initially, the world was easier to negotiate when they were still blind. They knew the geography. Sometimes they long to be back in the familiar world of the blind, in which they had learned how to cope. Others are overwhelmed by wonder. Annie Dillard tells of a young woman who was so dazzled by the brightness of the world when she was given back her sight that for two weeks she kept her eyes closed. When she opened them at first she could make no sense of what she saw but 'the more she now directed her gaze upon everything about her, the more it could be seen how an expression of gratitude and astonishment overspread her features; she repeatedly exclaimed: "Oh God! How beautiful"'.[7]

Similarly learning to see human faces is a slow business, wonderful and frightening. Jesus needed two attempts to open the eyes of the man born blind (Mk 8.22-26). After the first partial healing, he managed to see what looked like trees walking. In the gospel it symbolizes Jesus' struggle to open the eyes of the obtuse disciples. I often feel that I am half way through the cure. We do not easily see human faces but objects, obstacles, threats, useful things, allies and so on. We see people as sexual objects, useful or powerful objects. We do not always see a face that sees us. Our eyes need education. The old geography in which we just saw 'goodies' and 'baddies' was easier to negotiate. Jean Vanier says when people come to live in L'Arche for the first month they see everyone as saints; for the second month everyone looks like devils, and by the third month, they see people who are growing and struggling, just like themselves.

Discovered the Beauty and Terror of Science (London, 2008), p. 108.
[7] Annie Dillard, *Pilgrim at Tinker Creek* (New York, 1974), p. 29.

In *A Single Man*, the hero George, a gay man who is mourning the loss of his partner, comes across as an enigma. People do not know how to read him. His friends get him wrong and to his students he is a riddle. Faced with puzzlement, he says to a young student who wants to be of help: 'I'm exactly what I seem to be, if you look closely'. One of the gifts of the saints is to look closely and read people's faces, to see our vulnerable selves, pushed this way and that, our mixed motives, our deep hungers, our buried goodness. The more we are seen in our very particularity, our uniqueness, the more we shall be seen as the brothers and sisters of Christ. And so if we see people as they really are, then of course, we shall glimpse God who has made his home in them. Gerard Manley Hopkins, the nineteenth-century Jesuit poet, wrote: 'For I greet him the days that I meet him, and I bless when I understand'.[8]

In the novel *The Elegance of the Hedgehog*, Muriel Barbery describes the life of a highly intelligent Parisian concierge who is invisible to the wealthy people in her block of flats. They cannot grasp that a dowdy poor person like herself could feel as they do. She says:

> To rich people it must seem that the ordinary little people – perhaps because their lives are more impoverished, deprived of the oxygen of money and savoir-faire – experience human emotions with less intensity and greater indifference. Since we were concierges, it was a given that death, for us, must be a matter of course, whereas for our privileged neighbours it carried all the weight of injustice and drama.[9]

---

[8]'The Wreck of the Deutschland', Stanza 5, ed. W. H. Gardner, *Poems and Prose of Gerard Manley Hopkins* (London, 1985), p. 14.

[9]Muriel Barbery, *The Elegance of the Hedgehog*, trans. Alison Anderson (London, 2008), p. 70.

The light shed by the Risen Christ on the faces of our fellow human beings is growing dimmer. It is symptomatic of a secular age that the poor are increasingly seen with contempt. Owen Jones[10] has shown how members of the working classes

> are demonized by the tabloid press and by popular television shows as feckless welfare junkies, who drink too much, smoke too much, eat too much, breed too much and make bad parents. They have become regular butts in the media's theatre of cruelty. The television personality Jonathan Ross once asked his audience: 'Do you think that some people shouldn't be allowed to be parents? Like people from council estates'.[11]

The pagan night returns. Unless Christianity brings its light to bear on these brothers and sisters of ours, then Western society will be in danger of collapsing, with consequences which it is terrible to imagine.

Etienne Grieu wrote:

> A world dominated by competition engages in a formidable task of classification, not only of performances but also of people. Right at the bottom of the chart are those who aren't efficient enough. They thus become invisible in the eyes of others, as they are unable to demonstrate their usefulness in any of the various businesses undertaken. Therefore, they are without a fulcrum, reduced to living on welfare and not called on to make their contribution to building the world. They also feel humiliated as they scarcely have the means to say who they are, so as to get people to notice

---

[10] Owen Jones, *CHAVS: The Demonization of the Working Class* (London and New York, 2011).

[11] Andrew Gamble, 'A Tribe Betrayed', *Times Literary Supplement*, 19 and 26 August 2011, p. 14.

the unique treasure they bear. Charity cannot accept this kind of situation.[12]

This is a perception of the world in which everything must be measured, assessed, weighed and judged. It reflects the mechanical perception of the world which came to dominate the European imagination from the seventeenth century onwards. Such an imagination could not spot the child born in obscurity, whose witnesses were the shepherds, who did not count for anything, and the angels who could not be counted.

How can we learn to see those gathered around the fire in the light of Christ? To start with, we need to accept that we are, to some extent, responsible for how we see others. Sight is not just the passive reception of stimuli on the retina. We inherit from our society ways of seeing but we also make choices which shape our perception. Brian Davies OP wrote: 'For Aquinas, people have freedom of choice since they can interpret the world in different ways and act in the light of the ways in which they interpret it'.[13] When Kim en Joong, the Korean painter, was a baby, his parents followed tradition in putting before him silver coins, a book, a thread and so on. What he chose would reveal his future. But he refused to choose any of the objects on the table. Instead he reached out for the light of the candle which illuminated them. That will be his destiny, to choose the light, becoming a painter, a Christian and a Dominican.[14]

If I choose never to discipline my greed then I shall see the world of a greedy person, and fall upon my food without care for my health. If I chose to live a life of unbounded sexual promiscuity, I

[12] Etienne Grieu SJ, 'Discovering who God is in Caritas', in Oscar Cardinal Rodríguez Maradiaga (ed.), *Caritas: Love Received and Given* (Rome, 2011), p. 18.

[13] Brian Davies OP, *Aquinas* (New York and London, 2002), p. 108.

[14] Verboven, *The Dominican Way*, p. 155.

shall see other people in terms of the satisfaction that they can offer to my desires. Herbert McCabe gave up smoking when he realized that every time anyone walked into the room, he wondered if it was someone from whom he might be able to bum a cigarette. He saw people as possible purveyors of cigarettes. As the saying goes, 'To a pickpocket, the whole world is a pocket'.

We are called to choose the light. It is an article of our faith that God sees us as we are and sees us lovingly. We believe that truthful sight is therefore inseparable from a loving look. Equally, I only really see lovingly in so far as I see truthfully, and cleanse my eyes of the distortions of infatuation or disgust. Pope Benedict wrote:

> Truth needs to be sought, found and expressed within the 'economy' of charity, but charity in its turn needs to be understood, confirmed and practised in the light of truth. In this way, not only do we do a service to charity enlightened by truth, but we also help give credibility to truth, demonstrating its persuasive and authenticating power in the practical setting of social living.[15]

So baptism implies that we choose to look lovingly so as to see truthfully, and to look truthfully so as to learn to love.

When Anna Karenina, in Tolstoy's novel of that name, falls out of love with her husband, then she begins to see him differently. She no longer really sees his face. Her perception is dominated by his ears: '"Great heavens! What has happened to his ears?" she thought, gazing at his cold and commanding figure, and especially at the gristly ears which now so struck her, pressing as they did against the rim of his hat'.[16] His ears almost become characters in the drama, popping up into prominence at their hostile encounters. When we dislike

---

[15] *Caritas in Veritate*, para. 2.
[16] Tolstoy, *Anna Karenina*, p. 103.

someone, then it is harder to see their faces, like the blind man who at first saw just trees. Someone's nose may seem to dominate their face, or their lips seem repulsive. Charles Dickens brilliantly uses some part of the person to stand for their whole personality, usually unpleasantly. People shake their jowls and prod with their stomachs and poke with their noses.

How do we learn to see a human face? Perhaps we begin to wipe our eyes clean by acknowledging that if someone seems repulsive or contemptible to me, or even unattractive, it is because I do not yet see them properly. I suggested in the last chapter that saints do not much care what people think of them because they know that their identity is hidden in Christ. We cannot know who we are, for we are God's own children. This must be even more the case when we look at other people. The posh Parisians thought that they knew the concierge who looked after their building. And so when she went to dinner in an expensive restaurant with a famous Japanese film maker, whom they all longed to befriend, they could not see her there. It was inconceivable that such a glamorous person could take that insignificant servant out to dinner. So the beginning of seeing well is accepting that the irritating/attractive/stupid/arrogant/shabby/frightening/brilliant person before you is God's own beloved and shares in his mystery. If you think that you have got them nailed, then you are wrong.

The story is told of a monastery that was on the way to extinction. There were no vocations. Morale was low and the future was bleak. No one who visited the place ever wanted to stay. In desperation the abbot went to see a wise friend, a rabbi, to ask his advice. The rabbi commiserated and admitted that the rabbinic schools were also short of students, but as the abbot was leaving the rabbi said to him very quietly: 'One of you is the Messiah'.

The abbot went back and shared this puzzling statement with his monks, who could not think what to make of it. None of them seemed plausible candidates. Old Benjamin was delightful but terribly lazy and so it could not be him. Anthony was a good man but over fond of the bottle and that ruled him out. Edward was very obedient to all the rules but gloomy, and so he could not possibly be the Messiah. But it must be one of them.

But, the story goes, they began to look at each other in a new way. They began to see signs of holiness and kindness that had previously escaped their notice. Slowly the monastery became a gentler and happier place. People who visited stayed on and the community began to grow again. So the old abbot went back to the rabbi and said: 'Thank you for your words: "One of you is the Messiah". We never discovered who it is, but we are flourishing now'. And the rabbi laughed: 'But I said, "*None* of you is the Messiah"'.

If I do not know who I am, then who am I to judge anyone else? The desert fathers were unambiguous in their rejection of our right to dismiss others. Abba Moses the Black said, 'The monk must die to his neighbour and never judge him at all in any way whatever'.[17] When he was invited to a meeting to judge a brother who has sinned gravely, he came with a leaky jug dribbling water behind him. When they ask him why he is doing this he replies: 'My sins run out behind me and I cannot see them, yet here I am coming to sit in judgment on the mistakes of someone else'.[18] So the beginning of sight is a sort of blindness, at the very least a modest humility in our perception of others. It is like the *via negativa* in our knowledge of God. This I *do* know about that face across the Vigil fire, that he or she is *not* to be despised or dismissed as stupid, bad or contemptible. Who they are is yet to be revealed.

---

[17] Williams, *Silence and Honey Cakes*, p. 24.
[18] Ibid., p. 29.

So the first step is a negative one, a choice not to look at people cynically. But how can we learn positively to see their goodness? In the words used at baptism, we are told that we must carry our candles as we go to meet Christ with all the saints. This evokes the parable of the wise and foolish virgins. The wise virgins kept enough oil in their lamps so that they could go and meet the bridegroom when he came (Matt. 25.1-12). It is a loving encounter, the culmination of a wedding feast. The lamps are carried to light up the beloved. Loving opens a sort of knowing. In *The Shack*, God, who appears as a large Afro-American woman, says: 'So many believe that it is love that grows, but it is the *knowing* that grows and love simply expands to contain it. Love is just the skin of knowing.'[19]

Ian McGilchrist argues that what makes us human is an enormous capacity for empathy, which he puts down to the right frontal expansion of our brains, 'the latest great evolutionary development of the human brain'.[20] This empathy is the ground of human consciousness. He wrote: 'We deeply want and need to share experience: babies as little as forty-five minutes old imitate facial expressions, and babies and small children take pleasure in sharing experience for its own sake. What makes us human is the capacity for, and the sheer delight in, the sharing of experience'. So all knowledge, our human consciousness itself, is rooted in this innate capacity to emphasize with other people, to become one with them, to feel as they feel. We try to get under their skin. Dominique Pire, a Belgian Dominican who won the Nobel Peace Prize after the Second World War, loved to say: 'One must be ready to fill oneself with the other'.[21]

---

[19] William Paul Young, *The Shack* (London, 2008), p. 155.
[20] Ian McGilchrist, 'Digital Display', in *The Times Literary Supplement*, 18 June 2010, p. 10.
[21] Francesco Compagnoni OP and Helen Alford OP (eds), *Preaching Justice* (Dublin, 2007), p. 141.

This empathy, the foundation of all consciousness, can ripen into compassion. 'Compassion is the optic nerve of Christian vision'.[22] The Good Samaritan has compassion for the man who was robbed and left wounded by the roadside. His compassion opens his eyes to see this person not as a Jew, his enemy, nor as a nuisance, but as his neighbour. 'The priest and the Levite did not let themselves be affected by his plight. Any inchoate feelings of pity or shock were neutralised by wariness, disgust, or fear – or perhaps they felt nothing at all'.[23] Compassion makes one vulnerable. One's plans will be derailed. Again, the familiar theme of much of this book, one's control of one's life will be shaken. Instead of spending that money on a gift for his wife, the Samaritan has to spend it on this stranger. Compassion subverts one's egocentric perception of the world. Presciently, the last song that the Beatles recorded together, before they went their separate ways, was 'I, Me, Mine'.

This compassion for another implies that we dare to discover who we are with them. The test of a genuine love is that that person brings into existence some aspect of myself which otherwise could not even have existed. And so we must let ourselves be surprised not just by the other person but by who we are with them. In conversation, I become someone I have never been before. Together we find the words to make sense of who we both are. In his marvellous book on Dostoevsky, Rowan Williams quotes Bakhtin: 'Dialogue… is not a means for revealing, for bringing to the surface the already ready-made character of a person; no, in dialogue a person not only shows himself outwardly, but he becomes for the first time that which he is – and we repeat, not only for others but for himself as

---

[22] Spohn, *Go and Do Likewise*, p. 87.
[23] Ibid., p. 89.

well'.[24] And Williams comments, 'If I am hidden from myself, it is not because there is a buried identity which sustained introspection and careful self-observation can exhume, but because my identity is in the future, unfolding itself as it is formed in speech, and thus in encounter'.[25] The Church is lit by the light of Christ, because in conversation with each other, we are open to surprise, even surprise at ourselves.

Around that fire in the garden on an Easter night, we do not just see individual faces. We see a nascent community, drawn together by the fire, strangers perhaps, but cohering in our shared attraction to the light like moths. This is a tiny image of God's drawing the whole of humanity into unity. Jesus says in Jn 12.32: 'And I, when I am lifted up, will draw all things to myself'. Simon Tugwell wrote, 'He is the single One in whom we become single. He is the oneness of God expressed in human oneness; he is the One who comes forth from the One to create and recreate oneness in us'.[26] In the West, our churches are often filled with immigrants: Poles, Nigerians, Filipinos, Vietnamese and so on. Clustered around the Vigil fire, the faces of these unknown brothers and sisters are an image of the Kingdom which is coming to be.

When the Catholic hierarchy was restored in Britain in 1850, Archbishop Wiseman made a rather ill-judged statement about how he had been appointed to govern parts of southern England. This produced an uproar. Questions were asked in Parliament; indignant leaders appeared in the *The Times*, effigies of the pope and bishops were burnt and England prepared itself to repel these foreigners who dared to claim that they ruled freeborn English people!

---

[24] Rowan Williams, *Dostoevsky: Language, Faith and Fiction* (London, 2008), p. 133.
[25] Ibid., p. 136.
[26] Tugwell, *Beatitudes*, p. 13.

Then Archbishop Wiseman published 'An Appeal to the Reason and Good Feeling of the English People on the Subject of the Catholic Hierarchy', in which he wrote:

> Close under the Abbey of Westminster there lie concealed labyrinths of lanes and courts, and alleys and slums, nests of ignorance, vice, depravity, and crime, as well as of squalor, wretchedness, and disease; whose atmosphere is typhus, whose ventilation is cholera; in which swarms a huge and almost countless population, in great measure, nominally at least, Catholic; haunts of filth, which no sewage committee can reach – dark corners, which no lighting-board can brighten. This is the part of Westminster which alone I covet, and which I shall be glad to claim, and to visit, as a blessed pasture in which sheep of holy Church are to be tended, in which a Bishop's godly work has to be done, of consoling, converting, and preserving.[27]

He shed a light on the thousands of neglected and forgotten and claimed them as his own in Christ. Wiseman became recognized as a great champion of the poor, and, when he died, the whole country mourned. The shedding of light on these people was more than just recognition of their rights and dignity. It required that act of imaginative compassion which discloses their humanity and our own. Love must ignite our imagination.

Father Boyle describes the challenge, beautifully illustrating Paul's observation that we are the aroma of Christ, but how we smell depends on how we relate to Christ (2 Cor. 2.15). His local church, in a poor part of Los Angeles, became a sanctuary for illegal immigrants. The women and children found refuge in the

---

[27] Nicholas, Archbishop Wiseman, 'An Appeal to the Reason and Good Feeling of the English People on the Subject of the Catholic Hierarchy' (London, 1850), pp. 30–31.

convent nearby. Hundreds of homeless men slept every night in the Church and so it came to stink of smelly feet. People noticed but no one said anything until Boyle decided to face the issue in his sermon.

> 'What does this church smell of?' Finally a brave soul shouted out the truth: 'Smelly feet!' 'Why?' 'Because homeless people are living here'. 'Why is this?' 'Es nuestro compromiso'. It is what we promised to do. And then it began to smell differently. What does it smell like? 'It smells like our commitment'. Finally, a woman shouts out: 'It smells like roses!' The packed church roars with laughter and a newly found kinship embraced someone else's odour as their own. The stink hadn't changed, only how the folk saw it. The people at Dolores Mission had come to embody Wendell Berry's injunction: 'You have to be able to imagine lives that are not yours'.[28]

Kinship is the key word here. We are more likely to see someone with clarity, if we see them as our kin. When I was a young priest, my married friends thought that I ought to be educated into the joy of changing their babies' nappies. I am glad that stage in my life has passed. I have the impression, and am open to correction, that nappy changing is not so terrible for the parents; this poo comes from the child who is flesh of their flesh. When we are kin, then our perception changes. Even the unpleasant things are not so offensive because they are part of someone who is part of us. They do not assault us from the outside, as it were, because they are part of our identity.

---

[28] Boyle, *Tattoos on the Heart*, p. 74.

Lead kindly light

Eventually the paschal candle gets lit without immolating the priest, who marks the candle saying: 'Christ yesterday and today, the beginning and the end, Alpha and Omega, all time belongs to him, and all the ages'. This evokes the very beginning of everything when God said 'Let there be light'. It symbolizes the light that was lit on Easter morning, the dawn of the new creation.

It is also the light that illuminates us as we walk in procession into the Church to begin the Vigil. We go forward with the fire in front of us, like the Israelites who cross the Red Sea and set off into the wilderness, hoping eventually to arrive at the Promised Land. The Israelites took a long time arriving at their destination. On the way they bickered, succumbed to idolatry, were tempted to go back to the onions and cucumbers and garlic of Egypt and to slavery, demanded meat and got angry with their leaders. Finally when they got to its borders and saw that its inhabitants were tall and strong, most of them lost their nerve.

In the Letter to the Hebrews,[29] we are seen to be like them, travelling in the wilderness, waiting to enter the Promised Land which is God's own rest. The Church remains much like the people of Israel in the Sinai desert. We seem to be going around in circles, bickering, demanding strong leadership and then rejecting it if we get it. We too suffer from crises of confidence and of faith, fear that God has forgotten us, and may even be tempted to give up the whole adventure and settle for whatever Egypt offered us. So the newly baptized have not joined a triumphant group. Jean Vanier said that

---

[29] Richard Ounsworth OP, 'On the Threshold of the Promised Land', *Religious Life Review*, March/April 2011, pp. 67–78.

we advance more like rabbits sniffing our way forward than like giraffes who can see a long way ahead.[30]

Pilgrims cannot be weighed down by much baggage. We shall have to shed much if we are to travel, beginning with images of God. Eckhart said, 'If you think of anything He might be He is not that'.[31] We may have to let go of images of the Church. It does not turn out to be the community of radiant charity that we hoped for, but a crowd of unimpressive people who are often unsure and afraid, inclined to make shameful compromises and do not dare to tell their doubts and questions truthfully. God's holy people do not seem so holy after all. But this stripping away of illusions is also part of our journey to the Promised Land, and we must give each other courage for the way.

There was a bag lady who lived near S. Sabina, my home in Rome for nine years. She was utterly destitute, but weighed down by innumerable bags containing old clothes, ancient newspapers, empty tins. These gave her the illusion of security and wealth. But her poverty immobilized her. I often thought that if only she could recognize that she really was poor and free herself of all that stuff, then she could walk more easily and maybe even find a new life. One day I spotted her in St Peter's Square, smartly dressed, looking ten years younger and with nothing but a small hand bag. The Church can be like that at times, weighed down by unimportant things that seem to give us security and importance, but impeding our easy journey. We can let much go so as to travel lightly. In my own Church, some are nostalgic for the imagined cucumbers and garlic of a pre-Vatican Council Church that probably never existed. Others fret because the Promised Land of a renewed Church seems farther away, just like the Israelites in the wilderness. To believe is to plod on.

---

[30] Vanier, *Essential Writings*, p. 104.
[31] Sermon 23 in Walshe no. 54 Vol. II, p. 254, cited in Woods *Meister Eckhart*, p. 86.

In 1833 the young John Henry Newman was becalmed off the coast of Sardinia. He was depressed, exhausted and could not see his way forward. And so, with nothing else to do, he composed poems, most famously the hymn 'Lead, kindly light'.

> Lead, kindly light amid th' encircling gloom,
> Lead thou me on;
> The night is dark, and I am far from home,
> Lead thou me on.
> Keep thou my feet; I do not ask to see
> The distant scene; one step enough for me.

So we are baptized as pilgrims on the way to the Kingdom. For this we need courage, which is why the baptism of adults is followed immediately by confirmation. They were originally one single rite of initiation.

In the baptism of children, after the Our Father, the parents, godparents and the whole congregation are blessed. The child is at the beginning of the journey, and may well have to struggle with doubts, tough questions, may wander all over the place, like those Israelites in the desert, and so we are blessed that we may give him or her and each of us the courage as we travel, unafraid of anything: 'May God watch over your life, and may we all walk by the light of faith and attain the good things he has promised us'.[32]

---

[32] One version of the final blessing.

16

Did you receive the Spirit?

Confirmation follows immediately after the baptism of adults and mature children. Originally these two sacraments were part of the single process of initiation into the Christian life, culminating in the Eucharist. Unfortunately in the West they came rather unstuck, which resulted in a lot of confusion as to the nature of confirmation. Please forgive a few unavoidable words on the meaning of confirmation before I conclude in the next chapter by looking at what it means to live our confirmation day by day.

In the early Church most Christians were baptized during the Easter Vigil or at Pentecost. The whole local Christian community was gathered together in the cathedral so that the bishop, as the successor of the apostles, could receive them into the community of the universal Church. But in the fourth century, after the conversion of the Emperor Constantine and the end of persecution, this became ever more difficult. There were too many Christians to fit into any single church. This was a problem first of all in the megacity of Rome, with its tens of thousands of Christians. St John Lateran, the cathedral of the bishop of Rome, was enormous but there was not enough space for all the candidates.

How then could the Church continue to symbolize the link with the bishop, and through him membership of the whole Body of Christ? To vastly oversimplify, in the East,[1] the priest baptized and confirmed everyone, even babies, using chrism which the bishop had consecrated. This emphasizes the original unity of Christian initiation. In the West, another solution evolved. The parish priest baptized and the bishop then confirmed as he made the rounds of his diocese.

So what is the relationship between baptism and confirmation? The Church always maintained that the baptized received the Holy Spirit and so what is the point of confirmation? This is still being argued vehemently by theologians, and I hesitate to plunge into the debate lest I be torn to pieces by enraged liturgical experts.

When the Duchess of Cambridge was confirmed, the newspapers described it almost without exception as the sacrament of commitment. The idea was that baptism is when your parents sign you up for membership of the Church, and confirmation is when you make that decision your own. That would suggest that you only become a real Christian when you make that personal decision. But the main Christian Churches all deny that. The baptized are fully Christian. We may take years to embrace the decision of our parents and live it as our own deepest identity, but that is a matter of accepting what we are rather than of becoming Christians for the first time. Part of the difficulty is that 'confirmation' seems to suggest that we are 'confirming' our baptism, signing the contract our parents made. But *confirmatio* means 'strengthening', 'firming up'. It invigorates us.

---

[1] For a good summary of the history of confirmation see Austin Milner OP, *The Theology of Confirmation* (Dublin, 1972).

A Charles Adam cartoon showed two women looking at a big lump of jelly on a chair with two saucer-like eyes. One says, 'We are still waiting for Stanley to set'. The Holy Spirit is given to us in confirmation so that we may set and become mature as God intended. In the beginning, 'the earth was without form and void, and darkness was upon the face of the deep, and the Spirit of God was moving over the face of the waters' (Gen. 1.2). At confirmation, we bring to God all that we are, our strength and vitality, but also our muddle, our chaos, all that is as yet without form and void, so that the Holy Spirit will make us strong. One of my Irish brethren, Liam Walsh, has described it as the sacrament of 'growing up'.

This does not mean that it must be given when we are grown up. It 'empowers us to *start* undertaking the responsibility of being mature in Christ'[2] which is why it makes sense even to give this sacrament to babies. Sometimes when they are baptized their ears and mouths are blessed – this is called the ephepheta (Mk 7.34) – as a sign that even as babies they are being prepared for adulthood, to speak and hear.

We began this book by arguing that one reason why it makes sense to baptize infants is because we are all called to become children of the Most High. The really grown-up person is the one who has to become childlike, and who has put aside silly illusions that he or she runs the world. We are made to play with God for all eternity, and someone who thinks that they are too grown up to play is missing out on the joy of being a human being. So it is fine to baptize infants, because they remind us of what we are all called to become. Similarly confirming infants has a certain sense since it blesses their growing up in Christ. Herbert McCabe asserts that 'we are not just human

---

[2]Richard Conrad OP, *The Seven Gifts of the Holy Spirit* (London: Catholic Truth Society, 2009).

beings but human becomings.'[3] To be human is be evolving, changing, maturing. Most animals quickly reach maturity, but we take time to unfold into our humanity. Newman famously said: 'To live is to change and to be perfect is to have changed often'. Confirmation blesses our vast human capacity to become and that is appropriate at any age.

St Thomas Aquinas maintains that when we are immature we live for ourselves, but it is a sign of growing up that we are turned outwards towards others, members of the wider community, and so we are confirmed to become public witnesses to the faith, playing our part in the preaching of the gospel. This is foreshadowed when the baby is anointed as priest, prophet and king.

We are anointed on the forehead with the chrism, consecrated on Maundy Thursday by the bishop: 'Be sealed with the gift of the Holy Spirit'. These are words that have been in use since the fourth century and are first found in a Byzantine rite.[4] The forehead is anointed because it was believed to be the place of shame, where we blushed. We are anointed there so that we may go into the public forum and confess our faith without shame.

Being sealed (Eph. 1.13) means that we are marked as belonging to Christ. When I was a child it was still customary to seal envelopes with wax. I remember well the hot and slightly acrid smell. The deep red wax was melted with the fire of a candle, dripped onto the envelope and stamped with a seal so that it could not be surreptitiously opened. It proclaimed that this letter was from the bearer of the seal. We are sealed with the Holy Spirit as a sign that we belong to God. We are his people and he is our God.

Belonging to God does not deprive us of our own identities. We

[3] Herbert McCabe, *God Still Matters* (London and New York, 2002), p. 189.
[4] Milner, *Theology of Confirmation*, p. 78.

do not become ecclesiastical robots without a thought in our heads. We belong to God who gives us the grace of becoming ourselves. The Church should set us free to be so. A young man came running to Jordan of Saxony, the second Master of the Dominican Order in the thirteenth century, and cried out, 'I belong to God'. Jordan accepted him immediately into the Order. No long interviews and selection processes in those days. And Jordan said, 'Since you belong to God, then in his name we make you over to him'. The Order exists so that through God's grace the brethren can become the people whom God had created them to be, which is why we are so different from each other. Any organization which dehumanizes people and suppresses their individuality is not working with the Spirit of Jesus. At the Nuremberg rallies, Hitler's spirit, so as to speak, took over people, and they surrendered their identities. They became faceless members of a mob. The twentieth century was filled with mass movements which eradicated people's humanity and individuality. In these movements, led by Hitler, Stalin, Mao Tse Tung, Pol Pot and others, people are depersonalized. But the Spirit of the Lord comes upon us so that we may become ourselves.

We are anointed with chrism. St Thomas says that 'it is mixed with balm for the sake of the sweet fragrance which affects others'.[5] It is like a deodorant. If one is to represent Christ publicly, then one does not want to smell nasty. As one grows up one is taught how to care for one's body and, if you are a clean-shaven man, use aftershave. One of my brethren maintains that using it is an act of charity if you are to be squeezed close to the brethren in choir early in the morning. If we are anointed to grow up spiritually, representing Christ, the anointed one, in the public arena, then it is good that we have the ecclesiastical equivalent of aftershave and deodorant.

---

[5] *Summa Theologica* III q.72.2.

Jeremy Driscoll OSB wrote:

When Jesus said, 'When you fast, anoint your head and wash your
face and do not look gloomy' (Matt. 6.16-18), we can see from this
that Jesus was aware of and sensitive to the niceties of grooming.
He would know from his own experience what it means to 'anoint
your head and wash your face'. I love to think of him anointing his
head and combing his hair and looking into some kind of mirror
or into the lake to see if it looked okay.[6]

My brethren would be surprised to read me affirming that appearances
matter. I am always told that I look shabby and dishevelled. If this is
so, then it is despite my best efforts to the contrary. But what is at
issue is much more than being neatly dressed. According to the
Council of Florence, in 1439, we are anointed with the 'aroma of
good reputation'.[7] We are public representatives of Christ and so what
we do and how we are touches his reputation and that of his Body,
the Church. We can bring shame on Christianity or open people's
eyes to its beauty and attractiveness. We never act as purely private
individuals anymore. And we also have care for the reputation of
the Church. This does not mean burying unpleasant and scandalous
truths. It does imply that we care for the Church's good reputation,
and do not spread malicious gossip, and give the most charitable
interpretation to what our fellow believers do. And if the Church is
shamed, sometimes rightly, we are anointed to bear that shame with
her, as Christ bore our shame on the cross. So when we are ashamed
of what Christians do, especially our own Church, then we can bear
this as a sharing in Christ's cross.

---

[6] Jeremy Driscoll, *A Monk's Alphabet: Moments of Stillness in a Turning World*
(London, 2006), p. 50.
[7] Milner, *Theology of Confirmation*, p. 73.

Staying in the guest room of a friend, and unable to sleep after giving a lecture, I turned on the ancient television, which could only manage one channel. I watched a comedian making fun of religion. It was not malicious, indeed quite funny, but the general message was clear: you have to be really stupid to believe all this stuff: the Resurrection of the dead, Hell – anyone with a bit of common sense can see that these are rubbish. That is of course untrue. The naïve people are those who believe that the only valid truths are those which are obvious to common sense and can be understood literally. But in that moment, his wit swept up the crowd. He looked around the vast auditorium in which hundreds of people were sharing his contempt and asked if anyone was a Christian. A pleasant and innocent-looking young man put up his hand. There was someone who was prepared to bear the shame. He was living his confirmation.

'Virtue' comes from a Latin word which means 'strong'. So it is not surprising that there is an old association between confirmation and the virtues. Becoming virtuous is not about submission to the rules and regulations of the Church. It is growing up, becoming free to do spontaneously what is right. It is learning the pleasure and freedom of doing God's will. In the West we see a profound moral crisis. Bankers stuff their pockets with vast bonuses even when they lose money. Some Members of Parliament tried to sell their influence for cash; others fiddled their expenses. There is a vast crisis of trust, of the police, of lawyers, doctors, and, alas, of the clergy too. We try to respond to this by more and more legislation, checks, assessments, secret cameras: the culture of control. But what we need surely is a culture of virtue, in which we learn to act well not because it is required by the rules, but because of who we are. The bishops of England and Wales issued a statement prior to the election in 2010:

The practice of virtue helps to shape us as people. By the pursuit of virtue we act well not because of external constraint but because it has become natural for us to do so. The virtues form us as moral agents, so that we do what is right and honourable for no other reason than that it is right and honourable, irrespective of reward and regardless of what we are legally obliged to do.[8]

The Holy Spirit is given to us at confirmation so that we may become virtuous, and virtue is less about what we do than who we are called to be. Meister Eckhart told his Dominican novices: 'People ought never to think too much about what they could do, but they ought to think about what they could be. If people and their way of life were only good, what they did might be a shining example.'[9] We are confirmed so that we may be vigorously ourselves in Christ.

> I bind unto myself today, the strong name of the Trinity.
> By invocation of the same, the Three in One and One in Three.
> I bind unto myself today, the power of God to hold and lead:
> His eye to watch, his might to stay, his ear to hearken to my need;
> The wisdom of my God to teach, his hand to guide, his shield to ward;
> The Word of God to give me speech, his heavenly host to be my guard![10]

---

[8] The Bishops' Conference of England and Wales, *Choosing the Common Good* (London, 2010), p. 11.

[9] 'Talks of Instruction', in *The Essential Sermons, Commentaries, Treatises and Defence*, ed. and trans. B. McGinn and E. Colledge (New York, 1981), p. 250.

[10] St Patrick's Breastplate from the breviary.

But did you receive the Spirit?

Here we must face a widespread objection. If the Spirit is given at baptism and confirmation, then why does nothing seem to happen? Why don't people run around speaking in tongues and performing miracles as at Pentecost? This touches what threatens to become a deep division within Christianity. Vast progress has been made in healing the divisions between Western and Eastern Christians and the fragmentation caused by the Reformation. In the twentieth century, we have moved closer together. But at the same time a new split is threatening to open up and its roots lie precisely in this question of what it means to receive the Spirit.

Pentecostalism is the fastest growing form of Christianity. There are believed to be about 380 million Pentecostals today.[11] When you walk through African cities such as Ibadan in Nigeria, or through the barrios of Latin America, you see literally hundreds of Pentecostal chapels, many of them just huts with a handful of adherents, others with enough faithful to fill a football stadium. If you disagree with your pastor, or feel the call of the Lord, then there is nothing to stop you founding your own Church. There are also millions of members of the traditional Churches who would regard themselves as Pentecostals. For example, it is reckoned that there are some 100 million Roman Catholic Pentecostals.

This is a movement of enormous vitality which is transforming the lives of millions. Its expansion in mainland China is phenomenal. It attracts people because here one can see the power of the Spirit at work. Part of its success in Latin America is in healing broken families, getting men off drink and stopping them beating their

---

[11] Cf. Allen, *The Future Church*, pp. 375–413.

wives, thus enabling them to climb out of poverty. It makes most mainline Churches look tepid and ineffectual. It makes a difference. One understands why many Pentecostals think that the rest of us are not really Christians at all, and that we have not received the Spirit at baptism and confirmation.

Pentecostalism takes many forms, but in most versions the key moment is when we stand up and confess our faith in Jesus Christ as our personal saviour and receive a powerful manifestation of the Holy Spirit, usually through talking in tongues. The baptism of babies does nothing, it is asserted, because nothing seems to happen and nor does it at confirmation.

Pentecostals challenge us to live our faith in a vibrant way. But we, in turn, need to share with Pentecostals the good news that baptism, even of babies, really is a sharing in the life, death and resurrection of Jesus and the reception of his Spirit, despite the apparently semi-comatose state of many Christians. It is God who first loves us. We assert the absolute priority of God's grace and not of our response. As I argued in the first chapter, that is why, from the very beginnings of Christianity, babies were baptized. To say that baptism cannot work until we are old enough to make the commitment personally is to subvert our faith that it is God who draws near to us before we draw near to him, even when we do not experience this. Remember those words of Meister Eckhart: 'Even if you cannot conceive of yourself as near to God, you should still regard God as near to you'.[12]

But must there not be some experience of the Holy Spirit? Must there not be some evidence in people's lives that God's grace is at work? God comes to us as we are. Humans grow into divinity in a way that respects the slow pace of human ripening. Some animals

---

[12] *Talks of Instruction no 17*, quoted in Woods, *Meister Eckhart*, p. 163.

have barely emerged from the womb when they begin to behave like the adults of their kind. Within a few seconds of birth, young antelopes are staggering around on their spindly legs in a drunken manner. Human babies need years before they can begin to walk and talk and act like human beings, even though they are human. Our redemption respects the rhythms of our created nature. 'The Kingdom of God is as if someone would scatter seed on the ground, and would sleep and rise night and day, and the seed would sprout and grow, he knows not how' (Mk 4.26-29).

Sure, there must be some experience of the Holy Spirit in our lives, but the most profound experiences are not necessarily dramatic. We can fall deeply in love through long years, slowly opening our eyes to the beauty and attractiveness of another until we are ready to give our hearts without reserve. Sudden infatuations may pass quickly. If one counts a vivid experience of the Spirit as the only valid sign that one is sharing the life of God, then when there are arid periods, as always happens, one can easily become disillusioned. The tragedy is that so many Christians who leave their own Churches and become Pentecostals eventually cease to believe in anything at all. If one relies on powerful experiences to sustain one's faith, then it will be hard to last the course. The Israelites may have had a wonderful experience of liberation at the Red Sea, but then they endured years of dull plodding in the wilderness.

Of course it would be odd if a Christian never had any significant religious experience, but experiences may take many forms. We may be touched by the beauty of the liturgy, or moved by compassion for the suffering, or bowled over by a theological insight which changes how we see the world, or filled with a passion for justice when we see how oppressed are many of God's children. John Wesley, the founder of Methodism, warned us against making a 'shibboleth'[13] of any particular spiritual experience as *the* sign of being a true Christian.

The Spirit is the love of the Father and the Son, and, according to St Thomas Aquinas, the only sure test of the Spirit is that it draws us into unity.[14] Paul tells us that we may speak in tongues and perform miracles but if we do not love and build the unity of Christ's Body, we are not doing the work of his Holy Spirit (1 Cor. 13).

Now let's conclude in the final chapter by thinking about how we live confirmation day by day.

---

[13] *Plain Account of Christian Perfection* 1952, pp. 91-92. Quoted by Simon Tugwell OP, *Did you Receive the Spirit?* (London, 1972), p. 89.
[14] *De Veritate* q.12 a.5 ad 2.

17

Growing up

Before that brief interlude on the relationship between baptism and confirmation, we left the baptized wandering in the wilderness, finding their way forward with the light of Christ, sometimes feeling that they are lost and even nostalgic for the fat and easy days of slavery in Egypt. We are strengthened by confirmation for that journey through the wilderness, so that we may come to the Promised Land. At their first Eucharist,[1] the newly baptized and confirmed sometimes drank from a chalice filled with honey mixed with milk, a symbol of the goal of our journey. We are confirmed to be brave travellers in the wilderness. To understand a little more about what this means, let us look at Jesus' own time in the wilderness. We shall take Luke's version.

'Jesus, full of the Holy Spirit, returned from the Jordan and was led by the Spirit into the wilderness, where he was tempted by the devil' (Lk. 4.1-2). 'Tested' would be a better word. Surely Jesus was not tempted to worship the devil or do something as idiotic as jump off the Temple. And temptation concerns what you do, as when you give up whisky for Lent and succumb to the offer of a beautiful single

---

[1] Hippolytus in Yarnold, *Awe-Inspiring Rites*, p. 35.

malt. To be tested shifts the emphasis to who you are. We test metal to disclose its strength and weakness. Test matches show the strength of the English cricket team, sometimes. These three testings in the wilderness show what it means for Jesus to be the strong Son of God. Rather they show him avoiding three ways of misunderstanding strength. Children mature by testing their parents, trying out their strength, testing the boundaries, and so learning how to grow up. How many times can they refuse to go to bed before their mother's patience is at an end? These testings of Jesus in the wilderness show us what it means for us to become truly the strong sons and daughters of God.

Satan gives Jesus three commands: turn this stone into bread; worship me; throw yourself down from the Temple. He wants obedience not conversation. He wants to exercise control over Jesus, for he is 'the strong man' whom Jesus has come to bind, and he prevails when he shuts us up. Satan's name means 'the accuser', and accusation silences us. In the Jewish tradition, the demon presiding over Hell was called Duma, Silence.[2] This is not the intimate silence in which we are close to God, but the empty, sad silence in which we are afraid to speak. A contemplative silence opens our ears. An oppressive silence shuts our mouths. That is why the desert was believed to be filled with horrible and hairy demons, because it is a place of terrible silence and so the kingdom of Satan.

Jesus has been driven by the Spirit into the wilderness to wrestle with Satan on his own ground. This he does first by refusing to be silenced. The first gift of the Holy Spirit in the wilderness is speech. This is confirmation's gift to us. St Thomas says that confirmation is the gift of communicating: 'When [the candidate] arrives at maturity

---

[2] Simon Tugwell OP et al., *New Heaven? New Earth?: An Encounter with Pentecostalism* (London, 1976), p. 131.

he begins at once to live in communication with others, while previ-ously he lived almost solely for himself'.[3] So, he writes, confirmation gives someone 'the power to publically, as it were, *ex officio*, proclaim Christ in his speech'.[4] We pray at confirmation that the candidate will receive the seven gifts of the Spirit,[5] 'the spirit of wisdom and understanding, the spirit of right judgment and courage, the spirit of knowledge and reverence. Fill him/her with the spirit of wonder and awe in your presence'. They attune us to the Holy Spirit, and form us as people able to speak with authority about faith in the Church and in the public sphere.

The first disciples spoke boldly, Luke tells us in Acts (e.g. 9.29; 14.3). This is *parrhesia* which Simon Tugwell defines as 'being able to say everything and anything'.[6] Our Churches are filled with words: innumerable documents, position papers, episcopal declarations, theological dissertations, sermons, learned articles, journalistic reporting. But there is not always open speech in which we say what we most deeply believe, and share our doubts and fears, and open our ears to views other than our own. St Catherine of Siena gave the cardinals who were with the Pope exiled in Avignon a good dressing down: 'Be silent no longer. Cry out with a hundred thousand voices. I see that the world is destroyed through silence'.[7]

The Church should form the confirmed to speak well, openly and with confidence. This is not a matter of saying the first thing that

---

[3] *Summa Theologica* III q.72.a.2.

[4] *Summa Theologica* III q.72.a.5 ad 2.

[5] Richard Conrad OP, *The Seven Gifts of the Holy Spirit* (London: Catholic Truth Society, 2009).

[6] Ibid., p. 138.

[7] Letter 16, ed. Pierro Miscitelli, *Le Lettere di S. Caterina da Siena*, Vol. I (Siena, 1922), p. 68.

comes into our heads. Every confirmed Christian should receive a
basic theological training, knowledge of the scriptures and of the
Church's teaching. Confirmation has often been linked with the age
of reason, and we need to be taught how to think hard about our faith
and grow in confidence that though it reaches beyond what we can
know by reason, it is never irrational.

Robert Barron, an American theologian, said that when he visited
his niece who was preparing for university, he was impressed by the
weighty tomes that she was studying on Homer and Shakespeare, the
books on advanced physics and chemistry, but when he asked her
what books of theology she had, she showed him a book of cartoons
fit for a ten year old. He went immediately and bought her a copy of
Aquinas's *Contra Gentiles* in Latin! It was said of Louis Pasteur, the
famous scientist, that 'he had the faith of a Breton peasant'. Donald
Nicholl comments: 'While it is all very well for a Breton peasant to
have the faith of a Breton peasant it is not really praiseworthy for a
modern scientist to hold the faith in the same manner'.[8] Pope Paul
VI said, 'The world is in trouble because of a lack of thinking'.[9]
Indeed, and so too is the Church sometimes.

Jesus says: 'When they bring you to trial and hand you over,
do not worry beforehand about what you are to say; but say what
is given you at the time, for it is not you who speak but the Holy
Spirit' (Mk 13.11). But we prepare for these spontaneous words by
study and prayer just as a tennis player practises for hours so as to
perform spontaneously. We need to be taught how to defend our faith
rationally, intelligently, as grownups. This is how we open ourselves
to the Spirit's gifts of wisdom, knowledge and understanding. It is

---

[8] Nicholl, *Holiness*, p. 15.
[9] Quoted by Pope Benedict in *Caritas in Veritate* para 53, quoting *Populorum Progressio*.

said that when Herbert McCabe was six years old, his mother repri-
manded him for some naughty deed. She said, 'Now you have been a
very wicked boy. It is so bad that it might even be a mortal sin'. And
young Herbert is supposed to have replied, 'Mother, it is impossible.
I cannot commit a mortal sin until I have attained the age of reason.
According to the Church I have not done so at the age of six. Your
reasoning is therefore faulty'.

It takes time for people to find their voices, especially if they are
unused to speaking. They are likely to rant and posture, make ridiculous claims, and generally show up their ignorance. The solution is
not to silence people, Satan's reaction, but to help them find the words
for which they are searching. In a Dominican community, one of the
roles of the Prior is to help those who have awkward and uncom-
fortable things to say to find a better way of saying them, especially
when they are disagreeing with him! We are at the service of the Spirit
of love when we assist others to express the fears and reservations and
hesitations that they feel, and most especially when they are not our
own. When I was Master of the Dominican Order, there was only
one rule in the discussions of the General Council. We could disagree
with each other as much as we wanted as long as we never dismissed
another's views as absurd or nonsensical. A person is rubbished if
their views are dismissed.

To reiterate a constant theme of this book, if the Church is to
become a community for grownups then we must not be too afraid
of things getting out of control. When people are trying to find their
own voice and share some new insight, it is very likely that they will
not find the best words at first, and may even make assertions that are
evidently wrong or contrary to our faith. But rather than reaching for
the panic button, we need patiently to discover the true insight that
is struggling to get out. The Holy Spirit is poured upon the Church at
Pentecost and so it will not be brought tumbling down just because

some people have gone a little astray in their pursuit of the truth. Judaism teaches that we must attend to the minority view, even if we reject it, because one day we may need its wisdom.[10] A community which is unable to cope with disagreement and imposes uniformity will be ill-prepared for the future.

Let us now look at each of these testings and see what they teach us about what it means to be strong. I will loosely link these with the cardinal virtues. I do not believe that there is a systematic relationship, but it may suggest how the moral life is not so much about submission to rules as growing in vigour. We already covered similar ground to my brief treatment of Christian life as a struggle in Chapter 6, but this time the focus is on growing up rather than the healing of our love.

Command this stone to become a loaf of bread

'He ate nothing at all during those days, and when they were over, he was famished. The devil said to him "If you are the Son of God, command this stone to become a loaf of bread." Jesus answered him, "It is written, 'One does not live by bread alone'"' (Lk. 4.3-4).

If you are the Son of God, then you can do whatever you want. You can change stones into loaves and bread, and rocks into arm chairs or fridges. Herod says in *Jesus Christ Superstar*: 'Prove to me that you're divine. Change my water into wine'. In *War and Peace*, the Rostov children test the power of prayer but asking that the snow be turned into sugar. Some of the early apocryphal gospels show Jesus as a spoilt kid doing horrible things to his playmates because he has the power.

---

[10] David Brown, *Tradition and Imagination* (Oxford, 1999), p. 146.

He can get his own way and so why not? He is the Son of the Big Boss. As the Australians say, 'If you've got it, flaunt it'. LulzSec, the band of computer hackers, had the motto, 'We do it 'cause we can'.

The location of each testing is significant. This one occurs in the wilderness, the place in which God seems absent. When God is not around, one may be tempted to take things into one's own hands. What is the alternative? This, therefore, is the temptation which is especially seductive for our contemporary secular society. With the development of the culture of control our forebears came to see the world in mechanistic terms, and so there was little space for God's providence. Even God had to submit to the laws of cause and effect. If you think of the world as a great machine, typically a clock, then once the divine engineer has got it ticking, he becomes rather irrelevant. We must get on with running the world ourselves.

The strong are those who can impose their will, seduced by Nietzsche's 'will to power'. If one is alone in the universe, then what is to restrain one's exercise of power? If genetic manipulation means that one can make strange new beings, then why not? I can reshape the world as I wish. This is not of course to deny the immense blessings of modern medical research, from which I have personally benefited enormously. But a culture which is shaped by the desire to control and dominate will tend to see God's power as competing with our own. Atheism became an attractive option in the nineteenth century because people felt the need to be freed from God's oppressive shadow. We recreate God in our own image, and project upon him our own aspirations to unlimited power. Jesus comes to be seen as either irrelevant or as 'the Great Prohibitor'.[11]

Jesus replies to Satan: 'It is written, "One does not live by bread

---

[11] Alister McGrath, *The Twilight of Atheism: The Rise and Fall of Disbelief in the Modern World* (London, 2004), p. 140.

alone"'. He is not squashing Satan with a neat proof text. He is quoting the Book of Deuteronomy, where Moses reminds the people that once they had hungered in the wilderness. God 'humbled you by letting you hunger, then by feeding you with manna, with which neither you nor your ancestors were acquainted, in order to make you understand that one does not live by bread alone but by every word that comes from the mouth of God' (Deut. 8.3). In the desert, when they were weak, they were given food which they had not produced and which was pure, inexplicable gift.

So the point is not that our power is constrained by God: we may be powerful but there is someone who is even more powerful than we are! Rather, the point is that we are strong in relationship with the Strong God, whose word nourishes us as we journey towards the Promised Land. Strength is not the solitary will imposing itself. In the wilderness the Israelites were weak and would have perished but God's word gave them strength.

This applies to power within the Church. The empowering of the laity does not mean the disempowering of the clergy. The hierarchy needs to be strong to strengthen the laity, and vice versa. Otherwise the Body of Christ suffers from a disabling sickness. Sometimes the clergy and the laity suffer from a mutual suspicion, even a competition for control, which is mutually disempowering.

One cardinal virtue that this testing evokes is temperance. We must temper our desire for power, not because we should not wish to be too strong, but because an adult, mature approach to power is tempered by awareness of others and how we can sustain them. We temper the violence of the will. Faced with hunger Jesus knows what he most deeply desires. He is free for his mission because he is not enslaved by small desires such as getting his own way. Temperance sounds boring. You invite a friend around for a nice bottle of wine and after a single glass he primly suggests that is enough. But temperance is learning to desire well, to enjoy wine as wine, and not as a means of oblivion, and to enjoy the Word of God even more. It is delighting in things as they are, relishing and savouring them. Savour is linked to *savoir*, knowledge. If we savour our wine, then we may learn to savour the Word of God.

We need to temper the voraciousness within us, the consuming not just of food and drink but each other and the planet. Temperance tames the violence of desire which blinds us to what we consume. When I celebrated my 21st birthday during my novitiate, I asked my father to send some good plonk but nothing special since some of the novices would just swig it without savouring it. But unfortunately he sent a case of superb claret, which one of those novices downed by the pint as if it was Coca Cola. That was intemperate not so much because he drank too much, but because he did not appreciate it. Temperance simplifies life, they tell me, because each thing is enjoyed as itself and not to fill the vacuum which only God can satisfy. G. K. Chesterton claimed that there was more simplicity in the person who ate caviar spontaneously then someone who drank grape juice on principle!

It is bizarre that in a society which is obsessed with consumption and dieting the Church has largely forgotten the liberating discipline of fasting. We have an ancient wisdom to offer a world that swings between binge eating and anorexia. The world's young are being weakened by either starvation or obesity. Fasting is about being freed to desire more deeply, to hunger for what gives life. In Ian McEwen's most recent novel *Solar*, the hero, a world famous scientist, is unable to resist the snack before his eyes: 'What defeated him was always the present, the moment of vivid confrontation with the affirming titbit, the extra course, the meal he did not really need, when the short-term faction carried the day'.[12] But if you are a pilgrim journeying to the Kingdom, then you need to keep vivid an awareness of your final goal, the land of milk and honey, and not fall captive to the immediacy of the desire for the onions, cucumbers and garlic of servitude in Egypt.

Worship me and it will all be yours

'Then the devil led him up and showed him in an instant all the kingdoms of the world. And the devil said to him, "To you I will give their glory and all this authority; for it has been given over to me, and I give it to anyone I please. If you, then, will worship me, it will all be yours." Jesus answered him, "It is written, 'Worship the Lord your God, and serve only him'" (Lk. 4.5-8).

This temptation takes place neither in the desert, where God seems absent, nor in the holy place of the Temple. It is a neutral place, the world, and it is a worldly temptation, that of 'realism'. Obviously worshipping the devil is not a real temptation for Jesus, but it is a testing in that it reveals a little more about what it means to be strong. On the face of it, the devil is making an attractive proposition. Clearly it is better for Jesus to run the world than the devil. Think of all the good things that he could do. Of course, it is not right to worship the devil, but it might be justifiable, one could argue, given the results. The end justifies the means. This is the seduction of expediency, living in the 'real world'.

When Jesus raised Lazarus to life, the chief priests and some of the Pharisees called a meeting of the council and asked 'What are we to do? This man is performing many signs. If we let him go on like this, everyone will believe in him, and the Romans will come and

---

[12] Ian McEwen, *Solar* (London, 2010), p. 118.

destroy both our holy place and our nation' (Jn 11.47). But Caiaphas told them: 'You do not understand that it is expedient for you to have one man die for the people rather than to have the whole nation destroyed'. He is urging them to be realistic. The death of Jesus is expedient, advantageous, the only option.

It is expediency that drives us to do what we suspect may be wrong, because, regrettably, that is the way that the world works. Lady Thatcher's nickname was TINA: There Is No Alternative. Expediency led to Guantanamo bay, special renditions and the use of torture. In the Vietnam War, there was the famous regret: 'We had to destroy the village to save it from the Communists'. Get real, people say. It has recently come to light that British colonial rule suppressed the Mau Mau resistance in Kenya with hideous torture. No doubt to those involved it seemed the only realistic response to the horrible deeds of these terrorists. It was regrettable, and even shameful, but we must be realistic. At least we can try not to shock the public back home. The Kenyan Attorney General of the time wrote, 'If we are going to sin, we must sin quietly'. One can even imagine people thinking that there was something noble in being the ones who carry the heavy burden of these terrible deeds for everyone else. Someone must work 'on the dark side', as Dick Cheney put it.

Jesus replies, 'It is written, "Worship the Lord your God and serve only him"'. He is making a more subtle point than that we are commanded to worship God rather than Satan. In its original setting in Deuteronomy, the Israelites are reminded that it is God who brought them out of slavery in Egypt. God's providence does not let us down. Even though God appears to forget the Israelites wandering in the desert, yet he will bring them to their home if they will but trust him. Expediency is a failure of trust, a sort of despair.

It is not likely that any of us have been offered world domination in exchange for worshipping the devil, but expediency tempts us all.

Clergy may feel it expedient not to preach too strongly about the option for the poor when there is a wealthy potential benefactor in the front bench. It would be regrettable if he were to give his money to another cause. Think of all the good that we could do with it. Or they might be tempted not to speak too boldly on controversial issues. It might reduce their chances of becoming bishops, and of course they would be wonderful bishops! 'If I keep quiet now, then I can speak more effectively when I have got my diocese. I owe this to the Church!'

The two cardinal virtues that spring to mind here are justice and prudence. According to St. Thomas, justice is giving to each what is due to them. And the foundation of all justice is giving God what is due to God, which is worship. We worship God by doing what is right even when it seems pointless, even if it will lead the benefactor to give his money to someone else, because we trust that God's providence will bring us to our goal. We hallow his name and refuse to bend the knee to expediency.

Expediency often leads to the corrosion of law and so of the justice that is owed to our neighbours. Laws are rewritten so as to justify acts of brutality. In Kenya, according to David Anderson, an Oxford historian, 'the files reveal that changes were commonly made retrospectively to "cover" practices that were already "normal" within the camps and detention centres'.[13] And so expediency undermines the worship that we owe in justice to God and the respect for law that we owe to each other.

Prudence sounds a rather feeble virtue. It suggests caution, holding back, failing to be daring. No one could be heroically prudent. But prudence, as understood by Aquinas, was a more

---

[13] Quoted by Ben Macintyre, 'Torture device no 1: the legal rubber stamp', *The Times*, 12 April 2011.

exciting virtue. It is daring to live in what is indeed the real world, which is God's world. It is true realism. Prudence means that we should not act without thought, but having reflected we may see that bold action is required, 'a reckless tossing away of anxious self-preservation.'[14] If we acknowledge that God rules the world and that his will indeed will be done, then it is only prudent to do what is right and just. The pseudo-realism of this world, which invites us to cut corners, is blindness to God's rule. It is realistic to act justly because God's providence is quietly bringing us to himself, and no unjust action will get us nearer.

On the 23 March 1980, the day before he died, Oscar Romero, the martyred archbishop of San Salvador, preached on the woman taken in adultery. It is a beautiful text about freedom. The woman is freed to become a moral agent once again: 'Go and sin no more' (Jn 8.11). She is free to walk away from the place of death. She is welcomed back into the community, her accusers gone. And we see here Romero's freedom to say what is right, even though it would bring him into conflict with the powers of this world, and lead to his death.

He said: 'I have no ambition for power and for that reason, with complete freedom, I say to power what is good and what is bad and to whatever political group I say what is good and what is bad; it is my duty'. He concludes by summoning the soldiers to step into their freedom, to become fully moral agents, to refuse to be puppets of an unjust regime: 'Brothers, you are of our same people, and kill your own peasant brothers and sisters but over an order to kill given by a man ought to prevail the law of God which says: Do not kill. No one has to obey an immoral law. Now is the time to reclaim your conscience and obey your conscience rather than the order of sin'. This was one of the great invitations to freedom of the twentieth

---

[14] Josef Pieper, *The Four Cardinal Virtues* (Notre Dame, 1966), p. 21.

century. It may look idealistic, but it is living in the real world, which is God's world.

We live in an imprudent world of spin and image. Behind Blackfriars, where I live, there is a vast building site with a sign saying, 'Improving the image of construction'. Not, one notes, improve construction, just the image. And when Catalonia, in northern Spain, wanted to promote tourism, they showed a photo of a beautiful beach, but it was actually in Perth, Australia! The company that did this specializes in 'communication strategy', i.e. smoke and mirrors.

Our financial meltdown is surely rooted in imprudence. This is not just because we have not checked our figures or taken silly risks, or not had enough economic reserves, but because we have allowed our economy to become detached from reality. House prices had less and less to do with the value of houses as bricks and mortar and places where people lived. In fact the value of everything ceased to have much to do with what things are, but just what they would fetch on the market. Money bought and sold money, and zoomed around the planet in split seconds, ever more remote from the real world. Pope Benedict's Encyclical, *Caritas in Veritate*, focuses on the assertion that loving people is inseparable from living with them in the truth. He writes, 'Only in truth does charity shine forth, only in truth can charity be authentically loved. Truth is the light that gives meaning and value to charity'. (3)

Throw yourself down from here

'Then the devil took him to Jerusalem, and placed him on the pinnacle of the temple, saying to him, "If you are the Son of God, throw yourself down from here, for it is written 'He will command his angels concerning you, to protect you'. And 'On their hands they will bear you up, so that you will not dash your foot against a stone.'" Jesus answered him, "It is said, 'Do not put the Lord your God to the test'" (Lk. 4.9-12).

Jesus replies to the devil: 'It is said, "Do not put the Lord your God to the test."' Once again we are taken back into the story of Israel's wandering in the desert, when the people demanded that Moses produce water: 'Why did you bring us out of Egypt, to kill us and our children and livestock with thirst?' (Exod. 17.3). It is Moses' fault that they are not still in Egypt with the water of the great Nile, and with its orchards and vegetable gardens. He is to blame for this crazy bid for freedom. It is not their responsibility that they are in this tight spot. They never asked to be free. They want to run away from the terrifying burden of responsibility. At least as slaves in Egypt, they did not need to bear that burden. This is the argument of the Grand Inquisitor with Jesus, in Fyodor Dostoevsky's story of the Grand Inquisitor, who asserts that 'nothing has ever been more insufferable for humanity and society than freedom... In the end they will lay their freedom at our feet and say to us; "Better that you enslave us, but feed us".[15]

This last testing takes place on the roof of the Temple itself, the most holy place of Israel, and it is suggestive of how religious people may especially be inclined to get power wrong. Jesus has told the devil that we must trust God, and so let us trust God completely. He is our Father in heaven who will take care of us whatever happens. We can be gloriously irresponsible. We could even jump off the top of the Temple and not worry, because God will catch us. In the first test, we saw that Jesus' sonship does not mean that he grabs power.

[15] *The Brothers Karamazov*, trans. Richard Pevear and Larissa Volokhonsky (San Francisco, 1990), pp. 252–53.

Here we discover that neither does it mean a flight from power. The first feeds upon our will for power and the second on the wonderful liberation of not having any at all. So there is a terrible earthquake in Haiti. How awful! But it is not my responsibility. It is our heavenly Daddy who will look after the victims so much better than I could. The economic system is creating vast inequalities of wealth. What a pity. It is God, or maybe the market, which is to blame. Not me in any case. The Church is in a mess, but there is nothing that I can do about it. Stephen Cherry writes about 'Teflon' people, on whom no blame can ever stick. It is always someone else's responsibility. 'It is more common than ever to come across people with the sort of sloping shoulders on which no responsibility can rest'.[16]

The devil tempts Jesus with the sin of presumption, which is a form of hopelessness, a mirror image of despair. Presumption says that there is nothing that I can do, because it will all be alright. Despair, on the contrary, says that there is nothing that I can do because it will all go wrong. Both are flights from an adult grasping of responsibility. Despair is a sort of senile resignation and presumption a form of infantile impotence; both are opposed to adult maturity.

So we see in these stories three ways of misunderstanding what it means to be strong. The first test showed up the hollowness of a strength which is the imposition of one's will. The second test confronted us with the seduction of power which compromises with this world, a pseudo-realism, and this final test shows that we cannot take the easy way out and just flee power and responsibility, presuming that God will look after everything.

---

[16] Stephen Cherry, *Barefoot Disciple* (London, 2011), p. 55.

The courage of the confirmed

To confront this final test, we need the fourth cardinal virtue, which is courage, the courage for each of us to take up our own responsibility for the life and the mission of the Church. We shall only be able to face the challenges of today if the baptized and confirmed are strengthened in an adult use of power, neither grabbing it, nor competing for it, nor fleeing it. When I was a child we received a slap on the cheek from the bishop at confirmation, as a sign that we must be brave in the proclamation of our faith. God does not want his children to be wimps.

What strong courage do we need in the internal life of the Church? Aquinas believed that the greatest courage is that of endurance. We show courage by hanging on when our faith is attacked or we are disappointed by the Church, when it appears to be drifting in a direction that we dislike, and when we may feel embarrassed to belong to it. Why do so? Because Jesus gave himself irrevocably to a group of weak and foolish disciples, and remained bound to them even when they rejected him. How can we then dare to distance ourselves from the Church if God does not? And who am I to claim any superiority? It would make me look like a Pharisee shocked at Jesus' eating and drinking with tax collectors and prostitutes. And where would I go anyway?

When Jesus asked Peter if he would go he said: 'Lord, to whom shall we go? You have the words of eternal life' (Jn 6.68). Our endurance is sustained by hanging on to those words of eternal life, mediating on the gospels, rather than always fretting about ecclesiastical politics and churchy gossip. We have to reclaim our own identity, as a communion of abundant life, of grace and forgiveness, rather than as a power structure or a campaigning lobby. And if we do so, then we shall sit more loosely to all ideological parties in the Church, which are often powered by fear and panic.

We need the courage to open ourselves to people in our Church who are moved by other dreams and hopes. If someone pushes for something that I find incomprehensible – the Tridentine rite for the Eucharist for example – rather than indignantly throwing my hands in the air, I must use my imagination and intelligence to discover why, and what is attractive and even legitimate in this desire. I may go on disagreeing but at least I may understand why that other person holds views that are so different from my own, and even have enlarged my heart and mind to make space for what touches his or her deep desires.

Iris Murdoch, the English writer and philosopher, said that if you wish to understand another person, ask of what they are afraid. What are the fears that polarize our Churches and how can we give each other courage? Many traditional Christians are disturbed by the fear of chaos. The known world is shaken, and the future is uncertain. They want a Christianity that embodies clear order, a safe and secure world. Ways of speaking and acting that for some of us are evocative of freedom are for others threatening symbols of chaos. In *To the Lighthouse* by Virginia Woolf, a small hole in the sock of a young woman profoundly disturbs the fastidious philosopher who walks behind her. It evokes all his fears of a world come to pieces: 'How that little round hole of pink heel seemed to flaunt itself before them! … It meant to him the annihilation of womanhood, and dirt and disorder and servants leaving and beds not made at mid-day – all the things he most abhorred'.[17] Indeed I have even seen my undisciplined hair provoke distress in some as if it were a wilful challenge to orthodoxy!

---

[17] Virginia Woolf, *To the Lighthouse* (London: Penguin, 1996, first published 1927), p. 252.

Liberal Christians must understand this fear of chaos, respect its legitimate concern, be careful not to provoke it unnecessarily, like children throwing stones as lions in the zoo. But we must also share our confidence that chaos has been finally defeated. The world did indeed collapse on Good Friday, the sun was darkened and the veil of the Temple ripped in two. But on Easter Sunday, the world was made new again. The Leviathan has been slain and chaos defeated. The rainbow covenant means that floods shall not overwhelm the earth. We need not fear.

But what do liberal Christians fear? There is a deep unease that the Church is stuck or even retreating. To take again the example of my own Church, after the Vatican Council many Catholics dreamed of a Church that would be radically transformed. Almost fifty years later, this has not happened, at least not as many hoped. Does this mean that we will be stuck forever with a Church that is over-centralized, authoritarian, patriarchal, and felt by many to be exclusive of women? I do not believe so, but nowhere does the Bible teach us that the life of the Church shall be marked by smooth progress. This is a doctrine of the Enlightenment and not of our faith. History shows us that the Church often gets stuck in the wilderness like those Israelites for decades after the glorious Exodus. But we believe that God's providence is at work, bringing us to the Kingdom in ways that we cannot anticipate. We need not fear.

We need Church leaders who have the courage to hold us together and to care for the whole flock, especially those on the edge. They need to have the calm confidence that if the Holy Spirit is poured upon the Church, then they do not need to control everything, insist always on their way, but trust that the Spirit is at work in the whole community and not just in its leaders. Throughout this book I have referred to the rise of a culture of control during the Enlightenment which is secular in origin and due to the loss of a belief in God's providence. So we need leaders who have the courage to let things happen, to let God's unpredictable grace work in our community. Leadership is about ensuring that *no one* can grab control, because God's grace is in everyone.

When I was a young Dominican student, there was an attack on our priory of Blackfriars in Oxford. An extreme right-wing group, which disapproved of our stance on various issues, planted two very small explosives on the front of the priory, which detonated at 2am. We all woke up and rushed to the front of the house, to find all the glass of the windows shattered. The police and ambulances came. But where was the Prior, Fergus Kerr? The youngest friar was despatched to his room to wake him. 'Fergus, there has been a bomb attack!'; 'Anybody killed?'; 'No'; 'Anybody wounded?'; 'No'; 'Then go away and let me sleep, and we can think about it in the morning'. This was my first lesson in leadership! Christ has died, Christ is risen, Christ will come again. There is no need to flap or fear.

Our leaders need to show confidence in the young. God appeared among us as a new-born baby. Every year we celebrate his birth. God is forever young, fresher and more vigorous than we are, and so we must trust the young, in whom God is present, and who will be open to a future which we cannot imagine. When St Dominic sent out his young novices to preach the gospel, the Cistercian monks were convinced that they would get mixed up with women and never be seen again, but St Dominic said, 'I know for certain that my young men will go out and come back, will be sent out and will return; but your young men will be kept locked up and will still go out'.[18]

We also need courage *ad extra*, in our mission to the world. The gospel spread throughout the world because our predecessors in the faith were extraordinarily brave. More than half of the Spanish

---

[18] Simon Tugwell OP ed., *Early Dominicans: Selected Writings* (New York,1982), p. 90.

Dominicans sent to preach the gospel in Asia in the sixteenth century died before they even arrived. I have visited graveyards in Nigeria filled with the bodies of the young Western missionaries who died in their twenties and thirties, often of malaria.

We need another sort of courage, to leave our small and cosy ecclesiastical world, and immerse ourselves in the questions of our contemporaries and expose ourselves to their convictions. For this mission, we need, again, confidence and humility. We need to preach the great adventure of our faith, which will cost everything, even our lives. God became human so that we might become divine. A cosy and inoffensive spirituality, a bit of psychology lightly stirred in with a hint of morality, is not enough. Unless Christianity is seen to be a radical invitation to share God's own life, a wise folly, then why would anyone bother? Let's have more fools for Christ!

We also need the courage to listen to our contemporaries, especially when they disagree with us. They too call us to conversion. We must be prepared to get out of our depth, address questions to which we do not have the answers, and not be afraid to admit that we need help in finding them.

We must not be so obsessed with our ideological purity that we fear to get involved in this messy world. Jesus associated with everyone, whatever their morals, so that he might offer them his wide-open hospitality. When Amnesty International began to support abortion, then of course many Christians were deeply disappointed and rightly so. But is it good to withdraw our collaboration with this movement which stands up for life so strongly just because they do not share our convictions on everything? If we only associate with those who are pure, then we shall be more like the Pharisees than the followers of Jesus.

We need to have the courage to make bold gestures, as Jesus did constantly. Church leaders talk about many complex moral issues, about homosexuality and abortion, about euthanasia and bioethics. Often our words will simply not be understood by anyone who does not already agree with them. It is only if we open our homes to the people who struggle with these issues, offer and accept hospitality, make friendship, that there can be a context in which we can discover words that have any authority, gospel words. Of course we shall be misunderstood. The media will systematically misrepresent us. We may suffer. But there is a chance that we shall say something. Jesus took that risk; one can argue that he died in part because he was misunderstood, and was bound to be, but he rose again.

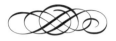

Epilogue

Every ritual enacts a story. The Eucharist, I have claimed elsewhere, is the three-act drama of faith, hope and love. What is the drama of baptism? It is harder to detect. Often it has seemed to me a rather confusing ritual, and I must constantly check the book to see what comes next. But I believe that it is not, in fact, a haphazard succession of events. It is a narrative with its own dynamic development.

The beginning and the end are clear. We start with the question: 'What name do you give your child?' We saw that all Christians are called to be childlike, though not childish. If we are to flourish and be strong in Christ, then we need to be renewed in the playfulness, spontaneity and imaginative creativity of a child, which is a participation in God's eternal freshness. We end with confirmation, which blesses our growth into spiritual maturity. Being childlike and true maturity are inseparable, otherwise we fall into either infantilism or weary, old cynicism. One cannot be truly childlike unless one's way is open to becoming adult, nor truly adult unless one remains young in God: Only playful human beings can share the life of our playful God.

So this is the Alpha and Omega of grace. But what happens in between? How does the sacrament bring us from the freshness of grace's beginnings to spiritual maturity? It does so, it seems to me, by embracing us in a love which is unconditional and unmerited but, as we move through the sacrament, we discover that this love is ever more demanding and transformative. As children of the font, we learn confidence in a love which is unshakeable. But as adults in Christ, we discover how it will turn our lives upside down and remake us. This love is transforming because it is God's friendship, and no true friendship ever leaves one unchanged.

We begin by being named in love, an unmerited love which precedes any response on our part. But this love is also Christ's claim, which summons us to belong to the spacious community of his friendship. God's love liberates us from the confines of our family, and invites us to belong to the whole Church, indeed the whole of humanity. All our loving must be touched by the universal outreach of God's care. In the litany of the saints, we discover that our community includes those who died.

Then we discover that becoming loving involves a struggle and a choice. Our hearts need to be purified of violence if we are to be truly young in Christ. Then at the blessing of the waters, the love of God invites us to share in God's own creativity, above all speaking words that give life, healing and nourishment.

Now we are ready to choose Christ rather than Satan, the history of humanity as a love story rather than doomed to futility. We then take the plunge, daring to be stripped of all masks, accepting to be loved as we are, be touched by God's grace, and be freed from the dominion of death. We are clothed in white to show that we are now members of God's holy people, not because we have suddenly become very good, but because we share the life of the Trinity. But this implies responsibility in the life and mission of the Church, because we are anointed priests, prophets and kings (or queens). Then we are given the light of Christ, so that we may see the wide embrace of God's family, the hidden dignity of every human being. And finally confirmation blesses our becoming, our growing up in Christ.

This is the love that makes us strong children of God, to whom the future is entrusted. It touches on the drama of being a human being, blessing our birth and death, our falling in love, our moments of failure, our struggle to understand the meaning of our lives, and our slow ripening into maturity. It also involves fundamental elements of the cosmos in which we live and of which we are made: oil, water and fire. It may be a brief and common ritual, whose significance is usually hardly noticed, but it is the drama of being fully alive in Christ. If we grasp the beauty of this simple sacrament, then the Church will flourish and be strong in offering the good news to our world, which even if it does not know it, hungers for this love.

Bibliography

Alison, James, *The Forgiving Victim*. London, forthcoming 2012.

Allen Jr., John L., *The Future Church: How Ten Trends are Revolutionizing the Catholic Church*. New York, 2009.

Ancelet-Hustache, Jeanne, *Men of Wisdom: Master Eckhart and the Rhineland Mystics*. New York and London, 1957.

Arendt, Hannah, *The Human Condition*. New York, 1959.

Barbery, Muriel, *The Elegance of the Hedgehog*, trans. Alison Anderson. London, 2008.

Basset, Lytta, *Une spiritualité d'enfant*. Paris, 2011.

Bauman, Zygmunt, *Liquid Modernity*. Oxford and Malden, 2000.

Bellow, Saul, *Conversations with Saul Bellow*, ed. Gloria Cronin and Ben Siegel. Jackson, MI, 1994.

—*Caritas in Veritate*. 29 June 2009, Vatican website, www.vatican.va.

Benedict XVI, Pope, *The Light of the World: The Pope, the Church and the Signs of the Times. A Conversation with Peter Seewald*, trans. Michael J. Miller and Adrian J. Walker. San Francisco, 2010.

Bennet, Alan, *The History Boys*. London, 2004.

Bentley Hart, David, *Atheist Delusions: The Christian Revolution and Its Fashionable Enemies*. New Haven and London, 2009.

Bishops' Conference of England and Wales, *Choosing the Common Good*. London, 2010.

Boland OP, Vivian, *Spiritual Warfare: Fighting the Good Fight*. London: CTS, 2007.

Bonhoeffer, Dietrich, *Letters and Papers from Prison*, ed. Eberhard Bethge, trans. Reginald Fuller. London, 1967.

Bowker, John, *Problems of Suffering in the Religions of the World*. Cambridge, 1975.

Bowker, John W., *Before the Ending of the Day: Life and Love, Death and Redemption*. Toronto, 2010.

Boyle SJ, Gregory, *Tattoos on the Heart: The Power of Boundless Compassion*. New York, 2010.

Boyle, Nicholas *Who Are We Now? Christian Humanism and the Global Market from Hegel to Heaney*. Edinburgh, 1998.

Brand, Eugene, *Baptism: A Pastoral Perspective*. Minneapolis, 1975.

—*Tradition and Imagination*. Oxford, 1999.

Brown, David, *Discipleship and Imagination: Christian Tradition and Truth*. Oxford, 2000.

Brown, Peter, *The Cult of the Saints*. Chicago, 1981.

—*The World of Late Antiquity: AD 150-750*. London, 1993.

Burridge, Richard, *Imitating Jesus: An Inclusive Approach to New Testament Ethics*. Grand Rapids, 2007.

Campos Villalón OP, Luisa, *Pedro de Córdoba: precursor de una comunidad defensora de la vida*. Santo Domingo, 2008.

Cavanaugh, W. *Torture and Eucharist: Theology, Politics, and the Body of Christ*. Oxford, 1998.

Cherry, Stephen, *The Barefoot Disciple: Walking the Ways of Passionate Humility*. London, 2011.

Chesterton, G. K., *Orthodoxy*. London, 1996.

Cleave, Chris, *The Other Hand*. London, 2009.

Compagnoni OP, Francesco and Helen Alford OP (eds), *Preaching Justice*. Dublin, 2007.

Congar, Yves, *Journal d'un théologien 1946-1956*, ed. É. Fouilloux. Paris, 2000.

—*At the Heart of Christian Worship: Liturgical Essays of Yves Congar*, trans. and ed. Paul Philibert OP. Collegeville, 2010.

Conrad OP, Richard, *The Seven Gifts of the Holy Spirit*. London: Catholic Truth Society, 2009.

Cordelier, Jérôme, *Rebelles de Dieu*. Paris, 2011.

Craig, Olga, 'The boy soldiers of Liberia', *Daily Telegraph*, 14 September 2003.

Craven, Margaret, *I Heard the Owl Call My Name*. Toronto, 1967.

Davies OP, Brian, *Aquinas*. New York and London, 2002.

Deiss, Lucien, *Springtime of the Liturgy*. Collegeville, 1979.

Dickens, Charles, *Oliver Twist*. London, first published 1843.

Dickinson, Emily, *The Complete Poems*, ed. Thomas H. Johnson. London, 1975.

Dillard, Annie, *Pilgrim at Tinker Creek*. New York, 1974.

Donovan, Vincent J., *Christianity Rediscovered: An Epistle from the Masai*. London, 1978.

Doty, Mark, *The School of the Arts*. London, 2005.

Driscoll OSB, Jeremy, *A Monk's Alphabet: Moments of Stillness in a Turning World*. London, 2006.

Duffy, Eamon, *Faith of our Fathers: Reflections of Catholic Identity*. London, 2004.

Eagleton, Terry, *The Meaning of Life: A Very Short Introduction*. Oxford, 2007.

—*On Evil*. New Haven and London, 2010.

Meister Eckhart, 'Talks of Instruction', in *The Essential Sermons, Commentaries, Treatises and Defence*, ed. and trans. B. McGinn and E. Colledge. New York, 1981.

—*Sermons and Treatises*, ed. Maurice O'C Walshe. London and Shaftesbury. 3 vols. 1979, 1981 and 1985.

Edwards, Jonathan, 'A Personal Narrative', in J. E. Smith *et al.* eds, *A Jonathan Edwards Reader*. New Haven, 1995.

Eggers, Dave, *What is the What*. London, 2008.

Elie, Paul, *The Life You Save May be Your Own: An American Pilgrimage*. New York, 2003.

Finn OP, Richard, *Almsgiving in the Later Roman Empire*. Oxford, 2006.

Fitzgerald, Scott, *All the Sad Young Men*, ed. James W. L. West III. Cambridge, 2007.

Foster OP, Kenelm, *God's Tree: Essays on Dante and Other Matters*. London, 1957.

Foster OSB, David, *Reading with God: Lectio Divina*. London, 2005.

Gaita, Raimond, *A Common Humanity: Thinking about Love and Truth and Justice*. London, 2002.

Gamble, Andrew, 'A Tribe Betrayed', *Times Literary Supplement*, 19 and 26 August 2011.

Gesché, Adolphe, *La Destinée*. Paris, 1995.

Gibler, Linda, *From the Beginning to Baptism: Scientific and Sacred Stories of Water, Oil and Fire*. Collegeville, MN 2010.

Giertych OP, Wojciech, 'The Importance of the Study of Theology in the Dominican Tradition', in *Building Bridges: Dominicans Doing Theology Together*, Dominican Sisters International *et al.* Dublin and Manila, 2005.

Gilley, Sheridan, 'Holiness in the Roman Catholic Tradition', in *Holiness Past and Present*, ed. Stephen Barton. London and New York, 2003.

Green OSB, Bernard, *Christianity in Ancient Rome: The First Three Centuries*. London, 2010.

Grieu SJ, Etienne, 'Discovering who God is in Caritas', in Oscar Cardinal Rodríguez Maradiaga ed., *Caritas: Love Received and Given*. Rome, 2011.

Griffiths, Bede, *The Golden String*. London, 1979.

Guy, John, *A Daughter's Love: Thomas and Margaret More*. London, 2009.

Hart, David Bentley, *Atheist Delusions: The Christian Revolution and its Fashionable Enemies*. New Haven and London, 2009.

Heaney, Seamus, *Human Chain*. London, 2010.

Heller, Zoe, *The Believers*. London, 2008.

Hildegard of Bingen, *An Anthology*, (eds) Fiona Boiwe and Oliver Davies, trans. Robert Carver. London, 1990.

Hilesum, Etty, *An Interrupted Life and Letters from Westerbork*. New York, 1996.

Hitchens, Peter, *The Rage against God*. London and New York, 2010.

Holmes, Richard, *The Age of Wonder: How the Romantic Generation Discovered the Beauty and Terror of Science*. London, 2008.

Hopkins, Gerard Manley, *Poems and Prose*, ed. W. H. Gardner. London, 1985.

Jalland, Pat, *Death in War and Peace: A History of Loss and Grief in England, 1914–1970*. Oxford, 2011.

Jamison, Dom Christopher, *Finding Happiness: Monastic Steps for a Fulfilling Life*. London, 2008.

Jaspers, Karl, 'Le mal radical chez Kant', *Deucalion* 36, no. 4 (1952).

John, Paul II, Pope. Apostolic Letter, *Salvifici Doloris* (1984).

Johnson, Maxwell, *The Rites of Christian Initiation: Their Evolution and Interpretation*. Collegeville, MN, 1999.

Jones, David Albert, *Approaching the End: A Theological Exploration of Death and Dying*. Oxford, 2007.

Jones, Owen, *CHAVS: The Demonization of the Working Class*. London and New York, 2011.

Kavanagh OSB, Aidan, 'A Rite of Passage', in Gabe Huck ed., *The Three Days: Parish Prayer in the Paschal Triduum*. Chicago, 1992.

—'Unfinished and Unbegun Revisited', in Maxwell Johnson ed., *Living Water, Sealing Spirit: Readings on Christian Initiation*. Collegeville, 1995.

Keneally, Thomas, *The Widow and her Hero*. London, 2007.

Ker, Ian, *G. K. Chesterton: A Biography*. Oxford, 2011.

King SJ, Nicholas, *The New Testament with an Interactive Study Guide Freshly Translated*. Stowmarket, 2004.

Kingsolver, Barbara, *The Lacuna*. London, 2009.

Larkin, Philip, *Collected Poems*, ed. Anthony Thwaite. London and Victoria, Australia, 2003.

Lash, Nicholas, *Believing Three Ways in One God: A Reading of the Apostles' Creed* London, 1992.

—'Authors, Authority and Authorization', in Bernhard Hoose (ed.), *Authority in the Roman Catholic Church: Theory and Practice*. London, 2002.

Lawson, Mary, *Crow Lake*. London, 2003.

Lederach, John 'The Long Journey back to Humanity', in Robert J. Schreiter *et al.* (eds), *Peacebuilding: Catholic Theology, Ethics and Praxis*. Maryknoll, NY: Orbis, 2010.

Lee, Hermione, 'A Sly Twinkle', *Times Literary Supplement*, 4 December 2009.

LeJoly, Edward, *Servant of Love*. New York, 1977.

Lewis, C. S. *Surprised by Joy*. London, 1955.

Linden, Ian, *A New Map of the World*. London, 2003.

Louth, Andrew, 'St Gregory the Theologian and St Maximus the Confessor: The Shaping of Tradition', in Sarah Coakley and David Arthur Palin (eds), *The Making and Remaking of Christian Doctrine: Essays in Honour of Maurice Wiles*. Oxford, 1993.

MacCulloch, Diarmaid, *A History of Christianity*. London, 2009.

Macintyre, Ben, 'Torture device no 1: The legal rubber stamp', *The Times*, 12 April 2011.

Maritain, Raïssa, *Les Grandes Amitiés*. Paris, 1949.

Martin SJ, James, *The Jesuit Guide to Almost Everything: A Spirituality for Real Life*. New York, 2010.

McCabe OP, Herbert, *God Matters*. London, 1987.

—*God Still Matters*. London, 2002.

McEwen, Ian, *Solar*. London, 2010.

McGilchrist, Ian, 'Digital Display', in *The Times Literary Supplement*, 18 June 2010.

McGrath, Alister, *The Twilight of Atheism: The Rise and Fall of Disbelief in the Modern World* London, 2004.

McGrath, Thomas, *Selected Poems: 1938–1988*. Copper Canyon, 1988.

McTernan, Oliver, *Violence in God's Name: Religion in an Age of Conflict*. London, 2003.

Miller II, Richard W., *Lay Ministry in the Catholic Church: Visioning Church Ministry through the Wisdom of the Past*. Kansas City, 2005.

Milner OP, Austin, *The Theology of Confirmation*. Dublin, 1972.

Miłosz, Czesław, *Proud to be a Mammal*. London, 2010.

Mitchell, Ed Stephen, *The Enlightened Heart An anthology of Sacred Poetry*. London, 1993.

Murdoch, Iris, *Nuns and Soldiers*. Vintage Digital, 2008.

Murray OP, Paul, 'Recovering the Contemplative Dimension', *Acts of the Elective General Chapter of the Order of Preachers*. Rome, 2001.

—*These Black Stars*. Dublin, 2003.

—*I Loved Jesus in the Night: Teresa of Calcutta, a Secret Revealed*. London, 2009.

Newman, John Henry, *Lectures on the Prophetical Office of the Church*. London, 1874.

—*Parochial and Plain Sermons* III. London, 1885.

—*Meditations and Devotions of the late Cardinal Newman*. London and New York, 1893.

—*On Consulting the Faithfull in Matters of Doctrine*, ed. John Coulson. Kansas City and London, 1961.

Nicholl, Donald, *Holiness*. London, 1981.

O'Brien, Flan, *At Swim-Two-Birds*. London, 2001.

O'Donoghue, Bernard, *Selected Poems*. London, 2008.

O'Donohue, John, Interview with Martin Wroe, *The Church Times*, 14 January 2011.

Oelrich, Anthony, *A Church Fully Engaged: Yves Congar's Vision of Ecclesial Authority*. Collegeville, MN, 2011.

Olivera OSCO, Bernado, *How Far to Follow? The Martyrs of Atlas*. Kalamazoo, MI, 1997.

Orsy, Ladislas, *Receiving the Council: Theological and Canonical Insights and Debates*. Collegeville, MN, 2009.

Osborne OFM, Kenan B., *The Christian Sacraments of Initiation: Baptism, Confirmation, Eucharist*. New York and Mahwah, NJ, 1987.

Ounsworth OP, Richard, 'On the Threshold of the Promised Land', *Religious Life Review*, March/April 2011, pp. 67–78.

Pagola, José A., *Jesus, An Historical Approximation*. Miami, 2009.

Paschal, Blaise, *Pensées*, trans. A. J. Krailsheimer. London, 1966.

Patten, Chris, *What Next? Surviving the Twenty-First Century*. London, 2008.

Philibert OP, Paul, *At the Heart of Christian Worship: Liturgical Essays of Yves Congar*. Collegeville, MN, 2010.

Pieper, Josef, *Four Cardinal Virtues*. Notre Dame, 1966.

—*Faith, Hope, Love*. San Francisco, 1997.

Polman, Linda, 'Fear of the poor is hampering Haiti rescue', *The Times*, 18 January 2010.

Potter, Dennis, *Seeing the Blossom*. London and Boston, 1994.

Proust, Marcel, *Swann's Way*, trans. C. K. Scott Moncrieff and Terence Kilmartin, revised by D. J. Enright. London, 2005.

Radcliffe OP, Timothy, 'The Demands of the Mass', *The Tablet*, 1 December 1990.

—*What is the Point of being a Christian?* London, 2005.

—*Why Go to Church? The Drama of the Eucharist*. London, 2008.

Rahner SJ, Hugo, *On the Theology of Death*, Quaestiones Disputatae 2. New York, 1961.

—*Man at Play or Did you ever Practice Eutrapelia*, trans. Brian Battershaw and Edward Quinn. London, 1965.

—*Meditations on the Sacraments*. London, 1977.

Renan, Ernest, *History of the Origins of Christianity*. London, 1890.

Rilke, Rainer Maria, *Selected Poems with Parallel German Text*. New translations by Susan Ransom and Marielle Sutherland. Oxford, 2011.

The Rites of the Catholic Church: Study Edition. Revised by Decree of the Second Vatican Ecumenical Council. New York: International Commission on English in the Liturgy, 1983.

Roberts, Gregory David, *Shantaram*. London, 2005.

Robinson, Andrew, *Tears at Night Joy at Dawn: Journal of a Dying Seminarian*. Stoke on Trent, 2003.

Robinson, Marilynne, *Gilead*. New York, 2004.

Rumi, Jelaluddin Coleman Barks, *The Essential Rumi*. San Franscisco, 1995.

Ruston, Roger, *Human Rights and the Image of God*. London, 2004.

Sachs, Jonathan, 'China is reversing the decline and fall of Christianity', *The Times*, 21 May 2011.

Sakaki, Nanao, *Break the Mirror*, trans. Gary Snyder. Nobleboro, ME, 1996.

Scally, John, 'The Spiritual Legacy of John McGahern', *Doctrine and Life* 60, no. 10, December 2010.

Schlink, Bernard, *The Reader*, trans. Carol Brown Janeway. London, 1997.

Shannon, William H. *Seeds of Peace: Contemplation and Non-Violence*. New York, 1996.

Shortt, Rupert, *Christianophobia*. London, forthcoming, 2012.

Smith, Ali, *There but for the*. London, 2011.

Spohn, William C., *Go and Do Likewise: Jesus and Ethics*. New York and London, 2007.

St Augustine of Hippo, *Confessions*, trans. Henry Chadwick. Oxford, 1991.

St Benedict of Nursia, *The Rule of St Benedict*, ed. Timothy Fry OSB. Collegeville, 1981.

St Catherine of Siena, *Lettres de Sainte Catherine de Sienne*, trans. E. Cartier, Vol. III. Paris, 1858.

—*Le Lettere di S. Caterina da Siena*, ed. Pierro Miscitelli, Vol. I. Siena, 1922.

—*The Dialogue*. New York, trans. Suzanne Noffke OP. Mahwah, NJ, 1980.

St Ephrem, *Ephrem the Syrian*, trans. and intr. Kathleen E. McVey. New York and Mahwah, NJ, 1989.

St Thomas Aquinas, *Summa Theologiae*, ed. Thomas Gilbey OP. 61 vols. Cambridge, 2006.

Stackhouse, Ian, *The Day is Yours: Slow Spirituality in a Fast-Moving World*. Milton Keynes, 2008.

Steinbeck, John, *Cannery Row*. New York and London, 1992.

Stevik, D. B. 'Christian Initiation: Post-Reformation to the Present Era', in *Made, not Born: New Perspectives on Christian Initiation and the Catechumenate*. Notre Dame: Murphy Center for Liturgical Research, 1976.

Tankard, Paul, 'Forbidden Art', *Times Literary Supplement*, 11 March 2011.

Taylor, Charles, *A Secular Age*. Cambridge, MA and London, 2007.

Tilley, Maureen, 'One Wholly Catholic: Saints and Sanctity in the Post-Apostolic Church', Catholic Theological Society Annual Meeting, 9 June 2011. To be published.

Tolstoy, Leo, *The Death of Ivan Ilyich and Other Stories*. London, 2004.

—*War and Peace*, trans. Aylmer Maude and Louise Shanks Maude. Kindle, 2011.

Tugwell OP, Simon, *Did you Receive the Spirit?* London, 1972.

—*et al. New Heaven? New Earth?: An Encounter with Pentecostalism.* London, 1976.

—*The Way of the Preacher.* London, 1979.

—ed, *Early Dominicans: Selected Writings.* New York, 1982.

—Simon, *Reflections on the Beatitudes: Soundings in Christian Traditions.* London, 1984.

—*Ways of Imperfection: An Exploration of Christian Spirituality.* London, 1984.

Vanier, Jean, *Images of Love, Words of Hope.* Hantsport, 1991.

—*Essential Writings.* Selected and Introduced by Carolyn Whitney-Brown. London, 2008.

Verboven, Lucette. *The Dominican Way.* London, 2011.

Walcott, Derek, *Collected Poems 1948–1984.* London, 1992.

Watkins, Claire, *Living Baptism: Called out of the Ordinary.* London, 2006.

Wells, H. G., 'A Vision of Judgement', http://ebooks.adelaide.edu.au/w/wells/hg/short/chapter3.html

Wells, Samuel, *God's Companions: Reimagining Christian Ethics.* Oxford, 2006.

Whyte, Jamie, 'I don't believe that believers really believe', *The Times*, 16 September 2008.

Wiesel, Elie *Souls on Fire : Portraits and Legends of Hasidic Masters.* New York 1972

Williams, Niall, *As it is in Heaven.* London, 1999.

Williams, Rowan, *Open to Judgment. Sermons and Addresses.* London, 1994.

—*Writing in the Dust: Reflections on 11th September & its Aftermath.* London, 2002.

—*Silence and Honey Cakes.* Oxford, 2003.

—*Tokens of Trust: An Introduction to Christian Belief.* Norwich, 2007.

—*Dostoevsky: Language, Faith and Fiction.* London, 2008.

Wiseman, Nicholas Archbishop, 'An Appeal to the Reason and Good Feeling of the English People on the Subject of the Catholic Hierarchy', London, 1850.

Woods OP, Richard, *Meister Eckhart: Master of Mystics.* London, 2011.

Worth Jr., Roland H., *The Seven Cities of the Apocalypse and Greco-Asian Culture.* Mahwah, NJ, 1999.

Yarnold SJ, Edward, *The Awe-Inspiring Rites of Initiation: Baptismal Homilies of the Fourth Century.* Slough, 1971.

Young, William Paul. *The Shack.* London, 2008.

Zamagni, Stefano, 'The Catholic Ethic and the Spirit of Capitalism', in D. Finn ed., *The True Wealth of Nations.* Oxford, 2010, pp. 69–94.